formatio
TRADITION. EXPERIENCE.
TRANSFORMATION.

Formatio books from InterVarsity Press follow the rich tradition of the church in the journey of spiritual formation. These books are not merely about being informed, but about being transformed by Christ and conformed to his image. Formatio stands in InterVarsity Press's evangelical publishing tradition by integrating God's Word with spiritual practice and by prompting readers to move from inward change to outward witness. InterVarsity Press uses the chambered nautilus for Formatio, a symbol of spiritual formation because of its continual spiral journey outward as it moves from its center. We believe that each of us is made with a deep desire to be in God's presence. Formatio books help us to fulfill our deepest desires and to become our true selves in light of God's grace.

Sacramental Life

Spiritual Formation Through the Book of Common Prayer

DAVID A. deSILVA

IVP Books

An imprint of InterVarsity Press
Downers Grove, Illinois

InterVarsity Press
P.O. Box 1400, Downers Grove, IL 60515-1426
World Wide Web: www.ivpress.com
E-mail: email@ivpress.com

InterVarsity Press® is the book-publishing division of InterVarsity Christian Fellowship/USA®, a
student movement active on campus at hundreds of universities, colleges and schools of nursing in
the United States of America, and a member movement of the International Fellowship of Evangelical
Students. For information about local and regional activities, write Public Relations Dept., InterVarsity
Christian Fellowship/USA, 6400 Schroeder Rd., P.O. Box 7895, Madison, WI 53707-7895, or visit the
IVCF website at <www.intervarsity.org>.

Scripture quotations, unless otherwise noted, are from the New Revised Standard Version of the Bible,
copyright 1989 by the Division of Christian Education of the National Council of the Churches of Christ
in the USA. Used by permission. All rights reserved.

The quote on p. 87 is taken from "I Come with Joy" by Brian Wren ©1971, 1995 Hope Publishing Co.,
Carol Stream, IL 60188 in the United States and ©1971, 1995 Stainer & Bell Ltd., 23 Gruneisen Road,
London, N3 England. All rights reserved. Used by permission.

The excerpt on p. 185 is from Now the Silence by Jaroslav J. Vajda ©1969 by Hope Publishing Co., Carol
Stream, IL 60188. All rights reserved. Used by permission.

Design: Cindy Kiple
Images: Mark Jensen/iStockphoto

Typeset by the Livingstone Corporation (www.LivingstoneCorp.com)

ISBN 978-0-8308-3518-8

Printed in the United States of America ∞

 InterVarsity Press is committed to protecting the environment and to the responsible
use of natural resources. As a member of Green Press Initiative we use recycled
paper whenever possible. To learn more about the Green Press Initiative, visit
<www.greenpressinitiative.org>.

Library of Congress Cataloging-in-Publication Data

DeSilva, David Arthur.
  The sacramental life: spiritual formation through the Book of
common prayer / David A. deSilva.
      p. cm.
  Includes bibliographical references (p.   ) and index.
  ISBN 978-0-8308-3518-8 (pbk.: alk. paper)
  1. Episcopal Church. Book of common prayer (1979) 2. Episcopal
Church—Liturgy—Meditations. 3. Spiritual formation—Episcopal
Church. I. Title.
  BX5946.D47 2008
  264'.03—dc22

                                                              2008017365

P   18   17   16   15   14   13   12   11   10   9   8   7   6   5   4   3   2   1

Y   23   22   21   20   19   18   17   16   15   14   13   12   11   10   09   08

To the Rev. J. Wesley Vanaman and the Rev. Thomas A. Snyder,

spiritual fathers who nurture worship in the beauty of holiness

Contents

Acknowledgments

In my lectures on Luke's Gospel and its sequel, I tell my students that writing a book in the first century implies a network of support, friends and ample free time. This remains true of much twenty-first-century religious writing as well. I am grateful to the Board of Trustees of Ashland University and its president, Dr. Frederick J. Finks, for a year's research leave to undertake this and several other projects, and to the Evanglisch-theologische Fakultät of the University of Tübingen, Germany, for their kind hospitality during that year. My gratitude goes out also to several individuals who were important conversation partners at various stages in the writing of this book: to the Reverend James Cox and the Reverend Dr. Daniel Hawk for reading an early draft of the chapters on baptism, to my wife, Donna Jean deSilva, and to Cindy Bunch, Ulrike Guthrie, and Lori Shire, each of whom read the entire manuscript and made helpful suggestions.

I could not write about spiritual formation through the sacraments had I not been invited into those sacraments in ways that allowed me to be spiritually formed and nurtured an awareness of transcendence. Two ministers, both of whom I served as organist and choir director at different stages of my life, have been especially important for my development in this regard. The first is the Reverend J. Wesley Vanaman, former rector of St. George's Church in Helmetta, New Jersey, my mentor throughout my college and seminary years. The second is the Reverend Thomas A. Snyder, former pastor of Christ United Methodist Church in Ashland, Ohio, a dear brother in the faith and a model of liturgical aptitude and creativity in a denomination that too often forgets its Anglican roots. It is to these two men, who will always have front-row seats in my own "cloud of witnesses," that I dedicate this book with love and gratitude.

David A. deSilva
All Saints' Day
Ashland, Ohio

Introduction

Since I left the Episcopal Church after twenty-four years of being nurtured in that tradition, I have met many Christians who assumed I did so because I came to my senses about the emptiness of praying the same words from the Book of Common Prayer week after week. Some look on the liturgy from outside as just going through the motions or praying by rote. Others see receiving Communion every week as a mistake that makes the sacrament ordinary or routine. Of course, nothing could be further from the truth, both about my own spiritual journey and about the liturgies celebrated throughout the Anglican Communion (and its daughter denomination, United Methodism, in which I hold ordination). I am a person of faith today precisely because the liturgies of the Book of Common Prayer gave me a language and a context for encountering God in my youth that continue to be essential vehicles for my own spiritual formation.

Christian spiritual formation is the process of allowing God to bring our "unruly wills and affections" (Book of Common Prayer, 219) into order with what is healthful to our spirits and to the spirits and lives of those around us. It is the process by which Christ's mind takes shape within us, so that he might indeed continue his work in the world through us. It involves learning to love what God commands and to desire what God promises, so that we will be stable in our commitment to live for him who died and lives for us. It is to come to the place where to do what God wishes is our pleasure and desire. That is what it means to be fully formed in Christ, the one whose will it was to do God's good pleasure.

For Christians who worship in the Anglican tradition of the Protestant Episcopal Church, the Book of Common Prayer (BCP), together with the Scripture readings that it prescribes, is the foundational resource for spiritual formation. The rites in this book shape encounters with

God and guide interaction with God from the cradle to the grave, from baptism to burial. In the regular course of the year, celebrations of Holy Baptism and baptismal renewal keep the dynamics of spiritual growth fixed in our minds—dying to everything in ourselves, our world and the spiritual forces around us that opposes God's desire for us and for human community, and reaching out for all that God has for us and calls us to become. Week after week, worshipers are brought face-to-face with the Savior who gives his life to us in Holy Communion, filling us so that we are able to give our lives to others. Every liturgy for the Celebration and Blessing of a Marriage calls Christian couples to bring that commitment to other-centered living into their homes. And as we stare into the face of the mystery of death at funeral after funeral, the liturgies interpret that reality in light of God's good purposes for us and send us back into the world to continue to walk in the newness of life to which we were called at our baptism.

These rites put the words into the mouths of worshipers so that the intentions and commitments they express will sink down deep into the heart and come to expression in changed lives. They teach us what to desire and what to seek from the Lord, both trimming away what is self-serving and opening our minds and hearts to the full range of what God desires to work for us, in us and through us. They form in us the habits of the most significant spiritual disciplines valued by Christian disciples through the centuries—adoration, prayer, self-examination and confession, as well as listening to and being shaped by Scripture. By means of these disciplines, we draw closer to God and grow more attuned to the mind of Christ.

This book explores the rites of the Book of Common Prayer as devotional resources. These liturgies, prayers and Scripture readings

- shape our beliefs about God and our understanding of God's interventions in the world;

- facilitate our approach to, and encounter with, the Divine;

- identify the challenges to the life of faith, the spiritual and temporal dangers we face;

- train our desires and ambitions; and

- orient us to the people and systems around us.

The aim of this book is to help both those who worship regularly in liturgical traditions and those whose worship style is nonliturgical to engage more fully the spiritual disciplines nurtured by these liturgies and experience the spiritual direction that these liturgies provide.

The devotional exercises that punctuate this book are a key component to this engagement. These will help you apply what you have read, to practice spiritual disciplines and to begin at once to make progress in discipleship. Some invite you to self-examination and reflection on a particular question. Others provide symbolic acts by which you might grasp a particular gift of God or make a commitment to God more fully. Still others provide guidance for times of prayer or recommend acts of service and engagement with others. They provide, of course, only *suggestions* for how you might engage the material found in this book, but engaging them in *some* form is essential if reading this book is to be more than an intellectual exercise.

Some of these exercises are presented as most appropriate for individual use, some for use in a group or, especially in the section on marriage, as a couple, but most are easily adapted to a variety of contexts.

WHY THE BOOK OF COMMON PRAYER?

If we are to listen to liturgy as a vehicle for spiritual direction and formation, we need to seek out some *particular* liturgies to listen to. The liturgies found in the BCP recommend themselves for a number of reasons—beyond their peculiar importance in the spiritual journey of the author of this book!

The liturgies of the BCP particularly recommend themselves because of their inclusivity both in terms of time and denominational breadth. This inclusivity arises out of the process that led to the compilation of the very first Anglican prayer book in 1549. Thomas Cranmer, archbishop of Canterbury under Henry VIII and Edward VI, led the process of creating a new collection of liturgies and other resources to be used in the newly created Church of England. He brought together a simplified form of the Roman Catholic rites, liturgies from the Eastern Christian churches, as well as innovations introduced by the Reformers on Europe's mainland. A fruit of the reformation of worship on the Continent, Cranmer's Book of Common Prayer put the liturgy back in the language and in the hands of the common people, who were invited again to participate in all aspects of the service.

Mary Tudor restored Catholicism and initiated a brutal persecution of Protestants (which claimed the life of Cranmer himself), but the Book of Common Prayer returned to use under Elizabeth I and was significantly revised in ways that would restore unity among those of Catholic and those of Protestant convictions throughout her realm. Christian unity and inclusiveness was again in evidence as an essential principle in the formation of the BCP.

In the modern edition of the BCP, which represents only the current step in a long and ongoing evolution of liturgy, this inclusiveness across time and across denominations is even more fully in evidence. One can still recognize behind the services of baptism and Communion the framework of liturgies from the time of Hippolytus in the third century. Two of the options for the Great Thanksgiving, the prayer offered at the time of Communion, are adaptations of Communion prayers attributed to Hippolytus himself and to Basil of Caesarea, the fourth-century theologian whose liturgy was deeply influential in the Eastern Orthodox churches.

The BCP is also a *representative* collection of liturgies. There are extensive parallels between the principal liturgies found therein and the services of baptism and Eucharist in the *United Methodist Book of Worship*, the *Lutheran Book of Worship*, and the rites of the post-Vatican II Roman Catholic Church. These similarities extend from common liturgical elements and order down to the wording of specific elements. As a result, what is said in this book on the basis of the BCP could, to a very large extent, have been derived as well from the liturgies of these other traditions.

In the end, however, Wisdom must be justified by her children. The choice of the BCP as a foundational text for spiritual formation is ultimately grounded in my conviction that its prayers and liturgies capture and communicate essential facets of our formation as disciples and that these insights are thoroughly consistent with the spiritual counsel of Scripture itself.

Many readers might not have a copy of the Book of Common Prayer on their bookshelves at home. The complete text is readily available online at <http://justus.anglican.org/resources/bcp/bcp.htm> and can be downloaded in a variety of formats. Bound copies can also be ordered through any Internet bookseller or local bookstore, and are surprisingly affordable.

WHY *THESE* FOUR LITURGIES?

Theologians define a "sacrament" as a promise of God joined to a visible sign of the effectiveness of that promise. A sacrament is so named because it identifies a place where God has promised, on oath (Latin, *sacramentum*), as it were, to meet God's faithful people. Protestant Christians acknowledge only two such sacraments—baptism and Eucharist, or the Lord's Supper—since they find a clear command of Christ in Scripture regarding only these two. According to sacramental theologians, I should probably either have stopped with these two or else proceeded to treat all *seven* sacraments historically embraced by the Roman Catholic Church. But this is *not* primarily a book about the sacraments. It is a book about living the *sacramental life,* that is, living in line with the model of discipleship that the sacramental liturgies articulate and seek to shape within us, and availing ourselves more fully and more often of the resources God sets before us through these sacraments.

The first (and larger) half of this book, therefore, focuses on the spiritual formation and direction given in the liturgies connected with the sacraments of baptism and Holy Communion, the two principal rites of the Christian church throughout the ages. The second half goes on, however, to consider the liturgies of marriage and burial as two vehicles through which the BCP helps nurture the sacramental life in particular life contexts. These liturgies represent attempts to "flesh out" the significance of baptism and Eucharist (the second of which is, in fact, intended to be celebrated within the marriage and burial liturgies) for Christian marriage, into which many disciples enter, and for living life in the face of death, into which *all* disciples must enter.

I would encourage unmarried readers not to see the short section on Christian marriage as irrelevant to them, even if they are committed to singleness. One of the principal lessons to be derived from the marriage liturgy is the community context of the marriage covenant. As in the baptismal covenant, the whole gathered congregation promises to do "all in [its] power" to support the couple in their life together, even as it promises in baptism to support the new disciple in his or her new life in Christ (BCP, 303). What you read here can equip you and your congregation to fulfill this supporting role more fully, bringing healing to marriages in your midst.

Of course, the BCP contains far more liturgical material than this. There are liturgies for morning, noontime, evening and bedtime prayer, which together constitute the Daily Office. There are services for special days throughout the church year, particularly the progression from Ash Wednesday through Easter. There are also services for ministering to the sick, for setting individuals apart for priestly service and for various other occasions. However, the services of baptism, Eucharist, marriage and burial are those that people most often encounter in the life of the Anglican Communion and, indeed, *most* Christian communions.

The explorations of these liturgies in this book do not attempt to follow the order of service woodenly, but tend rather to follow a more topical arrangement. This is due to the more practical focus of this book, which is on the spiritual direction these liturgies provide and the spiritual disciplines they seek to form—not a commentary on the liturgies themselves. The principal aim of this book is to help you discover ways in which to bring the spiritual formation fostered by the liturgies of the Book of Common Prayer more fully into your daily life, whether you worship regularly in this tradition or are exploring it from the context of another liturgical tradition. A close, secondary purpose is to provide a resource that can help reinvigorate your own participation in liturgy as you grow in those spiritual disciplines it embodies and become more attuned to the work of the Spirit it seeks to facilitate.

Whether the words of the Book of Common Prayer are so familiar that you can recite them from memory or you are a new explorer of the spirituality of liturgical worship, I hope that, as you read and pray through this guide, you will discover afresh the ways in which the rites contained in the Book of Common Prayer facilitate a genuine encounter with God and a transforming experience of grace.

PART ONE

Baptism

Walking in Newness of Life

Christian Life as Baptismal Life

The Whole of the Christian Life, in Time and
In Eternity is, in a Sense, Encapsulated in Baptism.
The Christian Life is a Baptismal Life, and it is All About
Dying and Rising with Christ, in This World and Hereafter.

MICHAEL GREEN

The sanctuary is in total darkness, save for a single, tall candle being carried in procession while a cantor sings a historic hymn—sung by Christians on this, the night before Easter, since the fourth century—celebrating God's deliverance of God's people from sin and death in the great new exodus of Christ, our Passover Lamb. The lights come on, and the whole story of God's great acts of creation and redemption is told through a series of Scripture readings. The minister then brings this story home to each worshiper gathered in the sanctuary. She reminds us that we became part of this story in our baptism and proceeds to sprinkle generous amounts of water over the congregation with an evergreen tree branch and a bowl, walking up and down the central aisle and calling out, "Remember your baptism, and be thankful."

In this way, every year, the Great Vigil of Easter poignantly immerses me in the sweeping saga of redemption and in the mystery of Christ's death and resurrection, the saga and mystery into which baptism initiates us.

Our spiritual journey as Christians starts decisively at the baptismal font. For those baptized in late childhood or adulthood rather than infancy, the spiritual journey begins before baptism, to be sure. But whether we are baptized as an infant, child or adult, baptism marks the beginning of our *Christian* life. Christians may fiercely debate whether people ought to receive baptism as infants or as older believers who can make a public confession. They may argue about whether sprinkling, pouring or immersion constitutes the "correct" method of baptism. But Christians tend to agree that baptism is the fundamental rite of entry into Christ's body, the church, the initiation into the journey of transformation into Christlikeness.

Baptized at the age of three weeks, I cannot recall my experience of baptism. But, since then, I have participated in the baptism of many others, and the Book of Common Prayer has invited me each time, together with the whole congregation, to renew my own baptismal covenant (see BCP, 303). I was confirmed, again in the context of the baptism of others, in a rite that placed my own baptism and its significance again before my eyes as I formally committed to the baptismal life, asking God to "renew . . . the covenant made with [us] at [our] Baptism" (BCP, 309). Together with the annual renewal of baptismal vows at the Great Vigil of Easter, the rites have brought my own baptism and its formative implications for my life regularly before my eyes, encouraging me to live out my baptism a little more fully, day by day, until it has its full effect in renewing and transforming my life.

At first, this repeated emphasis on baptism might seem strange. Isn't it enough, after all, that we *were* baptized—and have the certificate to prove it?

Baptism has a dual nature. On the one hand, it is performed once and considered thereafter to be an accomplished fact. On the other hand, baptism provides an orientation to our selves, our world and our God that must be appropriated day after day. Martin Luther wrote that "in Baptism, every Christian has enough to study and to practice all his life. He always has enough to do to believe firmly what baptism promises and brings—victory over death and the devil, forgiveness of sin, God's grace, the entire Christ, and the Holy Spirit with his gifts." We are both baptized *and* initiated into a baptismal life. We are taken into a baptismal *covenant* in which we are called to walk each day.

Theologians often compare baptism with the Jewish rite of circumcision. Paul himself described baptism as "putting off the body of the flesh in the circumcision of Christ" (Col 2:11). Jewish males experience the rite of circumcision when they are a mere eight days old. Long before they are able to understand the meaning of circumcision, they are initiated into the people of God and into the covenant with God on the basis of having been born to children of the covenant, their parents. Taken into the covenant people, however, they are also now obliged to live in accordance with that covenant if they would enjoy its blessings. Without such obedience, as the Torah, the prophets and Paul all agree, their circumcision becomes valueless: Real circumcision is a matter of the heart (Rom 2:25, 29; see also Deut 10:16; 30:6; Jer 9:25).

Similarly, real baptism is a matter of the heart, the heart that now longs to live for God and in a manner that pleases God, following the leading of God's Holy Spirit. The rite confers essential spiritual gifts for the process of being formed into the likeness of Jesus, such as the presence of the Holy Spirit in the life of the baptized, the pledge of the support and nurture of the Christian community and close identification with Christ's death and resurrection. But we need to make full use of these gifts and fully offer these gifts to one another.

For baptism to be fully baptism, it must not stop when we leave the font. It must become more and more the mold that shapes our lives, until Christ lives in us and we live for Christ. It must become more and more the compass point from which we chart each day's course, until we follow the promptings of the Holy Spirit more naturally and readily than our own desires. In the words of Luther, baptism is to become "the daily garment which the disciple is to wear all the time, . . . every day suppressing the old person and growing up in the new."

The spirituality of the BCP is first and foremost a spirituality of remembering our baptism. We hold our lives constantly before the mirror of our baptismal vows and seek to bring our lives ever more fully in line with the vision these vows express. In so doing,

> we are entering (a little more each time) into what God has done in and for us in this sacrament, calling into the present the power of what, historically, happened in the past, deepening our understanding of what we could never fully understand at the time of our baptism as infants *or* adults, and appropriating more and more the grace made available to us.

We are called to live out the sacrament of our baptism day by day, so as to enter "a little more each time" into the new life that baptism opens up for us.

In the following chapters, we will explore the gifts that God offers to us in baptism, as these are expressed in the liturgies of the BCP and the Scriptures upon which they draw, as well as the promises we undertake in response to God's gifts. We will also use the baptismal liturgy as a means of plumbing the depths of the significance of our own baptism and seeking to embody it ever more fully day by day.

PUTTING IT INTO PRACTICE

Think back upon your experience of services of baptism and baptismal renewal. In what ways have these experiences impacted you? What is your understanding of the meaning of your baptism for your life now?

Set a small, clear bowl of water in a prominent place in your home and, if possible, your place of work. Whenever you see it, say to yourself (touching the water, or using it to mark yourself with the sign of the cross on your forehead, as in baptism, if you find this useful), "I have been baptized; I belong to God; I am new in Christ."

2

The Forgiveness of Sins

※

The rite of baptism is an initiation into the new covenant inaugurated by Jesus, ever extending this covenant to generation after generation of the newly baptized. In a covenant relationship, two parties make promises to one another, pledging to fulfill certain obligations. One of the most prominent promises of God connected with baptism is the forgiveness of sins, associated with the image of washing or cleansing. These prominent images highlight the connections between Christian baptism and its precursors: Jewish purificatory rites and John's offering of a "baptism of repentance for the forgiveness of sins" (Mk 1:4). These earlier rites of cleansing sought to prepare people to encounter God, whether in the rituals of the temple or in the coming of the Messiah that John announced. The removal of the pollution of sin permitted the worshiper to stand before God with a clean conscience, in the hope of being received favorably by God.

The baptismal liturgy repeatedly draws attention to this aspect of the rite. The celebrant prays for "those who here are cleansed from sin" (BCP, 307) and gives thanks to God "that by water and the Holy Spirit you have bestowed upon *these* your servants the forgiveness of sin" (BCP, 308). The lesson from Ezekiel recommended for baptism also emphasizes God's promise to cleanse his people from sin: "I will sprinkle clean water upon you, and you shall be clean from all your uncleannesses, and from all your idols I will cleanse you" (Ezek 36:25).

Pouring water over the baptized visually captures this aspect of baptism quite well. Sprinkling, the gesture used by the Jewish priests for cleansing away ritual defilements, also conveys this sense for those who recognize the significance of its background. The waters of baptism first represent, then, God's promise to cleanse us from our sins against him and his willingness to enter into a new, favorable relationship with us. They offer us a new start—a clean slate, as it were—and give us the knowledge of God's forgiveness, so that we can stand before him with confidence rather than fear and so that we can confidently receive all that God has to give us for our new life in him.

Realistically, we have all sinned since our baptism, whether we were baptized as infants or baptized yesterday. But this does not mean that our clean start has been ruined. Early Christian leaders recognized that repentance from sin and ongoing appropriation of God's forgiveness of our sins through Christ would be part of the disciple's experience all along the journey (see 1 Jn 1:9; 2:1-2). Such forgiveness accompanies the expectation that we will indeed regard our having been washed of all the thoughts, words and deeds that alienate us from God and bar us from God's kingdom as a decisive break with those ways of life. Putting on our baptism in its aspect of "forgiveness of sins" day by day, we are protected against forgetting "the cleansing of past sins" and its cost to our Savior (see 2 Pet 1:3-9). This, in turn, disposes us to live more fruitful lives for God, not returning to destructive behaviors, but seeking opportunities to grow in the virtues God's Spirit implants.

❋❋❋❋❋❋❋❋❋❋❋❋❋❋❋❋❋❋❋❋❋❋❋❋❋❋❋

PUTTING IT INTO PRACTICE

Fill a glass or ceramic basin with water. Pray and meditate in God's presence on your sins. Ask God to reveal to you how you have desired, spoken and acted contrary to what pleases him. Using a water-soluble marker, make a list of your sins insofar as you are aware of them. Pray a prayer of repentance. When you are ready, immerse the paper in the basin and read the following Scripture:

> Do you not know that wrongdoers will not inherit the kingdom
> of God? . . . And this is what some of you used to be. But you

were washed, you were sanctified, you were justified in the name of the Lord Jesus Christ and in the Spirit of our God. (I Cor 6:9, 11)

Give God thanks for his gracious forgiveness of all your sins in the waters of baptism, and pray for God's help to walk more and more in the ways that please him.

3

New Birth, New Life

❀

In baptism God also promises us a "new" birth. The Thanksgiving over the Water declares that "we are reborn by the Holy Spirit" through the water of baptism (BCP, 306). We are accustomed to connect being born again—or the slightly better translation "born anew" or "born from above"—with Christian conversion. Because baptism is also regarded as the point of entry into the Christian life, it becomes closely identified with "the new birth." Like the image of washing or cleansing, the image of a new birth also speaks of a fresh start. It speaks of our acceptance by God in even more intimate terms than the image of forgiveness, since he receives us into his own family as sons and daughters (see Gal 3:26-27; 4:4-7). What does the fact of this new birth say about my first birth and the life that continues to grow from that birth?

The idea of a *new* birth gives us some distance from our *old* birth, a distance that can be necessary for finding wholeness in Christ. The author of 1 Peter speaks of this new birth in terms of being "ransomed from the futile ways inherited from our ancestors" (1 Pet 1:18; see also 1 Pet 4:3-4). He looks at the attitudes and behaviors that we have learned along the way of being raised by fallible parents in a broken world, and tells us that Christ has set us free from walking any further down that path.

When we look at our lives in light of Scripture and the call of God, we realize that we have learned many things from our families of origin, from our schools and classmates, from our associates at work and from the omnipresent media that have shaped us—mis-shaped us, really—in the image of human brokenness rather than the image of divine fullness.

The new birth provides us with the gift of making a break from the effects of that mis-shaping process and its hold on our lives. It gives us the opportunity to find the freedom to become what we would most wish for ourselves in God's future for our lives. A man who had been taught that his self-worth is based on performance and achievement is freed from the compulsion to invest himself endlessly in being productive and discovers a more balanced life and other kinds of creativity. A girl who had learned to seek comfort and to affirm herself through buying new goods is freed to discover the spiritual practices that will fulfill the core longings that new shoes cannot reach. A woman who had been coached to see herself ever in competition with others for limited goods discovers that cooperation and looking after one another's interests is both possible and more fruitful. Whatever it is that you and I need to relearn, our baptism is a means of grace through which God continues to make available to us the ability to identify and to release these "life lessons," imprinted on us from our education by broken people in broken systems, and to discover a new way of being human together in God's presence.

Baptism makes us new in the eyes of God, in the eyes of the Christian community and, as we grow in our awareness, in our own eyes as well. A pastor relates this story about the transformative power of baptism: A teenage girl became pregnant and decided to have the baby, despite the fact that the father was not going to stay with her and that her plans for college would be derailed. Her family was having a very hard time with the situation, disappointed in her for being sexually active outside marriage and for dampening her chances for future education and employment by having a child at such a young age. They had very little to do with the child for the first few months of his life. He was a symbol of failure and disappointment and a token of shame.

After some months the girl brought her baby to the church to be baptized. In the process of preparing for baptism, the girl's family began to look at their daughter and the child differently. When the day for the baptism came, the family surrounded the girl and her son, and the gathered congregation made its acceptance of them clearly known. The

child was reborn, as it were, in that act of baptism. He was no longer
defined by his first birth, in shame and disappointment, alienated from
family, facing the challenges of being raised by a single mother. His new
birth redefined him as a gift from God to be received with thanksgiving,
a welcome addition to a larger family and network of support. Just as
baptism allowed that baby to be seen as a new person, by God's grace
baptism continues to make this newness available to us as we continue
to move out from the dysfunctional elements of our old life.

The new birth also signals a drawing near to a new family and new
formation. Through our natural birth we came alive to relationships
with family and began to receive nurture by them and, more and more,
the larger society. So also through our birth by water and the Holy
Spirit we come alive to God through the gift of the Holy Spirit and
the nurture of Christian community, our larger family in Christ. We
received a new "genetic code," as it were, as God implanted his Word of
truth in us as the seed by which we are born anew (see 1 Pet 1:22-25).
As we tend, and allow God to tend, our spiritual formation, God's Word
takes shape within us, overwriting the dysfunctional patterns imprinted
on us from our first rearing in brokenness. We are children once again,
sitting with and learning to imitate the character and mannerisms of
our heavenly Parent, who is present to us through his Holy Spirit: "all of
us, with unveiled faces, seeing the glory of the Lord as though reflected
in a mirror, are being transformed into the same image from one degree
of glory to another" (2 Cor 3:18; see also 1 Pet 1:14-16).

As children, we are unlearning what we have internalized of the
spirit of this age—racial prejudice, the limitations of gender roles, the
divisive ideology of nationalism, the idolization of wealth and consumer
goods, the worship of power and the like—and learning how to love,
to serve, to put others first as we interact with our Christian sisters
and brothers. We are being nurtured by our new family in Christ and
contributing as well to the nurture of others within this family as we
learn to show "sincere brotherly and sisterly love" toward them (1 Pet
1:22, my translation), investing in their lives as we would in the lives of
our natural families. The good news of this new birth is that it brings

also a new destiny, a new inheritance that carries with it none of the defects, the costly personal probate, of our first inheritance.

In baptism, we are born not only "of water" but also "of the Spirit" (Jn 3:5). The rites of baptism and confirmation lay special emphasis on being "sealed by the Holy Spirit," being strengthened with the Holy Spirit, being filled "with God's holy and life-giving Spirit," increasing daily in the Holy Spirit and being sent into the world "in the power of that Spirit" (see BCP, 305, 308, 309, 311, 418). The marking of the newly baptized with the sign of the cross, particularly when the oil of Chrism is used, ritually enacts this sealing by the Holy Spirit. The oil is a symbol of this inner spiritual reality of God's Holy Spirit dwelling within us, guiding, discerning, assuring, empowering.

The Holy Spirit is the decisive agent of our transformation. In the Old Testament lesson appointed for baptismal services, God promises the Holy Spirit to his people:

> A new heart I will give you, and a new spirit I will put within you.
> . . . I will put *my spirit* within you, and make you follow my statutes
> and be careful to observe my ordinances. *Then* you shall live in the
> land that I gave to your ancestors; and you shall be my people, and
> I will be your God. (Ezek 36:26-28, emphasis added)

God's solution for the problem of human disobedience and wayward-ness is the gift of his Holy Spirit, causing his own Spirit to dwell within us, giving us a new heart with new, holy longings reflecting the new life in Christ. The new birth is a coming alive to the presence of God's Holy Spirit. We live in this new life as we learn to discern the leading and empowering of the Spirit and to walk in line with the Spirit (see Gal 5:16).

The celebrant pronounces over each newly baptized person, "You are sealed by the Holy Spirit in Baptism and marked as Christ's own for ever" (BCP, 308). The presence of the Holy Spirit in our lives is also the foundation of our assurance that we belong to Christ and that Christ him-self will jealously preserve and protect what is his now and for eternity.

Putting on baptism in its aspect of new birth "by water and the Spirit" (BCP, 371), we are reoriented daily toward our new "upbringing" in

God as we leave behind those facets of our first upbringing that reflect human brokenness rather than God's wholeness. We grow more attentive to the guidance of the Holy Spirit and seek to walk in line with the Spirit away from the attitudes and pursuits that alienate us from God and one another and toward the transformation into Christlikeness that is our destiny as God's children (see Rom 8:5-6, 12-14).

❋❋❋❋❋❋❋❋❋❋❋❋❋❋❋❋❋❋❋❋❋❋❋❋❋❋❋

PUTTING IT INTO PRACTICE

Think about ways in which a Scripture, prayer, hymn or sermon has challenged a "truth" that you've clung to and lived by for a long time. What beliefs about yourself and others have you had to give up as you've grown in discipleship? What do you find yourself still believing and doing that you know you've learned from broken human teachers (parents, peers, the media and propaganda that surround us, your own maladaptive responses to life's challenges) rather than from Jesus' instruction through the Holy Spirit?

Read 1 Peter 1:14-16. Spend some time in prayer in God's presence. Ask God to show you one character trait of his, or one characteristic behavior of his, that God would want you to embody and reflect more fully at this time. Ask God to show you more about how he enacts that character trait and to show you how to embody it as well in your specific circumstances. Write down your impressions in your journal. Return to this entry and repeat this exercise during the week or weeks ahead until you begin to see more of this characteristic of your heavenly Parent in your own heart and walk.

4

Union with Christ

❋

Baptism initiates us into "the Christian mystery, the death and resurrection of Christ." This is perhaps the most profound facet of God's promises to us in baptism. We do not merely *apply* the power and meaning of Christ's death and resurrection to ourselves, confessing, for example, that he died for us and that we will at some point live again with him. We *participate* in his death and rising to new life here and now as we move through a process of dying to our "old self" and learning to "walk in newness of life."

This is by far the most prominent interpretation of baptism's significance in the liturgies of the BCP, as it was in the letters of Paul. In the water of baptism, "we are buried with Christ in his death," and by it "we share in his resurrection," living a "new life of grace" (BCP, 306, 308). Having been baptized into the death and resurrection of Jesus, the baptized life is one in which we "put away the old life of sin, so we may be renewed in the spirit of our minds, and live in righteousness and true holiness" (BCP, 252-53).

Baptism, then, first closely identifies us with the death of Jesus. In baptism we begin to die to our life apart from God, in rebellion against God. We die to our life of self-will, self-seeking and self-serving. When Jesus was approaching Jerusalem to *give* his life for many, James and John were still looking out for what they could *get* for themselves, asking him to give them the most prominent and powerful positions when he entered "into his glory" (Mk 10:35-45). Their request showed their self-interest at the expense of their relationship with the other disciples, who were alienated by their request. Looking ahead to his own suffering and death as his own "baptism," Jesus told James and John that they, too, would be initiated in his baptism, an immersion into his commitment to serve rather than to be served. It would involve a death to their self-seeking, to their attempts to advance their position over others, and a new orientation to serve as their Lord had served.

The essence of the baptismal life is that it is, first, a life of dying. It is commitment to losing one's life for Christ's sake more and more, in order to secure it for eternity and to being united with Christ "in a death like his" so that we will also "be united with him in a resurrection like his" (Mk 8:35; Rom 6:5). We are united with Christ in a death like his when we adopt the mind that he displayed in his incarnation, passion and death. That mindset involved becoming a servant to others and to the purposes of God, bringing life to many as he gave himself away (see Phil 2:5-11). For Christ's followers, it involves looking out not for our own interests, but for the interests of others, as Jesus did most dramatically (see Phil 2:3-4; see also Phil 2:19—3:21; 4:2-3). It involves serving those whom God places before us as Jesus did, stopping his triumphal entry into Jerusalem in order to care for a beggar, rather than brushing him off, or pausing on the night before his passion to wash his disciples' feet, rather than using them as his "support people" to serve his own ends. It means laying down our lives for one another by sharing sacrificially with those who are in need, as Jesus loved us in his death by laying down his life for us. The baptismal life is a commitment to show others the selfless love that Jesus showed us in his life and his death for us.

Being made like Jesus in his selfless death requires that we die to self in terms of who we are apart from God. Paul uses the image of the "old person" or old self to describe this aspect of our existence:

> You were taught to put away your former way of life, your old self, corrupt and deluded by its lusts, and to be renewed in the spirit of your minds, and to clothe yourselves with the new self, created according to the likeness of God in true righteousness and holiness. (Eph 4:22-24)

This image far more dramatically dissociates us from our identity apart from Christ than the image of "new birth." Here, we completely "put off" the old self—who we are apart from God—like a garment that doesn't fit us any longer. Our baptism does not kill the old self any more than it makes it impossible for us to sin. However, it does make the life of that old self ill-fitting, uncomfortable, too restrictive for who the Holy Spirit is calling us to become.

The "old self with its practices" is not a pretty sight (Col 3:9-10). It is greedy, covetous, lustful; it is angry, thinks and speaks ill of others, is not above using deceit. It seeks its own gratification and acts viciously to protect its own interests. It shows up in the man who does whatever it takes to get a promotion for himself, regardless of what it costs him in relationships, or the grown woman who abandons her family because she feels unfulfilled. You know your own old self. It erupts when others fail to do as you would wish them to do, and you resort to manipulation or simply curse them silently in your heart. It speaks in the messages you hear within you, demeaning others and yourself. It keeps drawing you to the painkillers you find in compulsive eating, needless spending or sexual addictions, masking the underlying wounds of your soul and distracting you from the One who can heal them. It poisons your relationships with defensiveness or unforgiveness.

And yet, we are often reluctant to relinquish that old self. Dying to the old self is difficult: "Death *means* death: . . . death to your hopes, dreams, and ambitions. It may mean death to a work you have built up and seen flourish. It will mean death, all along the line, to self-will. That is what it really means to say, 'I have been baptized.'" The sign of the cross made on our foreheads at baptism means we have been "consecrated to a crucified Messiah," and therefore that we, too, are bound by baptism to "crucify the old person and to bear the cross."

But the Christian mystery is not just about dying. It is about discovering a new kind of life on the other side of this death to the old self. The dying life carries with it this promise: "The more completely you die to self the more you begin to live to God." The new person, with which we clothe ourselves in baptism, exhibits the beauty of "compassion, kindness, humility, meekness, and patience," while our relationships exhibit the beauty of forgiveness, love and harmony (see Col 3:12-14). The new person is Christ living in us, and us living for Christ (see 2 Cor 5:15; Gal 2:20). It is to be created anew by God, our "best self" in him.

This union with Christ in his death and resurrection is a spiritual grace continually held out to us in our baptism. It is a precious gift from God, allowing us to leave behind whatever is destructive to human relationships, to community and ultimately to ourselves, and to move into a life with God and with one another that releases God's love into this world and preserves us with Christ for eternity.

Though rarely practiced in the more liturgical traditions, the ritual act of immersion captures the symbolism of this central mystery with special vividness. We are plunged into the pool, and the cold water closes over our heads in a symbolic death and burial; we are pulled up from the water and emerge on the other side of the pool a new person, to live a new kind of life. Whether we were immersed into water as adults or had water sprinkled or poured on us as infants long ago, the baptismal life summons us to spend the remainder of our lives applying this immersion to ourselves, becoming now "in actual practice those new creatures who have risen from the waters of death."

❁❁❁❁❁❁❁❁❁❁❁❁❁❁❁❁❁❁❁❁❁❁❁❁❁❁

PUTTING IT INTO PRACTICE

Read Colossians 3:5-17. Spend some time in prayer, asking God to show you those things to which you need to "die" in order for Christ to come alive in you more fully. What aspects of your old person does God want to work on with you at this point in your journey? You might wish to write in your journal about what things you are shown. Ask God to help you discern what spiritual graces you have already put on as part of the regular clothing of your new person. With what virtue or behavior does God want to endow you or cultivate in you more fully in this next step along the path? Pray for the grace and discernment to walk in the new person in this way more fully.

Find or even buy a nice new shirt, dress, robe or other garment (white would be symbolically appropriate). Set it on a hanger in a convenient place. Put on an old shirt or dress that has outlived its use. Spend some time in prayer before God, meditating on Colossians 3:5-17 and Galatians 5:16-25.

Take a marker and write those character traits or specific behaviors and responses that you recognize as a face of your old self on this old shirt (you may write these on pieces of paper and pin them to the shirt). Pray to God for grace and guidance to leave these things behind and to walk in newness of life. Strip off the old garment, and leave it in a heap on the floor. Pray for the specific graces of the new self that the Spirit has laid on your heart to seek, and put on the white garment. Read God's Word to you: "You have stripped off the old self with its practices and have clothed yourselves with the new self, which is being renewed in knowledge according to the image of its creator" (Col 3:9-10). Continue in prayer, asking God for help to live more and more from the new self with which God has clothed you in your baptism into Christ.

You might find it useful to retain these two garments, perhaps hanging the white garment in an elevated place and leaving the old garment crumpled below it, as a visible reminder of the transformation God is working within you.

5

A New Exodus

❋

The last facet of God's promises to us held out in the baptismal liturgy is a renewed experience of God's deliverance—a new passover and new exodus. In the "Thanksgiving over the Water," the celebrant declares,

> Through [water] you led the children of Israel out of their bondage in Egypt into the land of promise. . . . In it your Son Jesus . . . was anointed . . . to lead us, through his death and resurrection, from the bondage of sin into everlasting life. (BCP, 306)

The repetitive patterns of the prayer—"out of their bondage . . . into the land of promise," "from the bondage of sin into everlasting life"—suggest that these two acts of God, the exodus and our baptism into new life, are parallel and interpret each other's meaning. Our baptism is a passing over from death to life, an exodus from a life of slavery into the freedom of the children of God.

If in the actual baptismal liturgy this emphasis is somewhat muted, it resounds much more forcefully when baptism or baptismal renewal is celebrated within the context of the Easter Vigil service, where "the spiritual meaning of baptism is most fully expressed."

The Easter Vigil was an occasion especially chosen by the church in the third and fourth centuries for the baptism of new converts, linking the rite even more closely to the mystery of Jesus' death and resurrection that is the focal point of baptism. It is also the service that is most rich in recounting the saving acts of God from creation, to the deliverance of Noah through the flood, to the exodus from Egypt, to the restoration of Israel after the exile in Babylon, to the triumph of Jesus over death and the grave. The prayers after each reading during the Easter Vigil connect these events to the baptismal life again and again (see BCP, 288-91). When we experience baptism and baptismal renewal in the context of this service, we see our life before baptism (our life lived apart from Christ) and our life after baptism (our life lived in Christ) in terms of the passover and exodus.

As the new passover, baptism makes us acknowledge that the forces of death hang over all that we did, and continue to do, living out the life of the old person. As we die with Christ, applying his paschal blood to the lintels of our hearts, we are set free from the tyranny of death: "by the Passover of your Son you have brought us out of sin into righteousness and out of death into life" (BCP, 291).

As the new exodus, baptism indicts our life apart from Christ as a life of slavery to hostile forces that beat us down to serve their bidding. In part, we need deliverance from slavery to the forces that rise up from our own self-centeredness. But we also need to experience the deliverance of an exodus in regard to the forces that constrain us from outside, from the slave-making systems of sick societies, local and global. "You once delivered by the power of your mighty arm your chosen people from slavery under Pharaoh, to be a sign for us of the salvation of all nations by the water of Baptism" (BCP, 289). And if the view over our shoulders, departing from Egypt, looks bleak, baptism also holds before us the bright vision of the new life God has freed us to embrace.

The imagery of the new exodus saves us from the deception that the self-centered life is really the way to self-fulfillment, reminding us that there is no more abject slavery than to fail to master oneself. It keeps our eyes fixed on the newness of life that God imparts in baptism and throughout our life as we enter "a little more each time" into this work of God's Spirit within us.

PUTTING IT INTO PRACTICE

Read Titus 3:3-5 and Romans 6:6-13. Prayerfully ask God for

discernment concerning the forces that drive you, often to act against
what you would choose, forces that arise from within, but also impose
themselves from without. What enslaves your mind and drives your desires and actions, preventing you from walking in the way you know
God is calling you to walk? Pray to God to make your baptism effective for your deliverance from these enslaving beliefs, desires, values and
practices. Read Jesus' Word to you:

> If you continue in my word, you are truly my disciples; and you
> will know the truth, and the truth will make you free. . . . Very
> truly, I tell you, everyone who commits sin is a slave to sin. The
> slave does not have a permanent place in the household; the son
> has a place there forever. So if the Son makes you free, you will be
> free indeed. (Jn 8:31, 34-36)

6

We Renounce All
That Is Not from God

❦

When two parties make a covenant, *both* parties involved take on certain obligations toward the other. God promises to us "union with Christ in his death and resurrection, birth into God's family the Church, forgiveness of sins, and new life in the Holy Spirit" (BCP, 858). We, in turn, bind ourselves to God by solemn promises made at baptism, reaffirmed at confirmation and renewed throughout our lives. These promises begin with a threefold renunciation and threefold declaration of commitment, capturing the essence of the baptismal life as an ongoing "turning from" and "turning to." We turn *from* all that contributes to the corruption of human life and society; we turn *to* follow the way of Jesus in the power of the Spirit. In this chapter, we focus on the first set of promises we make to God, in which we renounce all that is not from God in ourselves, our society and our world.

As early as the third century, baptismal liturgies included the formal renunciation of Satan, his servants and his works, followed by the application of the "oil of exorcism" to seal these renunciations. A similar threefold renunciation is required in the BCP (302):

Do you renounce Satan and all the spiritual forces of wickedness that rebel against God?
Do you renounce the evil powers of this world which corrupt and destroy the creatures of God?
Do you renounce all sinful desires that draw you from the love of God?

The renunciations challenge us to become more spiritually attuned to the forces around us and within us that oppose the work of the Holy Spirit in us and through us. They call us to grow in our discernment of our own impulses and of the spiritual dynamics of larger systems, so that we will consistently make ourselves available to cooperate with the movements of God's Spirit, rather than the contrary movements of other powers.

WE RENOUNCE SATAN
A renunciation of Satan might seem quaint and even superstitious to some participants in the baptismal rite. To others, who have themselves participated in the occult, it will be a courageous and liberating act. We are cautioned by the liturgy, which names Satan only at this one place, against

> two equal and opposite errors into which our race can fall about the devils. One is to disbelieve in their existence. The other is to believe, and to feel an excessive and unhealthy interest in them. They themselves are equally pleased by both errors, and hail a materialist or a magician with the same delight.

The authors of Scripture and the theologians of at least the first seventeen centuries of the church's existence and mission understood "Satan and all the spiritual forces of wickedness" (BCP, 302) to pose a clear and present danger to perseverance in authentic Christian spirituality and to the spiritual, political, moral and social health of "the kingdoms of this world." Whether we adopt the spiritualistic worldview inherited from our Christian tradition or choose to engage these "spiritual forces of wickedness" in their demythologized forms, baptism enlists us entirely for God's cause against them.

Who is this Satan? Scripture presents Satan as the "deceiver of the whole world" (Rev 12:9), a being who seeks to keep people from "seeing the light of the gospel of the glory of Christ," using false teachings and perversions of true spirituality to accomplish his program of keeping people alienated from the reconciling and transforming love of God in Christ Jesus. He is called the "god of this world" (2 Cor 4:4) and "ruler of this world" (Jn 12:31), transforming politics and economics into systems of domination that exploit and corrupt. He is the tempter, luring people away from God's call through sinful desires, through arousing hostility against Christians and through breaking the fellowship of the church with his schemes. "You may be sure that the old Enemy is working by every means to frustrate your desire for good, and to entice you away from every spiritual exercise of devotion."

To live an authentic life with God, we must discard every counterfeit. If we desire to have communion with God, we must withdraw from all fellowship with Satan, discerning and cutting off every tendril he might use to ensnare. Paganism has always been a tolerant religion, but Christianity, like its parent religion, Judaism, has always been jealous to safeguard the devotion and allegiance due the One God (see Deut 6:4-6; 1 Thess 1:9-10). "What pagans sacrifice, they sacrifice to demons and not to God. I do not want you to be partners with demons. . . . You cannot partake of the table of the Lord and the table of demons" (1 Cor 10:20-21, my translation).

To live the baptismal life, we must persist in our renunciation of all competing and counterfeit spiritualities, recognizing behind them the subtle activity of the great deceiver. The voices of psychics or astrologers, the manipulative practice of magic, conversation with whatever "spirits" speak in séances and fascination with the "other gospel" and "other Jesus" of Gnosticism, have no place in the lives of those who have pledged to be led in all things by the Spirit of Christ.

WE RENOUNCE THE EVIL POWERS

The second renunciation calls us to discern and resist "the evil powers of this world which corrupt and destroy the creatures of God" (BCP, 302). We do not renounce the world, nor do we devalue what God has created. Rather, we are alerted to the forces *within* our world that twist and debase God's good creation and prevent *every* person from experiencing that creation as good. The "spiritual forces of wickedness" work against God's purposes for human community—peace, justice, wholeness in relationships—through what one author has called "domination systems." These systems are larger than any one individual. They are often larger than individual governments

and economic systems. Domination systems are social structures that have
taken on a life of their own, seeking their own preservation and pursuing
their own goals, no matter what the cost to human life, relationships or
environment. They infuse human society, and so induct us from our birth
into ways of thinking and valuing that legitimate and perpetuate the structures and behaviors that support these systems.

Militarism, for example, is a domination system that has historically
pervaded almost every human society. It co-opts the resources of
governments, industry, science and media to create ever more and ever new
weapons of destruction in the name of national security. It even co-opts
the voice of God as religious rhetoric is used to legitimate the expense of
lives and resources by anchoring it in some divine will. Its foundational
logic stands diametrically opposed to the logic of God, who proclaims
that nations will never be made secure by violence or the threat of violence,
but by the pursuit of global justice. Instead, militarism seeks our assent to
its fundamental premise that inflicting death and related hardships is an
acceptable and necessary means of ensuring peace. Militarism allows vast
amounts of resources to be diverted from other needs and uses, many of
which would be much more in keeping with the concerns voiced throughout Scripture for human community. For all this, militarism has become an
ideology hardwired into our thinking and as such represents an "evil power"
that has corrupted creation and rampantly destroys God's creatures.

Another powerful domination system centers on global economy,
with the creation and accumulation of wealth as its core value. Global
economy leads developing nations to invest their resources in luxury
goods that can compete on the world market rather than in the creation
of infrastructures that will eventually end poverty in their own lands.
The earth itself is regarded as a resource to be exploited, whatever
the consequences for future generations or for local-but-uninfluential
populations, rather than as a wonderfully balanced system set in place
by its Creator and to be carefully preserved by its tenants. As many as
believe that "more is better" and that participate in the agenda of ensuring the enjoyment of more by a privileged few, participate in this evil
power that corrupts and destroys the creatures of God.

The ideology of patriarchy, of course, continues to preserve the interests of males, while insidiously limiting the use of gifts by both men and women. This is a highly controversial domination system, since it has invaded even our own Scriptures (but, then again, so had militarism, as seen in the stories of the conquest of Canaan). By promoting the place of males and male thinking in the public arena, moreover, patriarchy has contributed greatly to the rise and perseverance of the other domination systems.

These are systems motivated by greed and self-interest, operated by exploitation, enforced and maintained by violence. Their self-preservation *as systems and ideologies* has become instinctual, a spiritual force. They are infused with, and promote, a "diseased spirituality" that surrounds us. The baptismal life calls us courageously to examine the spiritual powers in the world around us, which inevitably involve us in the evils perpetrated by these systems (if only as the heedless beneficiaries of their operation) and to walk forward in our renunciation of them. The baptismal life calls us, as John called those Christians who were benefiting from the violence and economic injustice of Roman imperialism, to "come out of her, my people, so that you do not take part in her sins, and so that you do not share in her plagues" (Rev 18:4-5).

Baptismal repentance has always involved "coming out" of participating in these domination systems as much as possible. John the Baptizer's call for repentance exemplifies this (see Lk 3:10-14). Those who had sought to get more for themselves were challenged to step out of the mindset of greed that drives economic domination systems and instead to share what they had with those who did not benefit from those systems. Tax collectors and soldiers were not to take advantage of the matrix of Roman imperialism and the power to exploit that they received as agents of empire, purging themselves of the logic and practices of domination in their post-baptismal lives.

The structures of modern domination systems provide us with many such opportunities for exploitation as well. We farm out work to people in developing nations to save on production costs and maximize our corporations' profits, denying local workers jobs and yoking foreign workforces to our corporate interests rather than the interests of their own country's development. We accept the rewards given to us as executives, even while our companies lay off hundreds of workers and place their families in frightfully vulnerable positions. We foreclose on homes to protect the interests of the financial institution for which we work because the "rules and regs" do not allow for the necessary grace period before a worker's compensation claim or application for unemployment can be processed. John the Baptist's call for "fruits worthy of repentance" (Lk 3:8) is just as relevant to us, if we want our baptism to be effective.

In the second- and third-century church, baptism could require a radical change of life. Those who made their living by making idols, for example, or by killing (that is, as professional soldiers), or by prostitution or magical arts had to change their occupation. They could not be engaged in business that would perpetuate the violent expansion and maintenance of the Roman domination system, the false religion that legitimated it, or any business that compromised their loyalty to God or obedience to his commandments in other ways.

As we move forward in living out our baptism, we, too, are called to such self-examination of our professions and our way of life, so as to oppose rather than cooperate with (and benefit from!) the "evil powers of this world that corrupt and destroy the creatures of God" (BCP, 302). Insofar as we fail to move forward in this regard, our spiritual growth is stunted.

WE RENOUNCE SINFUL DESIRES

The third renunciation focuses on the "sinful desires that draw you from the love of God"—both in the sense of the love we ought to have for God, expressed by desiring what pleases God, and the love we can experience from God, replacing this with the gratification of baser loves and desires. As we have seen, this is another means by which Satan perpetuates rebellion against God, drawing us away from cooperation with the Spirit of God.

This is a tough one. To walk in this renunciation means saying no again and again to what we want and are told by our society that we ought to want. It means growing in that difficult virtue of self-control, a virtue made possible by the gift of the Holy Spirit such that, as we give ourselves over to God's Spirit more and more, we attain self-control as the Spirit gains control over our passions.

In Scripture, particularly in Paul's letters, we read about the "desires of the flesh" and even of the "flesh" itself as a spiritual enemy (see Rom 7:14—8:14; Gal 5:13, 16-25). Just as we have distinguished between the "world" as God's creation (and therefore good) and the "evil powers" at work in the world, so also we need to distinguish between "flesh" as the material, created aspect of our bodily existence (which is good and which is related to our eternal body as the seed is related to the full-grown plant) and "flesh" as the aggregate of forces and impulses within that divert us from loving God, loving our neighbor and fulfilling God's righteous requirements for our lives. We renounce "flesh" in the latter sense, even as we commit ourselves to use our bodies for doing good and commit ourselves to care for the "flesh," that is the physical needs, by charitable acts toward those to whom God directs.

Persevering in resisting these sinful desires is particularly problematic in a culture that promotes self-gratification (from food to sex to no-money-down purchases) instead of the mortification of the passions for the sake of loving and serving Christ in all persons and places. Nevertheless, if we want to experience the authentic love of God and others, we must renounce the inauthentic connections forged by illicit sexual encounters. If we want to experience the authentic fulfillment of our core longings by God and Christian community, we must renounce inauthentic attempts to appease our deep hunger with spending or eating or other such shallow compensators.

By renouncing all these forces that ultimately threaten to make of our life a gross distortion of the image of God, we make room for God's Spirit to help us grow into the likeness of Christ, who is the image of God.

❋❋❋❋❋❋❋❋❋❋❋❋❋❋❋❋❋❋❋❋❋❋❋❋❋❋❋❋❋

PUTTING IT INTO PRACTICE

Prepare some means of disposing of small pieces of paper in a manner symbolically meaningful to you (perhaps burning or burying them).

Using the three examination questions on pages 41-42 pertaining to renunciation, spend some time in self-examination, asking God to show you involvements with the demonic, ways in which you are enmeshed in the false beliefs and community-corrupting practices of domination systems of this world and areas of your life where you make room for sinful desires that you have not yet renounced. (*You may wish to break up this exercise over several days or to incorporate it more regularly into your times of devotion.*) For example:

- Do you seek guidance or empowerment from any spiritual source other than the Spirit of Christ (like Ouija, psychics or Wiccan rites)?

- Do you know in what kind of companies you are investing your retirement funds?

- Do you know the political involvements of the larger stores that you support when you shop or the trade and manufacturing policies of your clothing companies or coffee providers?

- Are you engaged in online gambling, excessive shopping or pornography?

You might wish to reread some of the preceding paragraphs to help guide your self-examination, especially where some aspects of these vows of renunciation are new to you.

As God reveals these involvements to you, write each down on a small slip of paper. Pray for God's help to make a complete and decisive renunciation of these things. When and insofar as you are ready, make a formal act of renunciation of each item God has brought to your consciousness, destroying each slip of paper as a symbol of your breaking with that influence or practice. Ask God to break the spiritual power any of these might hold on you, claiming your death to all these things in your baptism. Pray for guidance concerning how to live differently so as to walk in line with this renunciation.

Pray for God's Holy Spirit to fill you afresh, occupying all the newly cleaned-out spiritual strongholds with his life-giving presence and with new, God-centered desires and practices.

Throughout the day, as you identify the presence of the influence of Satan, sick systems and your own sinful desires, be prepared to say, "I renounced this in baptism; I reaffirm that renunciation now." Invite Jesus into the situation, and receive his grace to walk in line with the Spirit instead.

7

We Reach Out for
All That Is from God

❦

Up to this point, the promises of baptism have been concerned with our turning *away* as we continue to strip off the old self. This is part of the process of dying with Christ, dying to "the futile ways inherited from your ancestors" (1 Pet 1:18). Now we look forward to consider what we are turning *to* as we walk toward newness of life.

> Do you turn to Jesus Christ and accept him as your Savior?
> Do you put your whole trust in his grace and love?
> Do you promise to follow and obey him as your Lord? (BCP, 302-3)

Looking away from the life that we led under the influence of "the world, the flesh, and the devil" (BCP, 149), we turn to Jesus—to *see* Jesus, and to see in him the image and character of God as love and justice. We determine to place our focus, our attention, our *intentions* on Christ and to say, "*this* is the direction I am going in the baptismal life *today*," each day, as long as we have a "today" (see Heb 3:13-15). The more Jesus fills our focus of vision, the less room there will be for those powers we have renounced to intrude on it again.

Savior has become such a familiar religious word that we can forget its power. A savior is a deliverer, a rescuer, someone who puts us out of the way of imminent and significant harm. To seek out a savior means that we recognize that our lives are in danger and need rescuing, and the renunciations we make at baptism well encapsulate the many dangers that beset us and threaten to drag us down with what the psalmists call "the cords of death" (Ps 18:4-5). Jesus rescues us from our sins and their consequences, providing for our reconciliation with God. Our new life is based on this reconciliation. Delivering his people from their sins is wrapped up in Jesus' very name (see Mt 1:21). God's cataclysmic confrontation with a world in rebellion against his rule is affirmed throughout the New Testament. Being "saved through [Jesus] from the wrath of God" as the provision of God's love is a dramatic feature of our rescue (Rom 5:8-9). We are, of course, not merely saved *from* disaster; we are also saved *for* an eternal life in the presence and favor of God, our heavenly homeland.

Jesus also rescues us from the sick and death-dealing systems of the world. Through his teaching *and* his example, he saves us from the diseased thinking that our value comes from having power over others or getting ahead of others, building our lives around destructive competition rather than cooperation and even serving others and getting "underneath" them to raise them up (see, again, Mk 10:35-45). Jesus rescues us from all that is destructive of relationships and community, and he introduces a new ethos that profoundly deepens relationships and community.

He does the same thing in regard to the diseased thinking that pervades us in regard to material gain and commodities. Possessions are not the stuff of life. We recognize this ourselves when we breathe with relief at the simplicity of life as we go for a walk with a loved one, play with a child or watch a sunset. Jesus tells us to stop masking our emptiness with possessions or pleasurable sensations. Rather, we are directed to seek God and God's justice in human relationships, since this alone will fill that emptiness, and he teaches us to put lives ahead of wealth and the acquisition of goods, spending what extra we have on hand now to relieve the pressing needs of others (see Mt 6:19-34).

And Jesus delivers us from the power of Satan, from the "spiritual forces of wickedness" that would keep us in bondage. The author of the letter to the Hebrews looks at this aspect of salvation as a new exodus: "He himself likewise shared [flesh and blood] so that through death he might destroy the one who has the power of death, that is, the devil, and free those who all their lives were held in slavery by the fear of death"

(Heb 2:14-15). Fear of death drives us to engage in futile attempts to defeat death and deny our own mortality. Sometimes this takes the form of becoming fixated upon making our mark, so as to give ourselves an illusion of permanence. Sometimes we gain for ourselves that illusion by building larger homes, acquiring more goods, displaying our wealth and significance. Sometimes we deflect our attention to trying to control our own lives and the lives of those around us. Fear of death binds us in slavish pursuits that can neither stave off death nor truly provide authentic or full enjoyment of what life we have. By dying and rising again, Jesus shows that the seeming finality of death is really an illusion, a smokescreen that Satan uses to keep us afraid of losing our lives—precisely so that we will not give them away and discover the fullness of life that God has for us in Christ!

When we affirm that we put our "whole trust in his grace and love," we acknowledge that Jesus is with us, invested in us, for the whole journey. His *grace* is his generosity, his desire and ability to help us extricate our lives from the tangle of the old person. He is disposed to give us all that is needed to enable us to become people who are wholly pleasing in God's sight, fully God's persons in this world, thinking and willing and doing his good pleasure. He invites us to "approach the throne of grace with boldness, so that we may receive mercy and find grace to help in time of need" (Heb 4:16).

His *love* involves the deep feeling for and commitment to a person that we naturally associate with the word, as when Jesus looked at the inquiring young rich man and "loved him," even as he issued the challenge that would turn the would-be disciple away (Mk 10:21-22). But his love is also his covenant loyalty *(hesed)*, his absolute commitment to us on this journey out from the power of darkness into his kingdom. If Jesus showed such love for us as to die on our behalf while we were yet unreconciled to God, what will Christ *not* do for us to make his death and resurrection effective for our lives, our transformation, our entrance into eternity (see Rom 5:10-11)?

Love and security—two of our most basic needs—are met here in Christ, enabling new life, free from the coping mechanisms and compensators that keep us bound to the old life and the evil powers that rule over it. Christ's grace and love enable, embolden and empower us to continue to live out our renunciations in the face of both internal resistance and the resistance we will inevitably encounter from others. Christ's love and grace are not withdrawn if we falter in this difficult journey. They remain the constant source of strength for rising again and setting out anew on the journey. As Thomas à Kempis writes, "If through weakness you sometimes fall, take greater strength than before and put your trust in My abundant grace."

The baptismal life also means embracing the lordship of this Jesus who saves us, loves us and upholds us. This third affirmation is perhaps the most difficult. Everyone wants someone to love them. No one would object to someone saving them. But who wants someone to tell them what to do or how to live? The baptismal examination in both its renunciations and affirmations is very much concerned with the questions "Who orders your life?" "Who sets the direction, the pace, the goals?" We might like to think of ourselves as our own masters, which is prized among our cultural ideals ("I'm my own boss"; "No one tells me what to do"). We are warned, however, that Satan, the systemic powers of human society and the sinful bent that pervades and perverts us are in fact our masters as long as we seek to preserve the illusion of running our own show.

The apostle Paul and his circle speak of a transfer from one master to another. God snatched us out from under "the power of darkness" so that we might become subjects in "the kingdom of his beloved Son" (Col 1:13). Once we were "slaves of sin" and now are set free from sin so that we may become "slaves of righteousness" (Rom 6:17-18). Paul does not doubt for a moment that we are at all times under the power of some force that is not "us." The only question is, will we be at the mercy of Satan, the world and the flesh, or will we place ourselves under the loving, shepherding hand of Jesus?

Jesus asks his would-be followers, "Why do you call me 'Lord, Lord,' and do not do what I tell you?" (Lk 6:46). The confession "Jesus is Lord" is empty if we are not willing to follow his commands and his promptings—that is, to do what he tells us! The promise we make for our baptismal life takes us frequently to the words of Jesus in the Gospels, where we can read fairly plainly what he tells us to do. It also leads us to train ourselves to become more sensitive to hearing his voice as he makes his leading known through the Holy Spirit (see Jn 14:25-26; 16:13-15).

PUTTING IT INTO PRACTICE

Enter into a time of adoration of our Lord. Use a hymn like "Jesus, the Very Thought of You," "Jesus, Lover of My Soul" or any other hymn or chorus that helps you to enter into an awareness of Christ's presence and to open yourself up to him. Ask for Jesus to open your eyes to more of his character and your heart to more of his love.

Converse with him about some of the things you have found challenging in the course of these spiritual exercises or reading, and ask for his help to continue to make progress in the life of the new person he is calling you to become. Read these words of Paul as though spoken to you: "I am confident of this, that the one who began a good work among you will bring it to completion by the day of Jesus Christ" (Phil 1:6).

Read some portions of Jesus' teachings. You might select part of the Sermon on the Mount in Matthew 5—7, the Sermon on the Plain in Luke 6, the teachings about wealth and discipleship in Luke 14 or part of Jesus' farewell discourse in John 13—17. Ask Jesus to help you see just how far you are *already* living in line with his instructions and how your thoughts, speech and action need to change in order to live *more fully* in line with his commands.

Particularly where his words provoke resistance in you, ask Jesus for grace to understand the source of this resistance, to see more clearly how he would have you embody his instruction, to trust the path that he shows and to honor his lordship by doing what he tells you (see Lk 6:46).

8

We Journey Together
Toward Christlikeness

❀

The baptismal life is not a solo venture. In the midst of these acts of renunciation and promises of adherence as individual Christ-followers, the baptismal liturgy directs our attention to our responsibility toward one another in Christian community in this ongoing process of turning away and turning toward.

Baptism assumes a corporate spirituality, in striking contrast to the tendency—even pressure—to privatize our faith and spirituality. The celebrant asks the gathered congregation, "Will you who witness these vows do *all* in your power to support [the baptized] in *their* life in Christ?" (BCP, 303). When the congregation answers "we will, with God's help," they pledge their investment of themselves in the spiritual formation of each newly baptized sister and brother. Where congregations embrace this level of investment, these acts become not only the duty we render our sisters and brothers, but also the gifts we receive from them as they invest themselves in our spiritual formation and our lives as well.

Writing in the mid-second century, Justin Martyr gives a fine illustration of the communal support that surrounded baptism itself: "As many as are persuaded and believe that the things we teach and say are true, and undertake to live accordingly, are instructed to pray and ask God with fasting for the remission of their past sins, *while we pray and fast with them.*" Those who prepare for baptism are already surrounded by the encouragement and support of the Christian community, who join with them in their preparation as a sign of the way in which they will continue to be involved in one another's spiritual journey toward maturity.

What would it look like for us to "do all in [our] power" to support one another in our life in Christ? First it involves doing no harm. Jesus warns us not to live in such a way as makes a fellow believer—particularly one more vulnerable in his or her faith—"stumble" (see Mt 18:6-7). Paul similarly cautions us against making use of our "freedom" in Christ or our "knowledge" about what is permitted to us in Christ in situations where it will cause others to act against their own conscience (1 Cor 8:1-13).

Do we work at being aware of the impact our speech and actions have on other believers, or do we insist on enjoying our own freedoms and rights? The so-called worship wars provide a case in point. Do we promote contemporary worship in ways that devalue the spirituality of those who continue to be fed by God through traditional hymnody? Or do we insist on the latter because we more highly value securing our own satisfaction and comfort than making room for others to explore alternative expressions of adoration? If people from more religiously conservative backgrounds visit our congregations, are we sufficiently sensitive to the religious culture in which they have been socialized (for example, cultures that stress abstaining from alcoholic beverages), or do we harbor—and communicate, however subtly—our disdain for their scruples and apply pressure to accommodate to our culture? These are but a few areas in which dying to self contributes to supporting others in the new life.

We are also encouraged to help one another identify ways in which the old self is hindering progress in newness of life. Jesus, Paul, the author of Hebrews, James and Jude all agree that we should come alongside a sister or brother who is not acting in line with the new life in the Spirit, help him or her examine the behavior and help restore him or her to the baptismal life (see, for example, Mt 18:10-15; Gal 6:1-2; 2 Thess 3:14-15; Heb 12:15-17; Jas 5:16, 19-20; Jude 22-23). We naturally shrink away from such responsibility toward one another, for fear that our observations will be angrily rejected and that we will come to be regarded as meddlers. We might also be inclined to resist such intervention by another Christian in our own lives. Nevertheless, since the role of the flesh, the world and the devil is to make us insensitive to our own descent into sin, it becomes all the more necessary for our Christian family to prompt our recognition of and repentance from the persistent old self.

We are charged with loving and serving one another, showing our love for Jesus by investing ourselves in tending his sheep (see Jn 13:12-17; 15:12-13; 21:15-17). This means caring for one another's physical and emotional needs, as well as spiritual. In the growing post-resurrection church, believers understood their call to care for the poor in their midst quite well. They helped them persevere in their spiritual journey by supplying what they needed to persist in their physical journey, especially their sisters and brothers who faced persecution because of their commitment to walk in their baptism (see Acts 4:32-35; Heb 13:3; 1 Jn 3:16-18).

The same spirit lives today in Christians around us. A widow whose children have grown up, finding herself with a lot of room in her house, began to open up her home to some foreign, female seminarians for only a share in the utility costs. She made real for them the promise of Jesus that his followers would find an abundance of homes, mothers and sisters (see Mk 10:29-30). A Christian businessman committed himself to keep in touch with several local pastors in Indonesia. When there was an outbreak of hostility against Christians there, he mobilized the resources they needed for medical help, for rebuilding in the wake of a violent pogrom and for subsistence until their means of production were restored.

In stark contrast to the contemporary stress on individualism and the boundaries between the private ("religious") and public (what "polite" people talk about with each other), Paul talks about the entire church—not just one congregation, but all congregations—as one entity, the "body of Christ." What each member is given, he or she is given for the sake of the support, nurture and edification of the entire organism (see 1 Cor 12:4-11). Each member is called to invest these gifts in one another "until all of us come . . . to maturity, to the measure of the full stature of Christ" (Eph 4:13). We do this as we "teach and admonish one another" in the wisdom we receive from God (Col 3:16), pray for one another, encourage one another and keep each other focused on our progress in "[walking] in newness of life" with reminders of our common faith and hope (Rom 6:4).

The voices that speak through the Scriptures agree. Congregational support—the personal investment of each member of a congregation in the other members—is essential for our growth in faith. Baptism is merely the beginning of a lifelong process of being conformed to Christ's self-giving death, a process in which we all must invest ourselves in one another, especially in the young-in-faith. We acknowledge that we perform the act of baptism in obedience to Christ's command, but this particular pledge reminds us of Jesus' full command, which is to "make disciples" not only by "baptizing" them but also by "teaching them to obey everything that I have commanded you" (Mt 28:18-20).

As we encourage one another, caution a sister or brother about some behavior observed, share our struggles against the old person or our excitement about the new person as it comes to life in fresh ways, and support one another in prayer, we give and receive the gifts God has given us in one another—the gifts of God we are to *be* to one another. As we join with one another in seeking God's word and serving together as he provides opportunities for bearing witness to his love in the world, we also discover deeper levels of Christian unity. Such unity arises most naturally as we move together in the same direction toward a common goal—the goal of Christlikeness, of dying to sin (Satanic, systemic and personal) and of embodying more and more of the new life in the Spirit. When our congregations reflect this level of generous and energetic investment in one another's lives, then we have done "all in [our] power."

PUTTING IT INTO PRACTICE

If you are using this book in the context of a group setting or if you are part of another group that would be open to this discussion, talk about experiences in which another Christian or group of Christians was instrumental in your spiritual growth, in your weathering of some spiritual or personal challenge, in your turning from a destructive path and the like. In what positive ways have other Christians made an impact on your spiritual vitality and development?

Talk together about the degree of sharing and accountability people in the group are comfortable with and why they might be so open, or open only so far. Perhaps lay out some ground rules that will allow for increased involvement, support and accountability in an atmosphere of safety and trust.

If you are not already part of a small group, think about the questions in the previous exercise, perhaps using your journal to record your thoughts. Think about how you might make a place in your life for more Christian communion (perhaps it would require creating opportunities for such interaction in your church, for example, through starting a small group for spiritual formation, study of Scripture and mutual prayer).

We Promise to Live Out Our Baptism in "Real Life"

❧

After reminding us of our own baptismal renunciations and affirmations, and of the communal matrix for living out the baptismal life, the baptismal service brings us to the renewal of our baptismal covenant. This takes the form of rededication to both faith and action, to both belief and practice, "for just as the body without the spirit is dead, so faith without works is dead" (Jas 2:26). On the one hand, we affirm what the "one holy catholic and apostolic Church" (BCP, 310) has held up as the essential content—and boundaries—of our reflections about God and his interventions in the world in the form of the Apostles' Creed. On the other, we commit ourselves afresh to particular actions that draw the parameters of a faithful response to those past, present and future acts of God affirmed in the creed.

In his discussion of the "Baptismal Covenant," an anonymous seventeenth-century Anglican theologian gave eloquent expression to this connection between professing and living the creed:

> Believing does not mean only consenting to the truth of the Creed, but also living like people who believe. Believing that God created us should lead us to give the service and obedience that creatures owe their creator. Believing that Christ redeemed us should make us give ourselves over to him as his purchase, to be used fully in his service. Believing in a judgment to come should make us careful so to live now that we will not be condemned in it. And believing in the life everlasting should lead us so to use our short time here that

our everlasting life may be a life of joy and not misery to us. Thus from every sentence of the Creed we are able to find the motivation for Christian practice.

At the heart of Christianity is a story about God's creative and redemptive activity. From the beginning of the church, Christians have sought direction and guidance for their response to God from this story, seeking to live in ways that are consistent with the story. "We know love by this, that he laid down his life for us." That much is story. "And we ought to lay down our lives for one another" (1 Jn 3:16). That is to live in line with the story of Jesus' giving of himself for us.

Our reaffirmation of belief in this story is followed by five vows. In the first of these, we pledge ourselves to a spiritual formation program, a body of spiritual disciplines that enable us to discover how to live in ways consistent with our beliefs and how to find strength in God and one another for persevering in those ways.

Will you continue in the apostles' teaching and fellowship, in the breaking of bread, and in the prayers? (BCP, 304)

The language of this vow comes from the description of the earliest Christian community in Acts: "They devoted themselves to the apostles' teaching and fellowship, to the breaking of bread and the prayers" (2:42). After their baptism, the converts' new life *together* in Christ becomes the new focal point for their lives.

Eager to learn more about Jesus and the new life, they make learning about the way of Christ a priority for their time and relationships. They hang out with those who hung out with Jesus. Twenty centuries later, this takes the form of reading Scripture, the repository of apostolic teaching, and then reflecting on Scripture with other believers. It also takes the form of hanging out with those who have spent significant time with Jesus, namely the spiritually mature who have traveled some time and some distance with Jesus and who can serve as spiritual mentors and friends ("the apostles' . . . *fellowship*"). In turn, as we mature in Christian faith, we, too, are called to offer this gift to sisters and brothers who are younger in

the faith. Recognizing the importance of this interpersonal dimension of
spiritual growth, the organization of United Methodist Men has adopted
the slogan "Have a mentor, be a mentor." They encourage disciples at all
times to learn from a spiritual friend and to offer themselves as spiritual
friends to others.

Eager for fellowship with Christ, the Christians frequently break the
bread, an act that has unmistakable eucharistic overtones even as early as
the composition of the book of Acts. The spirituality of the Eucharist
will occupy the next major section of this book. For now, let it suffice to
say that the baptismal life involves consistently receiving Christ's body
as "given for us," empowering us to give our lives for others for Christ's
sake ("serving Christ in all persons," as the fourth vow will express it
[BCP, 305]) as well as to confront the corrupting and debasing powers of
the world as Jesus did, leading him to *his* cross (as the fifth vow will call
us to do as well [BCP, 305]). This eagerness for fellowship with Christ
was accompanied by eagerness for joyful fellowship with one another (see
Acts 2:46: "they broke bread at home and ate their food with glad and
generous hearts"). Continuing "in the breaking of bread" calls us also to
strengthen and deepen our relationships with fellow Christians, building
intimacy through opening our homes to one another and making our
shared faith journey a focal point of conversation and binding feature of
our friendship.

Devoting themselves to "the prayers," the early Christians model the
desire for intimate communion with God, creating space for God to shape
them, speak to them, direct them and empower them. Making this space
and frequenting it often is essential to the fulfillment of the church's mission in the world, particularly in the face of the hostile forces we have
renounced (see Acts 4:23-31). In the setting of Acts, this would have
meant aligning themselves with the liturgical heritage of Judaism as they
gathered in the temple. This would have included praying the Psalms and
other traditional Jewish prayers. It would have also included praying in the
developing tradition of Christian prayer, especially the Lord's Prayer, but
also free intercessions on behalf of one another, both present and far away.
Paul attests, for example, to the Jerusalem church freely offering prayers

on behalf of believers in Greece (see 2 Cor 9:13-14). It would also have included, in Pauline circles at least, praying "in the Spirit" (my translation), a form of mystical, ecstatic prayer (see, for example, 1 Cor 14:15).

Praying the psalms, other Jewish liturgical prayers and the Lord's Prayer shaped their understanding of God's character and of their place in God. These prayers infused them with models of what to seek from God for themselves and for others, and provided a language that taught them how to approach God and open themselves up fully to him (see especially the often emotionally charged and embarrassingly honest language of the psalms). This, in turn, formed the channels in which the water of the Spirit could flow in extemporaneous intercession and even ecstatic prayer. The same benefits come from the thoughtful use of liturgical prayer today. The collects, the "Prayers of the People," the Lord's Prayer and other forms teach us what to desire and what to expect from God, give us language with which to approach him, and, through constant use, dig the spiritual aqueducts through which the living waters of the Spirit are released in our lives and in our prayers.

Taken together, these spiritual disciplines of study and meditation on Scripture, frequent sharing in the Eucharist and spiritual intimacy with one another in Christ-centered fellowship and with God in prayer become the means of grace for ourselves and for others in Christian community, so that we all make progress together in the baptismal life. They create the life matrix in which all the remaining vows become possible and fruitful.

From the second vow through the fifth, we pledge to live in ways that counter the forces we have renounced—our own sinful desires, the oppressive forces pervading our society and world, and the schemes of Satan.

> Will you persevere in resisting evil, and, whenever you fall into sin, repent and return to the Lord?
> Will you proclaim by word and example the Good News of God in Christ?
> Will you seek and serve Christ in all persons, loving your neighbor as yourself?
> Will you strive for justice and peace among all people, and respect

the dignity of every human being? (BCP, 304-5)

The second vow reminds us ever to walk in line with our renunciations and in particular to refuse to become comfortable again with sin. Rather, every time we recommit to this vow we are reminded of the importance of turning away from sin and back toward God's leading as soon as we become aware, or are made aware, of our straying from living the life of the new person. Our declaration that "we will" persevere in repentance and returning "with God's help" gives God permission to shake us up in this regard. Our success in keeping this vow will be proportional to our diligence in the spiritual disciplines. Spending time in the Word ("the apostles' teaching"), in prayer and in close and intimate fellowship with other Christians opens us up to discern when we have fallen into sin and to enjoy the support of the Spirit and other Christians as we move to repent and reorder our steps.

The baptismal life also involves us all in evangelism, proclaiming "by word and example the Good News of God in Christ." If Satan, the domination systems of the world and our sinful desires are busily promoting distorted views of the purpose of life and the ways to fulfill our core longings, those who are baptized are enlisted to tell the truth, and to tell it courageously. The Reverend Dr. D. T. Niles, Sri Lankan evangelist and one-time president of the World Council of Churches, penned the now-famous quotation "Evangelism is one beggar telling another beggar where he found bread." Evangelism need not be conceptualized as taking people down a prefabricated four-point path to salvation. It is, rather, our sharing with others what we have found in God, inviting others into our experiences of God's grace so that they, in turn, might have an opportunity to encounter more of God's grace.

We cannot make this good news known by word only, without the consistent display of attitudes and deeds that make our words credible. Neither can we make it known by example only, without the words that tell others what makes our attitudes and deeds possible and meaningful. Just as we do not pour water or lay out bread and wine without the words that make them sacraments, nor speak the words without the water, or bread and wine, that can be apprehended by our senses and bring the word into our flesh, so the witness of our lives combines word and visible sign. In this way, as we live out our baptism more and more, God makes our existence into sacramental lives that give those around us a means of grace to apprehend more of God.

The fourth vow guides us to consider how we will receive the people we come across today. Will we engage someone as long as it serves our pleasure or advances our goals? Will we neglect or dismiss other people as conducive to neither? Or will we receive them all as people whom God has brought into our path so that we might offer to Jesus some service by fulfilling his desires for them, insofar as opportunity permits? In a stunning vision of the last judgment, Jesus teaches that to give food, drink, clothing, shelter, welcome, companionship and care to the least esteemed members of the community is, in fact, to give it to Jesus, while to withhold the same is to withhold it from Jesus himself (see Mt 25:31-46). We have the opportunity day by day to give back to Jesus the love he lavished on us by receiving the person in need with the dignity, openness and love we would bestow on our unseen Lord.

John Wesley captured this facet of the baptismal life in his "Prayers for Daily Use":

> You have made all people in your own image, and each person is capable of knowing and loving you. Do not permit me to exclude any person from my loving care, but let me treat each person with that tender love and respect that is due all your children. . . . You established the worth of each human being by giving your precious blood for him or her: set the value you place on each person I shall meet today firmly before my eyes, and let me love as you have loved.

In approaching a person from this viewpoint, we counter whatever Satan, the world or our own flesh would say about that person and bear witness to God's truth about that person in our actions: the person before us is God's creation, so loved and valued by Christ that he died on that person's behalf to bring him or her into Christ's fellowship and the love of Christian believers. As we love thus more and more with Christ's love, we grow closer to the place where we can claim with Paul, "It is no longer I who live, but it is Christ who lives in me" (Gal 2:20), the place where we are well advanced on the journey to Christlikeness.

The fifth and final vow holds up before us our choices in regard to how we will encounter *systems* this day—the "evil powers of this world which corrupt and destroy the people of God" (BCP, 302). Will we live in the midst of them and even benefit from them? Or will we examine them, asking if they provide for the justice and peace of all people, or just for a privileged few? And if we subject them to such scrutiny, will we stand with Jesus and the prophets alongside those whose experience of justice and *shalom* is threatened or denied? Walking in newness of life includes investing ourselves beyond our interests and the interests of "our own," and looking out for the interests of those whose dignity is not being fully respected, whose enjoyment of God's gifts meant for all is being curtailed so that others may have more than is their due.

In sum, to live the baptismal life is to believe the story of what God is doing in the world and to walk in line with that story in every circumstance by seeking the justice and *shalom* of the kingdom of God. It is to live always with a view to reclaiming ourselves, our neighbors and our world from the "spiritual forces of wickedness" that have so long deceived, enslaved and ravaged God's creatures.

PUTTING IT INTO PRACTICE

What are your current, regular involvements in the spiritual formation disciplines suggested by the first of these five promises? (For example, do you regularly attend the worship of the congregation and the sacraments? Are you regularly involved in Christ-centered fellowship and acts of service?) How can you attend more fully to the spiritual disciplines in which you are currently involved (for example, to the hearing and contemplation of Scripture in the ministry of the Word within the regular services of worship)? How might your engagement with spiritual disciplines need to increase if you want to see more steady growth in the "new person"? Create a plan for yourself that you can try out for the coming month or quarter.

Review the day that is past in light of the second through fifth promises made at baptism. What opportunities were well used this day? Which were not? How could you have attended more fully to your baptismal vocation this day?

Now think about the coming day, as far as you can envision it. How can you approach the day's activities in a way that you will be attentive to your baptismal vows? What adjustments are you prepared to make in order to be faithful to God's agenda for your day where this might differ from your own agenda? How can you learn from the day that is past how better to use the coming day? Spend some time in prayer, thanking God for well-used opportunities, repenting for missed opportunities and asking for guidance and the Spirit's empowerment for the day to come.

10

A Sevenfold Prayer for
the Baptismal Life

※

The Book of Common Prayer appoints an elegant, sevenfold prayer
to be said over those who are about to be baptized or who are renewing
their baptismal commitment:

> Deliver them, Lord, from the way of sin and death.
> Open their hearts to your grace and truth.
> Fill them with your holy and life-giving Spirit.
> Keep them in the faith and communion of your holy Church.
> Teach them to love others in the power of the Spirit.
> Send them into the world in witness to your love.
> Bring them to the fullness of your peace and glory. (BCP, 305-6)

These petitions represent a logically unfolding, step-by-step process.
The first petition invites God to extricate those about to be baptized
from the old life matrix that has kept them bound to sin, sick systems
and death. The next three petitions ("Open . . . Fill . . . Keep") establish
the new life matrix for the nurture and growth of the new person. The
fifth and sixth petitions direct and enable ministry ("Teach . . . Send").
All these petitions together set those who are being baptized on the
course to their new destiny, the fullness of God's peace and glory, the
subject of the final petition ("Bring"). The baptismal life, however, also
involves constantly returning to each step of the spiritual process and
deepening our apprehension and embodiment of the same.

As these prayers represent the church's prayers on *our* behalf in our
baptism, we are invited to continue to pray them over ourselves again and

again until their substance is realized in us. It would be quite appropriate to incorporate them into a time of morning prayer, as we clothe ourselves afresh each day with the new person that we first put on in baptism. So used, they can orient us to engage each new day in a manner that is healthful for our own souls and for the good of others in the power of the Spirit, as we continue to strive to live out our baptism in newness of life.

The form of these prayers emphasizes God's actions on our behalf, not only at baptism, but throughout our lives as disciples. These petitions, like so many collects and other prayers in the BCP, proclaim our complete dependence on God for progress in discipleship and service. The rhythm of the verbs, falling on the strong beat of every petition, drums the action of God into our hearts and invites us to become more and more open to these ongoing actions of God on our behalf, delivering, opening, filling, keeping, teaching, sending and, through all of these combined, bringing us ever nearer our heavenly destiny. The more we return to these prayers, the more we invite these actions of God to become the rhythm of our lives, the cadence with which we fall increasingly in step each new day.

THE SEVENFOLD PRAYER AS A SPIRITUAL EXERCISE

Deliver me, Lord, from the way of sin and death. Jews and Christians have historically understood that there are two ways of doing things—God's way and the wrong way. At the climax of Deuteronomy, God declares to have "set before you life and death, blessings and curses," urging his people to "choose life, . . . loving the Lord your God, obeying him, and holding fast to him" (Deut 30:19-20) rather than the way that leads to death and curse. Toward the beginning of the second Christian century, the authors of the *Didache* and the *Epistle of Barnabas* both describe at length what it looks like to walk in "the way of life"—the way of the commandments of God and the teachings of Jesus—and "the way of death." The baptismal life is a constant dying to the way of death in which Satan, the systems of this world and our own sinful desires seek to confirm and enmesh us.

This petition holds ever before us our own threefold baptismal renunciations. The person who prays this prayer must be open to God's searching eye, as he makes us aware of how our ways intersect with "the way of sin" that kills abundant life. We pray with the psalmist, "Search me, O God, and know my heart; try me and know my restless thoughts. Look well whether there be any wickedness in me and lead me in the way that is everlasting" (Ps 139:23-24; BCP, 795). In response to God's probing, we must be willing to step out of the way of sin and death when the Holy Spirit convicts us, rather than trying to defend our involvement in that way. As part of the dying that precedes newness of life, this petition reminds us to be willing to die to our own desires, delights and dysfunctions for the sake of the new and abundant life God has for us as we follow him, firmly trusting that what he will give will exceed the pleasures or compensations of sinful behaviors.

Open my heart to your grace and truth. As we pray to be detached from the way of sin and death, we pray to find the fullness of what is ours in God. We ask to be opened up to the abundance of all that *God* has for us, knowing that this will satisfy our core longings and bring joy and fullness as our participation in the way of sin and death never could. We pray with Thomas á Kempis, "Let your love possess and raise me above myself, with a fervor and wonder beyond imagination." As we become more open to the gifts of God's favor, we *want* to leave behind the compensations of the way of sin and death more and more, so that we can experience more of the genuine and surpassing joy that comes from God. We also seek God's truth—about our heart, our affections, inclinations, desires, speech, actions (all in the context of God's gifts, gentleness and sustaining love, so that we can bear the truth and accept its implications). We ask to have our innermost person opened to God's truth about this world and our involvement in it, and about his good will for us in the context of what he wants to make of us, of his church and of his world, so that we can direct all our energies toward his designs.

Fill me with your holy and life-giving Spirit. In the context of baptism, being filled with the Holy Spirit is all about God coming to make his home within us, fulfilling his promise to "dwell" with his people (see Lev 26:11-12; Ezek 37:27; 2 Cor 6:16; Rev 21:3). The Holy Spirit, as we have already seen, is the presence and power of God within us to enable us to walk in newness of life. While we confess this Spirit to have been imparted in baptism, we pray daily to be continually refreshed in the Holy Spirit, even as Paul directed: *"Keep being filled* with the Spirit" (see Eph 5:18), be continually immersed anew in the Spirit so as to be able to want what pleases God *this* day, to be empowered for the new life *this* day, to have God's intimate companionship for the journey of *this* day, to experience the internal guidance of the Spirit *this* day and thereby to walk in the way of righteousness and life *this* day.

Keep me in the faith and communion of your holy church. As we pray this petition, we ask God to help us to keep talking to other Christians about our common faith and living it out in our shared circumstances. We ask God to keep us present in the praying, worshiping assembly and to open our eyes and minds to continue to discern new venues for, and new levels of, Christian intimacy and support. Remaining in "communion," or in Christian fellowship, is absolutely essential for perseverance and growth in the new life. Our fellow Christians keep reflecting back to us the character of the new life. Their enthusiasm is contagious. Their ability to discern our need and offer edifying support can be timely and life giving. Their awareness of God can rekindle our own when our vision of God has grown dim and our experience of his presence has grown cold. And, of course, it is the Christian community that keeps offering to us the means of grace to persevere (prayer, mutual support, the sacraments).

Teach me to love others in the power of the Spirit. As we consider the people whose paths we will cross this day, we pray that God would empower us to live out the mystery of "Christ in us." We pray to be empowered to love as Christ loved, to give ourselves as Christ gave himself, out of the fullness that we have received—and continue to receive—from God. Resting in God's presence, we ask to have our hearts so transformed that we will love the person God puts before us (or moves us to seek out) as God would have us love that person—not as, in our flesh, we might think it appropriate to respond to him or her (whether to disdain, disregard or love wrongfully). In the power of the Spirit and under the

Spirit's guidance, we pray that we will indeed seek the interests of others rather than our own (see Phil 2:4), for "when a person is self-seeking he or she abandons love."

Send me into the world in witness to your love. What is our purpose, our agenda, as we go out into the day ahead? Is it to get done the tasks we set for ourselves or that our job or situation imposes on us? Or is it, in the midst of all these and above all these, to connect people with the love of God by loving them in the power of the Spirit and inviting them to encounter God in the midst of their situation? The baptismal life calls us to take on, as our primary role, the office of ambassadors for Christ, taking the message of his self-giving for the life of the world out into our world by word and example.

Bring me to the fullness of your peace and glory. The final petition keeps before our eyes the "imperishable, undefiled, and unfading" inheritance that is ours in Christ (I Pet I:4), the fullness of the kingdom of God, where the light of God and the Lamb illumines our whole existence and the just reign of God makes perfect community possible. It reminds us where we are headed and therefore helps us to keep training our desires on God's promises, so that we will in fact arrive at our eternal destiny. It invites the Spirit to give us foretastes of that fullness, to whet our appetites and center our desires on God. The more that this petition reflects the undivided desires of our hearts, the more we will find integrity of faith and life.

Regular engagement of some foundational spiritual disciplines will also greatly help us to move toward the realization of these prayers. In particular, as we read Scripture we grow in our awareness of the particulars of "the way of sin and death" (confronting our own blind spots), our recognition of God's "grace and truth" and our insight into how to "love . . . in the power of the Spirit" (BCP, 305). As we meditate and pray over Scripture, we move from *informational* mode to a more *formational* mode, allowing God to bring home what we most need to hear, to open us up to what we most need to experience of him and to give us specific guidance concerning how he will "send [us] into the world in witness" (BCP, 306).

Christian community and conversation provides a third essential discipline. Other Christians can discern the way of sin and death at work in our lives in ways that we do not allow ourselves to see, as well as help us to see God's grace active in our lives. Our experience of being filled with God's "holy and life-giving Spirit" is sustained and deepened in concert with other Christians with whom we seek God's presence and guidance. And, of course, the church is the place where, at its best, we love and are loved in the power of the Spirit and where we discover our individual and collective call to witness and mission. The sevenfold baptismal prayer can be used to give focus to our engagement in these three spiritual disciplines, even as these disciplines will give depth and effectiveness to our efforts to allow God's full work to take place within us.

PUTTING IT INTO PRACTICE

Set aside some time each morning (if possible) to pray through the seven petitions of this baptismal prayer, substituting *me* for *them, my* for *their.* Pause after each petition. Allow God to direct your thoughts and to lead you into further contemplation and prayer on each point as God brings specific impressions or words or people or situations before you. You may wish to write down in your journal what you are shown and your prayers in response. Don't move on to the next petition until you are ready—or until the Spirit is ready! Continue this exercise each morning, as long as you find it useful. You may wish to return to the practice in special seasons.

Write the seven petitions on a small card that you can carry with you. Pray these petitions at various times throughout the day, pausing per-haps only a few seconds after each. Be attentive to and expectant of the impressions and leading that the Spirit gives.

Gather with your group for a time of worship, opening prayer and a reading of a passage from Scripture. Then spend some time individually reading through the passage alongside the seven petitions, meditating on any insights that arise from the Scripture text in regard to any number of the petitions, as the Spirit leads. What does the passage say about "the way of sin and death"? What does it say about what it looks like to "love . . . in the power of the Spirit?" (and so forth). Pray over these insights, and ask God how to apply them. (*This exercise is best done if you are part of a group exploring this book together, whether in the context of a regular class or small group, or with a "faith friend." You may, of course, adapt it for individual use.*)

At a predetermined time, come back together as a group and share with one another what you have learned through, or how you have been affected by, prayer and meditation on the Scripture text. What do you learn from one another's insights? Share with one another what one thing has arisen from this exercise that God impresses on you as the most important matter for prayer. Conclude by praying the sevenfold petition together (using *us*), the Lord's Prayer and for one another's specific prayer concerns.

PART TWO

Holy Eucharist

Nourishment for the New Life

II

Encountering Jesus in the Eucharist

If baptism charts the course for our journey, the Eucharist, or Holy Communion, provides our nourishment for the journey. In the Eucharist, God provides spiritual refreshment and empowerment to sustain us in our exodus from sin and from the corrupting powers of this world, even as God sustained the Hebrews throughout their wilderness wanderings in their own exodus from Egypt.

> Shepherd of souls, refresh and bless thy chosen pilgrim flock
> with manna in the wilderness, with water from the rock.

In terms of physical nourishment, coming to the altar to receive a small piece of bread and a sip of wine or grape juice does very little, if anything, for us. But, received as spiritual nourishment, it is "the health of soul and body, the cure of every spiritual malady. By it, our vices are cured, our passions restrained, temptations are lessened, grace is given in fuller measure, and virtue once established is fostered; faith is confirmed, hope is strengthened, and love kindled and deepened." All that we commit to do in our baptism, Holy Communion nurtures and empowers. It is no wonder, then, that spiritual directors in the Anglican tradition have consistently recommended the "frequent receiving" of Communion as "the most effective means of growing in grace."

It is not the simple act of receiving bread and wine, of course, that provides such a remarkable litany of spiritual benefits, but receiving the promises and gifts of God that have been joined to this bread and this wine, and, in particular, the intimate contact with Jesus that the rite facilitates. In this and the following four chapters, we will explore the meaning of Holy Communion through the various lenses held up to it by the liturgies of the Book of Common Prayer, so that we will be able to savor the sacrament more completely and receive all that God would give to us by this means of grace. In the remaining chapters in this section, we will explore the spiritual disciplines that the eucharistic liturgies invite us to practice and the ways in which each discipline contributes to our fulfillment of our baptismal covenant.

THE NEW COVENANT

The most consistent feature of the celebration of the Eucharist throughout the Christian church is the recitation of the words of institution:

> On the night he was handed over to suffering and death, our Lord Jesus Christ took bread; and when he had given thanks to you, he broke it, and gave it to his disciples, and said, "Take, eat: This is my Body, which is given for you. Do this for the remembrance of me." After supper he took the cup of wine; and when he had given thanks he gave it to them, and said, "Drink this, all of you: This is my Blood of the new Covenant, which is shed for you and for many for the forgiveness of sins. Whenever you drink it, do this for the remembrance of me." (BCP, 362-63)

The words of institution represent a harmonization of the various accounts of Jesus' speech over the bread and the cup at the Last Supper in Matthew, Mark and Luke, as well as in I Corinthians. In all four versions Jesus is remembered to have invested the pouring out of his blood with the significance of covenant, further specified as the "new Covenant" ("covenant": see Mt 26:28; Mk 14:24; "new covenant": see Lk 22:20; I Cor 11:25).

The phrase "new covenant" looks back to Jeremiah 31:31-34, the only passage in the Hebrew Scriptures to use the expression. There God promises to "make a new covenant with the house of Israel and the house of Judah." This will differ from the first covenant in that God will "put [his] law within them, and . . . write it on their hearts," and is accompanied by the promise that God "will forgive their iniquity, and remember their sin no more." Early Jewish readers understood this as a promise that God's commandments, laid out under the "old" covenant given to Moses, would be so deeply internalized by God's people that obedience would be natural and instinctive. It would be more of a renewal of the old covenant rather than a truly *new* covenant.

The author of the epistle to the Hebrews, however, understood this prophecy to announce a decisively new act on God's part that would forever change the way his people would relate to him. First and foremost, the new covenant involved a sacrifice of a different order than anything prescribed under the old covenant. Where the "blood of bulls and goats" (Heb 10:3-4) offered in the annual rite of the Day of Atonement provided a sacrifice that, in effect, amounted to nothing more than an ongoing reminder of the sins that kept the people at a distance from a holy God, the Son of God now provides his own blood as a unique, decisive atonement offering that would completely cleanse the consciousness of God's people and remove the very memory of sin from both the people and the holy God, fulfilling the promise of Jeremiah 31:34.

Jesus' death changes God's perception of us, as well as our perception of our own standing before God. As we receive the bread and the wine, we appropriate afresh the promise that God will "unite us with [his] Son in his sacrifice" and make us "acceptable through him" (BCP, 369). The words of institution assure us, speaking of the cup as the "new Covenant . . . for the forgiveness of sins" (BCP, 368) that God's promise is made real for us: "I will . . . remember their sins no more" (Jer 31:33-34, as quoted in Heb 8:12). We can enter God's presence—now in prayer and worship, hereafter for eternity—with full confidence of being accepted by God and finding favor with him.

The second major component of the new covenant concerns God putting his law in our hearts. For the early Christians, this was the role fulfilled by the Holy Spirit, God's promised gift that would enable his people to discern his instruction in the doing of his will day by day (see Jn 14:26; 16:12-13; 1 Jn 2:20-21, 27) and to fulfill the just requirements

of the law (see Rom 8:2-4). The promise of the new covenant gives us
the assurance that God will indeed supply all that is necessary for us to
enter into and walk consistently in "newness of life" (BCP, 393) as we
follow the leading of the Holy Spirit that God has sent into our hearts.

❋❋❋❋❋❋❋❋❋❋❋❋❋❋❋❋❋❋❋❋❋❋❋❋❋❋❋❋❋❋

PUTTING IT INTO PRACTICE

Reflect on your experiences of Holy Communion. When has it been
a particularly meaningful experience for you? What was the setting?
What impressions did you form as you participated in the liturgy and
received the elements? What did you take away with you?

Go to a place that is conducive to your being aware of God's presence.
Spend some time centering yourself on God. How do you feel about
being here? Are you comfortable in God's presence? Are you troubled
and uncomfortable?

Read Hebrews 9:24-28. Visualize Jesus offering you the bread and
the wine, telling you that he is making everything right between you
and God. Visualize Jesus offering himself on the cross, a gift *to* God to
atone for your sins, a gift *from* God to assure you that God loves you and
doesn't want anything to stand between the two of you. See Jesus entering into God's eternal realm, to sit at God's right hand as a constant
reminder to you and to God that nothing stands between you. Invite
God's Spirit to let you see yourself in God's presence as God sees you—
cleansed, made new, basking in his favorable acceptance.

Read Hebrews 10:19-22. Come back often to this place with God.

12

Remembering

❧

The act of remembering Jesus' giving of himself to us and for us is so important that it is given repeated attention in the words of institution both as found in the New Testament and as used in Communion liturgies. "This is my body, which is given for you. *Do this in remembrance of me*" (Lk 22:19, emphasis added). "This cup is the new covenant in my blood. *Do this*, as often as you drink it, *in remembrance of me*" (1 Cor 11:25, emphasis added).

We fix our gaze on Jesus' self-giving as one of the principal compass points by means of which we chart our course toward newness of life. The author of 2 Peter gives eloquent expression to the importance of remembering from what and for what we have been cleansed by Jesus' self-giving death. It is God's means of inviting us into "life and godliness," of communicating "his precious and very great promises," by means of which we escape "the corruption that is in the world because of lust, and may become participants of the divine nature." It is an invitation into a life of growing in faith, goodness, knowledge, self-control, endurance, godliness, mutual affection and love. Neglecting the new life offered to us, however, shows us to be "nearsighted and blind, and . . . forgetful of the cleansing of past sins" (2 Pet 1:3-9). Remembering that we have been cleansed of past sins means that we will not so casually allow ourselves to fall back into the ruts of the old person. Jesus died so that we would leave those well-worn paths behind.

At the climactic moment of the breaking of the bread, the celebrant declares that "Christ our Passover is sacrificed for us" and invites us to "keep the feast" (BCP, 364, reciting 1 Cor 5:7-8). As our passover

Lamb, Jesus dies to break the power of our captors—sin, death and Satan—so that we may live a life beyond their oppressive rule over us. But just as the Hebrews forgot the darkness of their lives in Egypt and longed to return to their bondage during their journey to the Land of Promise, so we stand in danger of returning to the life of our old self, unless we remember from what, and at what cost, Christ freed us.

Remembering also ensures that we will keep focused on *responding* gratefully to the provisions Jesus has gained for us "for life and godliness" (2 Pet 1:3) by making full use of those provisions. Every time we return in the sacrament to the story of Jesus' giving of himself for us, the answer to the question "How then shall we live?" is clarified. We shall live in such a way as honors Jesus' costly love for us and death on our behalf. We will live in such a way as moves us forward into the life with God that was Jesus' goal for us as "he stretched out his arms upon the cross" (BCP, 362).

Forgetting is the great danger to our souls. Forgetting is precisely the aim of the world, the flesh and the devil, as they seek to fill our consciousness with their distractions and clamor, so that we will respond to these rather than to Jesus in his self-giving love. The simple act of remembering—and remembering often—stands at the foundation of our ongoing spiritual formation

❋❋❋❋❋❋❋❋❋❋❋❋❋❋❋❋❋❋❋❋❋❋❋❋❋❋❋❋❋

PUTTING IT INTO PRACTICE

Set out bread and a small amount of wine (or dark grape juice, if you prefer) to serve as a visual reminder of the Eucharist. When you see it, thank Jesus for his love and his giving of himself for you, to open the way for you to newness of life. Ask Jesus, "How would you have me show here, this day, that I remember my cleansing from past sins?"

Throughout the week, remind yourself of the words of institution whenever you pick up a piece of bread to eat or lift a glass of wine to drink: "My Body, which is given for you"; "My Blood of the new

Covenant, shed for you and for many for the forgiveness of sins" (BCP, 362-63). As you practice this, in what ways do you notice that simply remembering shapes your attitudes, feelings and actions?

13

The Host Who Is the Feast

❋

The sacrament is more than a memorial of Jesus' inauguration of the new covenant. We come to the altar not only to *remember* Jesus, but also to *encounter* Jesus. We become present to Jesus and his self-giving love on the night before his passion, while Jesus becomes present to us in our churches as we, too, gather around a table. In Holy Communion, the two horizons merge.

The fact that the Last Supper was a *Passover* meal is significant. We remember Jesus' self-giving in the bread and the wine in much the same way that pious Jews remember God's acts of deliverance in the Passover and exodus. The annual celebration of Passover involved telling the story of their ancestors' deliverance over the sharing of flat bread, roasted lamb and bitter herbs, which gave each person the opportunity to "regard himself or herself as if he or she also came forth from Egypt." Generation after generation, practicing Jews experience that foundational event not as distant viewers, but as participants, saying, "*We* were slaves in Egypt." *They*, and not just their ancestors, were delivered by God from slavery in Egypt. It is with *them* that God has made a covenant. *They* must now respond faithfully to God as those who have experienced God's deliverance.

In a similar fashion, when we tell the story of Jesus' giving of himself to his disciples and share bread and wine, we become present with Jesus on the night on which he gave himself. The words of institution transport us back to the place where Jesus offers himself to his disciples. We share the table with the Lord acting as our host, breaking bread and offering wine, creating fellowship over the sharing of food. Now Jesus is offering the bread and the cup to *us* who gather around the table of the altar. Jesus holds out the bread and the cup to us, and says to us, "My Body, given for you; my Blood, shed for you," allowing us to receive and appropriate for ourselves that enormous expression of love. The celebrant speaks of how Jesus "stretched out his arms upon the cross" (BCP, 362), extending his or her arms in front of the congregation so that we might better visualize and grasp Jesus reaching out to us. Even though we were not present in body at the crucifixion, we grasp that we were present in Jesus' heart, intentions and embrace—an embrace we experience in the sacrament.

We do not simply remember, then, that Jesus died for his disciples, who were gathered in that upper room, or "for many" in general. Rather, we take the bread, hearing "Christ died for *you*," for *you* in particular, for *me* in particular. We lay aside "all thoughts of bread and wine and minister and everything else that is or can be seen" in order to see Jesus "offering us his own body and blood to preserve our bodies and souls to everlasting life."

The layers of mystery continue, however, as our host, to whom we have become present, becomes the feast. Each layer brings us into closer and closer connection with Jesus, from sitting at the table with him to the mystical taking of Christ into our very selves. In John's Gospel, Jesus is remembered to have said:

> I am the living bread that came down from heaven. . . . Those who eat my flesh and drink my blood have eternal life, and I will raise them up on the last day. . . . Those who eat my flesh and drink my blood abide in me, and I in them. (Jn 6:51, 54, 56)

Read by Christians who practiced the Eucharist, these words became an early commentary on the sacrament as one means by which we maintain and deepen our connection with Jesus, "in [whom] was life" (Jn 1:4) and from whom we receive the eternal life promised here. Jesus' words about eating convey very powerfully the level of intimacy he seeks with us. The physical connection established in sexual intercourse pales by comparison to the physical connection established by this mystical eating, whereby we take Christ fully into ourselves and whereby he becomes part of us (just as we say that "we are what we eat").

Jesus attaches the promise that he will abide in us and we in him to the visible and outward sign of eating this bread and this wine (see Jn 6:56). Jesus does not simply come to be "with us" in the sacrament. He comes to infuse us with himself, to take on flesh anew in us as his body, the church, to so unite us with himself as to bring us at last to the point where we can say with Paul, "It is no longer I who live, but it is Christ who lives in me" (Gal 2:20).

❋❋❋❋❋❋❋❋❋❋❋❋❋❋❋❋❋❋❋❋❋❋❋❋❋❋❋❋❋

PUTTING IT INTO PRACTICE

Attend a celebration of Holy Communion at your earliest opportunity (in addition to Sunday Eucharist, there may be weekday services of Communion in your vicinity). Allow yourself to experience the immediacy of Jesus' offering himself to you as the minister speaks the words of institution and offers you the bread and the cup.

The practice of "spiritual communion" was often recommended to those who were unable, for one reason or another, to attend the Eucharist. Center yourself with a time of quiet, focusing on Jesus. Read again the text from John quoted above. Pray: "Lord Jesus, I want to abide in you, and have you abide in me, more fully. Let me receive your flesh and blood spiritually into my heart and life. Infuse me with your Spirit; live in me; live through me." Remain in the moment, alert to the Spirit's prompting.

14

A Family Meal

❋

So far, we have focused mainly on our connection with Jesus in the sacrament. Indeed, this is a place where some people are most comfortable and beyond which they will not go. I remember talking with a friend about the almost nonexistent level of interaction between parishioners at a Communion service at her church. She remarked that she liked it that way. She could just come to the service, concentrate on God and leave undisturbed.

But there is another dimension to the Eucharist that we dare not neglect—the other people around the table. Holy Communion is an expression not only of our being joined inwardly to Christ, but also of our being knit together with one another into the *people* of the new covenant. Brian Wren captures this in his Communion hymn "I Come with Joy":

As Christ breaks bread and bids us share,
each proud division ends.
The love that made us makes us one,
and strangers now are friends.

Or, as Paul expressed the same truth, "Because there is one bread, we who are many are one body, for we all partake from the one bread" (I Cor 10:17). The unity of the loaf—which is Christ—remains intact, no matter how widely he is distributed in the bread and the cup. As we receive Christ into ourselves one-by-one in Communion, we are bound up together into a larger, unifying reality, namely the body of Christ. As Christ takes on flesh and blood in each one of us, he takes on flesh and blood in *all* of us collectively, unifying us into a single body.

This means that there can be no private Communion, no receiving of Christ without receiving one another as sisters and brothers who have also taken Christ's life into their lives. The way Paul addresses an abuse of Holy Communion in Corinth is instructive in this regard. The Corinthian Christians celebrated the Lord's Supper (as Paul calls it) in such a way that the social divisions between rich and poor, leisure class and working class, were reflected in the church's gathering. Instead of promoting unity and reflecting everyone's status as "new creation" in Christ, all sons and daughters of the Most High, their practice of the Eucharist tended to reinforce the divisions that were already present in the "old creation" of human society (I Cor 11:20-22).

If we participate in the Lord's Supper without having regard for *everyone* around the table, in any manner whatsoever suggesting that we are comfortable with the human-made barriers that separate us from one another, we violate the sacrament at its core. Paul warned that whoever "eats the bread or drinks the cup of the Lord in an unworthy manner will be answerable for the body and blood of the Lord" (I Cor 11:27-29). Disciples must "discern the body" in order to receive the bread and the cup to their advantage rather than judgment. Eating and drinking worthily or unworthily here is not a matter of our private consciences and preparation, but of our openness to the Spirit's desire to knit us more closely together with our sisters and brothers in Christ around the worldwide table of the Eucharist. "Discerning the body" is not about understanding that Christ is in the bread, but that Christ through the bread is in all those who share in the Eucharist, and Christ cannot be divided against himself.

I have occasionally lost sight of this spiritual truth. In two instances, I found myself in escalating conflicts with a fellow New Testament scholar and an editor. The details are not important, only that both conflicts reflected equally strong egos affirming themselves by beating down the opponent. Graciously, God intervened. In one case, it was through persistent dreams of reconciliation; in the other, through a more immediate impression made by the Spirit. The message of each intervention was that my "antagonist" and I were both *in Christ*, both fed by the same spiritual food and nourished by the same spiritual drink. We could not, therefore, persist in looking at one another through the lens of conflict, but must look through the sacramental reality that we were part of Christ's body and were bound to honor, even love, one another. In God's sight, the actual issues under dispute were not important. The fact that we lost sight of each other as part of one body, was.

❋❋❋❋❋❋❋❋❋❋❋❋❋❋❋❋❋❋❋❋❋❋❋❋❋❋❋❋❋❋

PUTTING IT INTO PRACTICE

Think about the people in, and visitors to, your church. How are people treated? Are any made to feel that they are less welcome or prized than others? Are there ways in which the church might need to adapt its schedule (for example, if the congregation or community has a number of third-shift workers) or manner of celebrating the Eucharist so as to put the body first and convenience or preferences second? Share your reflections with the leadership and be ready to take the lead in developing a new outreach.

When you next have opportunity to participate in the Eucharist, pay attention to each person in the congregation (as fully as possible), particularly as each is receiving Communion. Ask God to open your heart more and more to each person, especially those toward whom you have some aversion. If you sense any prejudice in your heart or rivalry or unforgiveness, confess this to God and ask him to help you release whatever in you threatens the unity of the body. Ask God to allow your shared experience of receiving Christ into yourselves to become an ever-stronger impetus toward solidarity and love.

15

An Appetizer

❀

In the Eucharist we look back upon Christ's giving of himself for us as a past event. We become present to him, offering himself to us in the present moment. But we also look forward to the consummation of Christ's self-giving, when his death for the life of the world will have had its full effect.

Jesus pointed in this direction at his last supper with his disciples. After offering them the cup, he announced, "Truly I tell you, I will never again drink of the fruit of the vine until that day when I drink it new in the kingdom of God" (Mk 14:25). Paul kept this focus alive, reminding his converts that "as often as you eat this bread and drink the cup, you proclaim the Lord's death until he comes" (1 Cor 11:26). The loaf is broken up and distributed to the members of the church in every place, uniting them in Christ. But those members, now scattered throughout the world and throughout time, will yet be gathered up and brought together in the future, the "loaf" of Christ's body restored to perfect unity and wholeness in the future kingdom of God.

Therefore we, too, continue to proclaim our hope in the context of the Great Thanksgiving. We look backwards: "Christ has died; Christ is risen." But we also look forward: "Christ will come again" (BCP, 363).

The author of 2 Peter, who had pointed his readers back to their "cleansing from past sins" (see 2 Pet 1:3-11) hence Jesus' death on their behalf, as the first compass point by which to chart their course forward, regarded this consummation as the other compass point. Knowing that God is bringing the present world order to an end, we are given the privilege of being forewarned and therefore of preparing to be welcomed into God's "new heavens and a new earth, where righteousness is at home" by "leading lives of holiness and godliness," seeking "to be found by him at peace, without spot or blemish," finding our "stability" in this life by growing in the new life of Christ (2 Pet 3:11-14, 17-18). Looking back to our cleansing from sin impels us forward to grow in grace and equip ourselves with all the virtues God seeks to nurture within and among us; looking ahead to Christ's final victory draws us forward on the same trajectory.

If we keep taking our bearings from these two compass points each day, we will enjoy stability in our discipleship and not be thrown off course. We will not be duped into investing our energies, our resources, indeed our very lives in building our own little kingdoms on earth that are destined by God to come to nothing, but will spend our time wisely now, investing ourselves in what will endure into the eternity of God's kingdom.

One of most poignant images of the heavenly banquet, of which Communion is a foretaste, is found in Revelation 19. The "marriage supper of the Lamb" (Rev 19:6-9) celebrates the union of the victorious Christ with his bride, the church, perfected at last through much trial and testing. In that consummation, the presence of God permeates and illumines all spaces, private and public, and all people walk by his light, seeing everything clearly in the light of God and of the Lamb. Wealth is no longer seen to be more valuable than the *shalom* and dignity of each and every person. The quest to gain power over others is laughable, as we walk together in the light of the Servant Messiah. The distractions of the empty, fleetingly pleasurable sensations to which we so often turn in the dark, private spaces of life are unthinkable when we can drink our fill from the living waters and experience fulfillment to the depths of our souls. The gates of the city are never shut (see Rev 21:25), for every division between an "us" against a "them" has been overcome, and all the nations—who for so long have ravaged each other in the quest for "national security" and "the preservation of our way of life"—can experience healing under God's gentle hand (see Rev 22:2).

But the invitation to the marriage supper of the Lamb, the

consummation of the Eucharist, comes only to those who respond to an earlier invitation, calling God's people out of Babylon: "Come out of her, my people, so that you do not take part in her sins, and so that you do not share in her plagues; for her sins are heaped high as heaven, and God has remembered her iniquities" (Rev 18:4-5). For John, "Babylon" was Rome, the city that had managed to dominate the entire Mediterranean by means of diplomatic partnerships and, where that failed, brutal military action; the city that reorganized the world's manufacturing and trade for the sake of its elite's endless enjoyment of luxury goods from across the provinces; the city that fostered famine in the provinces by encouraging the overproduction of goods for export and then was hailed for its beneficence when it sent famine relief to those same provinces; the city that spread its worship of the goddess Roma Aeterna, in concert with the worship of the emperors, across the Mediterranean, seducing city after city to believe in the myth of its own eternity and divinely given role as bringer of law, peace and prosperity to the whole world. Those who hoped to share in the marriage supper of the Lamb—indeed, to be married to the Lamb as part of the bride, the church—could not continue to get in bed with the great harlot.

Babylon has had many faces since Rome, even as she had many before Rome. She continues to take on flesh as nation after nation holds onto the ways of domination systems (see chapter six) rather than heed the voices of the prophets, Jesus and the apostles. Babylon thrives through our ongoing failure of trust. We hold on to violence as a means of ensuring peace, because we don't trust God to show us a better way, a less costly way. We hold on to the amassing of capital because we don't trust God's provision for tomorrow. We hold on to our gender or ethnic biases, because we don't trust God to give us a sense of identity and worth in a world without hierarchies or divisions.

John's message is clear. Looking ahead to the marriage supper of the Lamb means letting go of our grasp on Babylon—and Babylon's hold on us! It requires an act of trust. Feasting at the Lord's table means fasting from other tables. As Paul warned his converts that they could not share the table of the Lord and the table of demons (see

I Cor 10:21), John warned that we cannot feast on the fruits reaped by the domination systems that oppose God's vision for human community, that seek to forestall God's consummation, and then expect to celebrate that consummation. Our feasting at the Communion table calls us to fast from the tables spread out with the fruits of injustice in witness to our hope in and commitment to the coming messianic banquet.

PUTTING IT INTO PRACTICE

What is your understanding of the affirmation "Christ will come again"? How do your expectations of the last things (whether in your own story or in the story of the kingdoms of the world) shape your priorities for the here and now? In what ways do you find yourself *not* living in line with your convictions about ultimate things?

Center yourself on God and reflect on those good things that Holy Communion anticipates: walking in the light of God and the Lamb; the gathering of all Christ's own from every nation, language and denomination into a community of justice and peace; the healing of the nations. In what ways are you now walking in line with these values? What specific things might you do to make more room in your life for advancing these ends?

Spend some time in prayer. Ask God to reveal to you the ways in which you are sharing in the fruits of Babylon's table and holding on to the false beliefs that ultimately undergird domination systems. These might include

- "I can be safe only if I am more powerful."
- "I can never have enough to be truly safe from want."
- "I will be happy if I have more."
- "We have more wealth and more power because we are superior and more suited to dominate."

- "Other people and the earth's resources exist for my pleasure and to serve my agendas."

From what does God ask you to fast, in order that you may feast more fully at the table of the Lord and be free to take more of Christ's life into yourself?

16

Self-Examination and Confession

❦

The next eleven chapters explore the ways in which the eucharistic liturgies of the Book of Common Prayer nurture the habits of three essential spiritual disciplines: self-examination and confession of sin (chapters sixteen through eighteen); prayer and intercession (chapters nineteen through twenty-two); and worship (chapters twenty-three through twenty-six). Together with the meditative reading of Scripture, these form the core practices by means of which we invite the Holy Spirit to fully realize our death to the old self and our quickening to the life of the new person.

People from many different cultures and religious traditions have recognized, almost instinctively, that the presence of the divine is powerful, full of the potential for blessing, but also the potential for harm. Because of this, they have paid particular attention to making sure they approach the divine "correctly," in a condition that will not offend God or the gods. Before coming into the presence of the Holy, people have tended to cleanse themselves of anything they felt might jeopardize a healthful encounter with the Holy, so that they would enjoy the benefits of a favorable encounter with the divine.

Early Christians believed that the Holy God was most concerned about purity of life in terms of ethics. Our thoughts, desires and actions should be in line with what God wants for us and for human community. Where we are out of alignment, purification involves naming those aspects of our lives that are not in line with God's wishes as an act of dissociating ourselves—cleansing ourselves—from those defilements. The process of purification continues as we seek henceforth to reflect

God's holy character, desires and purposes more and more closely.

The Book of Common Prayer stands firmly in this tradition, pointing the way to the Lord's table through the gate of penitence. The two rites for celebrating Holy Communion are preceded both by "An Exhortation" to self-examination (BCP, 316-18) and two "Penitential Orders" (BCP, 319-21, 350-53). These direct our attention to the need to examine our lives for ways in which we have sinned against God *and* fallen out of walking in love with our neighbors. These resources are typically engaged only in Advent and Lent, the traditional seasons of penitence and preparation. Nevertheless, their presence in the BCP as prologue to both eucharistic rites serves as a constant reminder that the invitation to reach out for the new life that God offers at the Lord's table is also a summons to root out all that contradicts that new life within us.

You have already been exposed to several exercises in self-examination and confession in the section on baptism. Our baptismal vows, prayers and Scriptures about the old person in contrast with the new have served as vehicles for reflecting on our progress on the journey toward Christlikeness. In this and the following two chapters we will explore how the eucharistic liturgies further nurture these disciplines.

THE COLLECT FOR PURITY

Even if the Exhortation and formal Penitential Orders are rarely used, the eucharistic liturgies themselves begin with a brief prayer inviting God's searching and cleansing, called the "Collect for Purity":

> Almighty God, to you all hearts are open, all desires known, and from you no secrets are hid: Cleanse the thoughts of our hearts by the inspiration of your Holy Spirit, that we may perfectly love you, and worthily magnify your holy Name; through Christ our Lord. (BCP, 355)

A constant part of the Eucharist since 1549, this prayer lays an essential foundation for the work of cleansing that is prerequisite to our approaching God here in the sacrament and hereafter in eternity. It is an opening collect not only in that it begins the service, but more profoundly in that it invites us to open ourselves up to God as we enter the liturgy.

The focal point of the collect is "the thoughts of our hearts"—who we are and what we entertain in our most private selves. We have to learn how to let God into this place, to prune, tend and cultivate. The basic problem of our existence is a polluted, divided heart. We try now to serve God and later to serve Mammon (our greed and drive for self-gratification). We want to do the good, but are drawn to what harms and debases ourselves and others. In the words of James, we are "double-minded and unstable in every way" (Jas 1:8). We want a world in which violence is no longer necessary, but we also want to hold on to our privileges and our abundance, enjoyed at the cost of another's want. We want to be good parents and faithful spouses, but we also want to gratify our secret desires or pursue our selfish goals. We want to be filled with the love of God, so that we can, in turn, love in the power of the Spirit, but we don't want to give up the painkillers and quick fixes that, in the end, keep us from that fullness.

This collect trains us to become increasingly aware of our transparency before God, for only thus can God make us transparent to ourselves. It opens by declaring that God already knows all that is within us—even what we wish to hide from him, other people and even from ourselves. It speaks in unison with the psalmist who confessed, "LORD, you have searched me and known me. You know when I sit down and when I rise up; you discern my thoughts from far away. . . . Even before a word is on my tongue, O LORD, you know it completely" (Ps 139:1-2, 4). In this way, the collect teaches us an important dimension of the practice of the presence of God, the God who searches the heart and brings what is hidden—even from ourselves—to God's healing light.

It is threatening to have our hidden thoughts and intentions exposed. It means that we will be held accountable for them and that we will have to look critically at them. But even in the face of this discomfort, we can lower our defenses before God and his Word because we know that his desire is to free us from our divided heart for glad, single-hearted pursuit of new life in Christ. God is a partner in this exercise of self-examination, confession and repentance—a spiritual guide and healer, not a stern and disapproving probation officer. God works within us and alongside us to bring about the change he desires in us and that we desire for ourselves as we seek to walk in the newness of life opened up for us in our baptism. God uses his intimate acquaintance with our most secret selves for our good, not harm—to cleanse us and to heal us of our divided heart, so that our love for God will be whole and complete and our walk full of integrity.

And so we can pray with the psalmist: "Search me, O God, and know my heart; test me and know my thoughts. See if there is any wicked way in me, and lead me in the way everlasting" (Ps 139:23-24). We can accept our transparency to God and allow him to make us transparent to ourselves. We can bear the discomfort of genuine self-knowledge, because we do not bear our sins alone. Jesus has carried them for us to the cross already.

I still remember how a college friend went on about what it was like to be with a particular woman he had been dating. He spoke of the transparency they shared with each other, the ability to be open with one another—open *to* one another—so completely that they discovered more about themselves even as they discovered more about the other. For him, there was no better place on earth than that space of openness. This is the space into which God invites us, as we allow the collect to press deep into our consciousness: and so we pray, "you know my heart better than I do myself; you know all my desires, even what I would wish to keep secret from everyone; and you love me, and you believe in my transformation, just the same."

For such transformation, we are entirely dependent on the "inspiration of the Holy Spirit," the fulfillment of God's promise to "put my spirit within you" (Ezek 36:27), renewing us in that Spirit again and again until we do indeed walk in line with God's vision for our lives together. The BCP keeps us ever mindful in prayer after prayer of our dependence on God for all progress on the spiritual journey and in so doing keeps our hearts inclined to be more and more open to his presence and intervention wherever we find ourselves.

❋❋❋❋❋❋❋❋❋❋❋❋❋❋❋❋❋❋❋❋❋❋❋❋❋❋❋❋❋❋❋

PUTTING IT INTO PRACTICE

Pray meditatively through Psalm 139:1-11. Pause with each verse, allowing each new sentence and set of images to sink down into your awareness of God's knowledge of you and presence with you. When you are ready, pray through Psalm 139:23-24 and remain in that place of openness and transparency before God. Be attentive to the Spirit's prompting. Repeat this exercise at different times and in different settings throughout the week, until you can readily find that place of openness to God and become comfortable in that space.

Copy the "Collect for Purity" onto a small card so that it can be readily available throughout the day, or perhaps even memorize it. At various moments throughout the day, pray the collect. Use the first part to become aware of God's presence and your transparency before him. Then pray the petition that follows, being attentive to the changes in disposition that the Spirit may work in you. Keep this exercise mentally available for times throughout the day when you catch yourself indulging impure desires or acting out of line with love of neighbor.

The Confession of Sin

The confession of sin is an important hinge-point in our experience of the liturgy. As we move from opening collect to confession of sin, the opening half of the liturgy becomes an extended opportunity for self-examination. We enter God's presence with acts of praise acclaiming his justice, holiness and generosity, qualities that are meant to be reflected in our lives as his children. We hear God's righteous desires for us and claims on us in the reading and interpretation of the Scriptures. Even the prayers we offer can convict or confirm us, as we discern whether we have desired and acted in line with these prayers or have in fact contributed to the brokenness and harm from which the church prays for deliverance.

The entire service up to this point is crafted to give us opportunities to examine our conscience and our walk, to implant more of God's vision for human community and arouse our desires for the same, and thus to bring us to the point of confessing our sin as more and more of God's holiness dawns on our understanding. We find ourselves with Isaiah in God's temple, our eyes opened both to his just character *and* to our participation in injustice. But we also know that, like Isaiah, when we make our confession God will provide the cleansing of which we stand in need. Beyond this hinge-point, we move forward into peace and reconciliation with God and one another, are nourished by the body and blood and return to our world renewed and empowered to serve God and love our neighbor more fully.

GENUINE SELF-KNOWLEDGE
Between the invitation to confession and the prayer itself sits the simple

rubric "silence may be kept." How we use this silence and other times of silence throughout our week is vital if we are to grow spiritually. We are invited to find in this silence that deep sorrow for our sins that comes from recognizing and understanding the import of our sin, painful as that understanding might be, so that we will indeed be truly sorry, and our repentance heartfelt and decisive.

Self-examination is widely recognized as an essential part of preparation to participate in Holy Communion. Thomas à Kempis, for example, devotes the fourth book of his *Imitation of Christ* to preparation for and participation in the Eucharist. There he gives ample attention to the discipline of self-examination, offering a litany of spiritual weaknesses as a mirror for the soul: Do you master your own emotions, impulses and desires, or do you let them carry you away with them instead? How zealous and alert are you for your favorite television shows or attentive to gossip magazines, and how lax and inattentive when it come to prayer and acts of service? How much do you spend on yourself, versus your neighbor in need, whom you are to love as yourself? John Wesley, seeking to provide "the serious Christian" with a means of growing daily in specific Christian virtues in his "Prayers for Daily Use," made self-examination a part of both the morning and evening exercises each day.

The discipline, practiced regularly, helps us arrive at a more genuine knowledge of ourselves, in regard both to our strengths and to our shortfalls. Regular reflection on the motives and movements of our desires and emotions and on our behaviors and interactions also provides us with the opportunity for change and amendment of life. If we remain unaware of how we injure our own spiritual progress and interact hurtfully with others, we will not know how to focus our minds on specific areas and strategies for improvement or focus our prayers more specifically as we ask for God's help in these areas of weakness. Finally, self-examination leads us into greater humility and patience with others, both as we plumb more fully the depths of God's patience and forgiveness toward us and as we understand that we have far more in common with those who offend us.

The prayer of confession preceding the Great Thanksgiving leads us into a simple exercise of self-examination. Far from allowing us to remain content with external righteousness, it bids us examine not only our words and deeds, but also our thoughts (the words we tell *ourselves*, the deeds we *wish* we could do). Moreover, it teaches us not only to examine what we have done, but also to look at what we have chosen not to do or perhaps overlooked altogether. A person who does nothing overtly sinful, but still acts only for himself or herself and fails to give help to the neighbor in need, or lives oblivious to the pain of neighbors far and near, has fallen short of the mark of authentic humanity just as surely as the person whose life is entangled in obvious and less socially respectable sins.

The confession asks us to use two simple criteria in our self-examination. Have our thoughts, words and deeds shown love for God from our whole heart and the kin of love for other people that shows them to be as dear to us as ourselves? These were the two commandments Jesus lifted up as the heart of God's law, the motives and goals for all the rest. Jesus' summary of the law combined two portions of the Torah (see Mark 12:28-31). The "first commandment" stands at the very core of Judaism—the declaration that the God who revealed himself to Israel is God alone and the injunction to love this God with one's whole heart, soul and strength (see Deut 6:4-5). In this context, love is much more than a feeling. It signifies the commitment to be loyal from the heart to the Lord with whom this covenant agreement is made, performing the services that the Lord requires and remaining aligned with *this* Lord against all rivals. Love finds expression in choices, in allegiances, in avoidances, in actions.

Jesus brilliantly selects Leviticus 19:18 as the second commandment, calling his followers to love—to show the same kind of covenant loyalty—to their fellow human beings. This commandment comes from the heart of the holiness code of Leviticus. Loving one's neighbor as oneself is part of Israel's call to "be holy" as God is holy, reflecting his character (his holiness) in their interaction with one another and the world. Since God extends his loving kindness toward all and is especially known as the champion of the needy, his people are called to share this characteristic in all of their dealings as well. Keeping these two criteria in front of us will mean putting restraints on what we do—but it will also lead us to discover a life that is more free, full and unconstrained than a life centered on self and on the actions and attitudes society forces on us for its own ends.

As we reflect on our choices, thoughts, words and deeds done or not done, we could discover many ways in which we have failed to enact love. But self-examination is not merely a private, mental exercise. It is also a spiritual exercise into which we invite God's participation: "Search me, O God, and know my heart; test me and know my thoughts. See if there is any wicked way in me, and lead me in the way everlasting" (Ps 139:23-24). The silence of self-examination is not an opportunity for introspection so much as conversation with God about our lives and listening for his perspective on where we have shown love well, and where we have not.

In addition to Jesus' summary of the law, the penitential orders offer the Ten Commandments, a central part of the Old Testament law that is affirmed again and again by voices in the New Testament, as an additional aid for self-examination. The Ten Commandments ask us to examine ourselves in regard to our faithfulness to honor God in the ways that he has specified, our faithfulness to our obligations to other people (respecting the inviolability of their lives, reputations, possessions and covenant relationships; for example, marriage) and our regulation of our internal desires. The last is exemplified in the prohibition not only of acts such as stealing and adultery, but even of *wanting* what belongs to another, allowing our hearts to move in the direction where our actions cannot rightly follow.

We won't use these tools profitably if we approach them as a checklist by which to justify ourselves and affirm our moral accomplishments. I could read the sixth commandment and acquit myself, having never killed anyone. But Jesus urges me not to skip over this command-ment too quickly: "You have heard that it was said . . . 'You shall not murder.' . . . But I say to you that if you are angry with a brother or sister, you will be liable to judgment; and if you insult a brother or sister, you will be liable to the council; and if you say, 'You fool,' you will be liable to the hell of fire" (Mt 5:21-22). Murder is only the end result, the extreme manifestation, of many little ways in which we "kill" our fellow human beings. We murder their wills with our anger when they run counter to our own. We assault their self-esteem and reputation when we speak words that diminish them, killing them by inches. Who can now walk away from the sixth commandment acquitted?

We will grow through self-examination if we approach these commandments instead out of a healthy desire for a timely diagnosis, before we have done too much harm to our own souls' health, our relationships and God's creation. Following Jesus' lead in his commentary on the prohibitions against murder and adultery, and Moses' lead in the inclusion of the tenth commandment, we can meditate on the Decalogue, asking God to reveal to us the ways in which we have not lived fully in line with their full intent, even if we could otherwise acquit ourselves in regard to the letter. We do not want to avoid seeing the cancers in our souls and the toxins in our relationships!

With God, the diagnosis is never a judgment or a sentence. Rather, it is the beginning of the path toward our cure. It is the beginning of deliverance from the old person in some area of our life and relationships, and from the damage the old person wreaks, so that newness of life can begin to take root in that area. It is not something we need to fear or avoid, even though it will be uncomfortable, given our instinctive defensiveness. We can, instead, receive it as a gift from the loving Parent who continues patiently to train us to live in ways that will be fruitful and full.

GENUINE SORROW

Self-examination and confession is not just a mental exercise. We sin with our whole being; we need to repent with our whole being. We need to allow ourselves to feel genuine sorrow, engaging our hearts as well as our minds in this discipline. This does not mean subjecting ourselves to feelings of inadequacy or guilt, as if piety meant self-loathing. Rather, it is an exercise in appreciating the full import of our sinful choices, attitudes and lifestyles, so that we can comprehend the depth of God's mercy and compassion toward us and, experiencing a fuller measure of gratitude toward him, be catapulted into greater degrees of love toward God and our neighbor.

Again Luke's Gospel is instructive. While Jesus dines at the house of Simon the Pharisee, a woman who was known to have led a blatantly sinful life intrudes into the scene. She weeps at Jesus' feet, dries them with her hair and anoints them with costly ointment. Simon and his other guests feel nothing but contempt for this woman and disdain for Jesus for allowing her to defile him with her touch. Jesus, however, points Simon and us to the deeper lesson in her actions. She knows how much she affronted God by abusing his gift of life. She knows the immensity of the debt that has been waived when her sins were forgiven. So she is full of love and gratitude toward Jesus for that forgiveness. Simon and his guests lack sufficient awareness of their own sinfulness and so have little compassion for a fellow sinner like the woman. Her godly sorrow opened her up to the full experience of forgiveness, to a deeper level of gratitude for having been rescued out of a destructive lifestyle by Jesus and to a deeper level of love for God and neighbor.

A hymn text penned by Phineas Fletcher in the early seventeenth century invites us to enter into the experience of that unnamed woman and to make her experience our own.

> Drop, drop slow tears and bathe those beauteous feet
> Which brought from heaven the news and Prince of Peace.
> Cease not, wet eyes, his mercy to entreat;
> To cry for vengeance sin doth never cease.
> In your deep floods drown all my faults and fears,
> Nor let His eye see sin, but through my tears.

Godly sorrow, the sorrow for sins that leads to repentance, is truly a great gift. As we see our sins through God's eyes and feel fully the pain, the ugliness and the inauthenticity that our sins have wrought in our lives and the lives of others, we can begin to ask God to see our sins through our tear-filled eyes.

GENUINE INTENTIONS

We are assured of forgiveness, but not in order to return to the sinful attitudes and behaviors that we renounce in confession. Rather, the experience of mourning our sins and receiving God's forgiveness opens us up to the renewed freedom to find joy in the ways that please him, the ways about which he will reveal more and more as we keep returning to him. Those who "intend to lead a new life, following the commandments of God, and walking from henceforth in his holy ways" are the ones who will profit from repentance and confession (BCP, 330), and it is this new life that our sharing in the body and blood of Christ is intended to empower. We are freed from our sins so "that we may delight in your will, and walk in your ways, to the glory of your Name" (BCP, 360), moving anew toward being holy as God is holy, that is, toward reflecting his loving, generous, gracious and just character in our own interactions and pursuits.

In self-examination, we see how ineffective have been our attempts to satisfy the core longings of our hearts—acceptance, meaning, purpose, significance, intimacy—through twisted and sinful behaviors. We perceive the destructive effects of our attempts to mask our pain when our core longings have not been met. But we also have the opportunity to imagine how good, how full, how noble and ennobling are the ways that please God. Ultimately, wholeness (holiness) will come to us as we find our core longings met in God and in the doing of his will, as we fulfill in our lives the purposes for which he created us—to love and honor him and to love one another with free and generous hearts.

True repentance requires an act of faith. It requires believing that living in line with God's vision for human community really will result in greater fulfillment and delight than continuing in our sinful ways. When we step out in this faith, we discover that sharing what we have brings far greater wholeness than hoarding, for sharing creates community while hoarding reinforces boundaries between people. We discover that approaching an irascible colleague or a rival with concern that his or her deep needs be met alongside our own enhances cooperation and undermines enmity. When we look at a member of the opposite sex not as an object of desire, but as someone with whom to exchange encouragement regarding the fulfillment of core longings in God, we offer far more to one another than our society's typical dating and mating rituals suggest.

Confronted with self-examination, we can fall into two spiral patterns. One is the downward spiral of seeking to protect our sinful and self-centered strategies for self-fulfillment, which tend to be reinforcing over time. The other is the upward spiral of experiencing the delight that comes from living for God, a pure delight that impels us to choose more and more the path of covenant loyalty to him and love for one another. The upward spiral results in a life that honors God—that lives "to the glory of your Name." Such a life provides for us the gift of deep integrity, for we rise to the heights for which we were fashioned, giving back to our Creator the response of gratitude that we can and *must* make for the gift of life that we received. In this integrity is the peace that passes all understanding and the rest for restless souls.

※※※※※※※※※※※※※※※※※※※※※※※※※※※※※

PUTTING IT INTO PRACTICE

Use the Ten Commandments as a guide for self-examination. Begin by finding that place of transparency before God and inviting him to bring to your awareness the specific areas that he wants to change. Then read prayerfully through the commandments one by one. Pause after each, asking God to show you where you are not walking in line with this commandment. Be alert for what God's Spirit will raise to your consciousness; ask God to show you how this is not in line with his will for you. Ask for God's pardon and for the Spirit's assistance to walk in newness of life in this area. When you have completed the exercise, hear again the good news: "There will be more joy in heaven over one sinner who repents than over ninety-nine righteous persons who need no repentance" (Lk 15:7); "God proves his love for us in that while we were still sinners Christ died for us" (Rom 5:8).

Writing your discoveries in a journal would be an excellent complement to this and the following exercises.

On a new day, repeat the above exercise, this time using Jesus' summary of the law (found in Mt 22:37-40 or BCP, 319) as a guide. Conclude by praying the confession of sin found in the BCP, 320 or 360.

Read James 1:22-25. Scripture often holds up a mirror to our souls, helping us see what is out of line with God's desires for us and guiding us toward amendment of life. We see ourselves as we are now, but also as we can become as we follow the Spirit.

Select a passage of Scripture—perhaps the Sermon on the Mount (Matthew 5—7) or Sermon on the Plain (Lk 6), perhaps a brief epistle (such as Philippians, Colossians, James or I John), perhaps a brief prophetic book (such as Amos or Micah)—to use as this mirror for your soul over the next week or two. Before reading each day, as in the previous exercises, open up your soul to God's searching and pray for him to bring to your awareness what he wishes.

Read through a paragraph of text. Then reread the paragraph in shorter segments, pausing to examine how you see yourself reflected in it. Be attentive to sins of *omission* as well as *commission.* As before, confess your sins to God. You may use the "Confession of Sin" in the BCP (359-60) for this purpose, or pray in your own words.

Return once again to the Scripture passage. What vision for an alternative way of living do you see that moves you out of the old person and more fully into the new? Pray that you will be able to walk in line with God's prompting.

18

Solidarity in Sin,
Solidarity in Forgiveness

❦

A layperson once objected to the *we* forms of the confession of sin. He said that he could not speak for anyone but himself and preferred to pray this prayer with the pronouns *I* and *me*, not *we* and *us*. In this way, he turned the community's confession of sin into an individual prayer for pardon. The plural pronouns, however, far more appropriately capture our "solidarity in corporate sinfulness," including the sin that is woven into the society of which we are a part.

Paul had something like this in mind when he wrote to address a situation of tension between Jewish and Gentile Christians in Rome. The former could claim to be the privileged among God's people, insisting that the Gentile Christians, the latecomers to the people of God, follow their practices. The Gentile Christians could pride themselves on being the more enlightened among God's people, freed from the tribal prejudices and superstitions of the parent religion. Neither side was extending toward the other the welcome that they had themselves received from Christ (see Rom 15:7). Paul broke down these barriers to unity by explaining how neither could claim to stand in a superior position before God, since both had sinned and stood in the same need of God's mercy. Neither could boast over the other in God's household.

As we take to heart and confess our solidarity in sin—the fact that "all have sinned and fall short of the glory of God" (Rom 3:23)—we find more ground for patience with one another, humility and gentleness in our treatment of one another and the abandonment of all pretensions to be better than another. Moreover, our shared experience of God's forgiveness and renewal has the power to nurture an unflagging hope for the redemption of any and all we encounter.

"An Exhortation," which precedes the Eucharist (BCP, 316-17) stresses not only the importance of self-examination and confession, but also the importance of seeking reconciliation with one another and making restitution for wrongs that we have done. For Jesus, making our relationships with one another right was the highest priority in regard to living out our piety: "So when you are offering your gift at the altar, if you remember that your brother or sister has something against you, leave your gift there before the altar and go; first be reconciled to your brother or sister, and then come and offer your gift" (Mt 5:23-24). This is because our relationship with God is not, ultimately, a private matter. It is a communal matter. God is in relation with us together as his covenant people, and that is a dimension of our faith that we dare not neglect. We cannot be right with God when we are at odds with one another. Or, in the words of the BCP, it is those who are "in love and charity with [our] neighbors" that may approach the altar (BCP, 330).

Reconciliation and restitution might take the form of a simple apology that restores another person's dignity, or it might involve reversing, if possible, the damage that we have done through our negligence or willfulness. It is an offering that, once made to one another, makes our offerings to God acceptable. It is not by chance that the exchange of the peace immediately precedes the taking up of the collection in the service of Holy Communion. In this way, we are cleansed not only from our private defilements as individuals, but also from the ways in which we have defiled our relationships with one another. We are able to come before God with the clean conscience that Christ's sacrifice for our sins has provided (see Heb 9:13-14; 10:19-22).

The sharing of the peace that immediately follows the confession of sin and declaration of pardon is a liturgical opportunity both for the celebration together of God's acceptance of us *and* for reconciliation with those present. We are ourselves forgiven by God; those who have injured us stand forgiven by God. What God has forgiven, we cannot now hold against one another (see Mt 6:12, 14-15).

This liturgical act, however, is but a symbol of what we are called to do throughout the week, often at greater length than is possible in that brief moment of the service, extending forgiveness to those who have hurt us, humbling ourselves to seek forgiveness from those whom we have hurt. By these acts, we move closer to unity with one another and walk more freely in the forgiveness we have received from God. Thomas à Kempis regards such exchanging of forgiveness and releasing of "suspicion, ill-feeling, anger, and contention" to be a fitting part of our offering of ourselves to Christ as a "Sacrifice of Peace," giving up both our offenses and our grudges. Like all sacrifices, it is not without cost, but the costliness of this kind of sacrifice is honoring to God.

PUTTING IT INTO PRACTICE

Enter into that place of openness before God using Psalm 139 or the "Collect for Purity." Ask God to show you where you have not walked in love and charity toward your neighbors and in what ways you have caused pain to them. Pray to God for pardon, and ask him to send the Holy Spirit to prepare the way for reconciliation. Then, approach the person God has brought to your mind, confess how you have not acted toward him or her out of love and ask for pardon. In some cases, the person may express relief or gratitude for your apology and gladly put the offense behind him or her. In some cases, pardon may *not* be forthcoming. What is important is that *you* act in line with the prompting of God's Spirit.

Repeat this exercise, this time asking God to bring to your awareness those against whom you are holding some grudge or ill feelings, such that it has interfered with your relationship and your acting toward those persons with love and charity. Pray that, by the inspiration of the Holy Spirit, you will release those feelings and forgive them from the heart. If it is *necessary* in order to resume open relationship with that person, extend forgiveness. It is usually best to approach this subtly: "I have to confess that, after you said *this* or did *that,* I had some bad feelings that I didn't let go of for a while. I only mention this because I don't want there to be anything between us, hindering our relationship." More serious offenses, however, can only be dealt with more seriously and sometimes only after working through them with the support of a pastor, counselor or spiritual friend.

Prayer and Intercession

That they may obtain their petitions, make them to ask
such things as shall please Thee.

FROM THE COLLECT FOR THE TENTH SUNDAY
AFTER TRINITY *(1928 PRAYER BOOK)*

One of the most important contributions that the Book of Common Prayer makes to our spiritual formation is to teach us those things for which we ought to pray and which we ought to desire from God, so that we will grow into maturity as disciples of Jesus. This approach to prayer is not the most popular nor the most attractive to our consumer culture. Many preachers teach, on the contrary, that we can ask God for whatever we want—a better job, a bigger house, a parking place closer to the entrance of the mall, victory for our favorite political candidate—*and* be assured that God will give it to us. After all, Jesus himself says, "Very truly, I tell you, if you ask anything of the Father in my name, he will give it to you. . . . Ask and you will receive, so that your joy may be complete" (Jn 16:23-24). "God wants you to have what you want!" such preachers insist. "God wants you to be happy and prosperous! You're a child of the King, so start living like one!" Understood like this, praying for something "in Jesus' name" becomes a magical formula for making our wishes materialize, for turning God into a cosmic Santa Claus.

James, the leader of the church in Jerusalem, was acquainted with a similar (per)version of Christian spirituality. To this, he said, "You do not have, because you do not ask. You ask and do not receive, because you ask wrongly, in order to spend what you get on your pleasures" (Jas 4:2-3). God is not going to answer our prayers for things that we seek for our own gratification. God knows that giving us such things would harm our souls and further distort our lives, and he gives only "good gifts" to his children, such as the Holy Spirit (compare Mt 7:11 and Lk 11:13).

Praying is not about getting God to give us what we want; it is about learning to want what God wants to give. And he is not out to make us rich or powerful or successful. God is certainly not out to help us get our own way in everything. He wants to make us more like Jesus. The prayer life of a mature disciple reflects a desire to receive from God those good gifts that will help him or her reflect Jesus' heart and actions more closely, combined with the confidence that God will answer such prayers.

The Collect for the Fifth Sunday in Lent masterfully captures this vision for prayer: "Almighty God, you alone can bring into order the unruly wills and affections of sinners: Grant your people grace to love what you command and desire what you promise" (BCP, 219). The goal of spiritual formation is to learn to love doing what pleases God and to desire the promises he has given us. It is to be free from desiring the things that the world (the media, the ideologies of our economy and corporate practices, and the like) sets before us to distract us and perpetuate itself.

We learn to desire the life of covenant with God, according to which we are stewards of *God's* wealth for the sake of others rather than hoarders of our *own* wealth; in which we learn to serve those around us rather than seek power over them to make them serve our goals and desires; in which we learn to place sexuality within the bounds of lifelong partnership and commitment and not indulge it for its own sake apart from that bond (or even within that bond). We learn to desire fellowship with God forever and the reward of hearing him say at the last, "Well done, good and faithful servant" (see Mt 25:21, 23).

We seek to come to the place where to do what God wishes is our wish as well. To arrive there is to be fully formed in Christ, the one whose will it was always to do God's good pleasure, whose prayer was "Thy will be done."

We don't automatically *know* what we should be seeking in prayer. Our perception of our needs tends to be distorted by the cravings born of the desires of our old self, often learned from observing what the world around us chases after. But God knows "our necessities before we ask and our ignorance in asking." He opens up our lives to those good gifts "which for our unworthiness we dare not, and for our blindness we cannot ask" (BCP, 231). We rely on God to "put away from us . . . all hurtful things," even those things our old selves would find highly desirable, and to "give us those things which are profitable for us," trusting God to know precisely what those things are (BCP, 229). Growing into Christian maturity means allowing God to train our desires toward those things that he provides, raising our hearts above seeking what will not, in the end, satisfy our longing for abundant life.

Praying through the Scriptures is an essential part of this training. Scripture is a witness to what God wants to give us and accomplish in us, teaching us to pray in line with these things so as to cooperate with the work of the Spirit. It is also full of models for prayer. Praying with those who have learned from God and from the Scriptures what we should be seeking in prayer—such as those who have given us the BCP—until those prayers become our own is another essential part. These prayer resources help to trim away what we ask for wrongly, to spend what we get on our own desires, but they also open up our minds and hearts to the fuller range of what God desires to work for us, in us and through us—"those things which for our unworthiness we dare not, and for our blindness we cannot ask."

In the three chapters that follow, we will explore the collects, the "Prayers of the People" and the Lord's Prayer as resources that teach us how to ask God for "those things that are necessary for our life and our salvation" (BCP, 79). What do these models and forms of prayer hold before our eyes as truly needful and most desirable? As we allow these prayers to shape our desires, we will pray with greater confidence that we ask rightly, seeking what it pleases God to grant.

PUTTING IT INTO PRACTICE

Think about what topics normally occupy your prayers. Make a list of specific petitions you can remember offering to God or the sorts of things you find yourself praying about/for during a typical week. Look over your list. How would you characterize your prayer life? What does your list suggest about your "theology" of prayer?

Scripture helps us reflect on what God wants to do in our midst and within us. Choose one of the following passages for extended reflection: Ephesians 2:1-10; Philippians 3:10-21; 1 Peter 1:3-9, 13-21; 2 Peter 1:3-11. What does the text say about what God wants to give us or to do on our behalf or to see us do? What does it say about challenges on the way?

Now let the passage diagnose and illumine your situation. How fully are God's gifts, intentions and promises, of which the text speaks, realized in your situation? Where is there need for a fuller realization of these? Where do you recognize obstacles to the fuller realization of these? What does the text suggest that God would want to see happen in you, your attitudes, your attachments, your actions? Pray through your responses to these questions, seeking God's guidance and empowering grace.

Paul opens up several windows into his prayer life (see Eph 1:17-23; 3:14-21; Phil 1:3-11; Col 1:9-14; 1 Thess 3:11-13; 5:23-24). Select one of his prayers for closer reflection. What does Paul long to see happen in the lives of these Christians, both as individuals and as communities of faith? What would the fulfillment of these prayers look like in your life? In your congregation? What would change in your life and what would remain constant, so as to accommodate these longings and their fulfillment more and more?

Personalize the prayer for yourself and your congregation, and spend some time before God praying through this prayer. You may repeat the exercise with the other prayers as you find helpful.

20

The Collects of the Day

❦

The "collect" is a prayer that seeks to gather up and express the petitions of those who have assembled together. From the collects we can infer what the content of our longings and prayers ought to be, if they are indeed to be gathered in these collects. Over the course of the liturgical year, churches using the BCP are exposed to a different collect each Sunday and additional collects on special feast days. A number of themes emerge from the cycle, representing the overarching formative impression they seek to make on our prayer life and spiritual awareness.

First and foremost, the collects keep the importance of *attaining God's promises* ever before our eyes as the ultimate aim of *all* our endeavors, of which we must not lose sight:

> You have prepared for those who love you such good things as surpass our understanding: Pour into our hearts such love towards you that we, loving you in all things and above all things, may obtain your promises, which exceed all that we can desire.

God has prepared for us a life of such fulfillment as surpasses anything we might attain apart from following him with our whole hearts. As we grow to believe and experience this more and more, this foundational conviction empowers our full commitment to discipleship, guiding our investment of our thoughts, our energies and the precious time allotted to us each day. We will cease to chase after the distractions that seem so fulfilling for the moment and will seek wholeheartedly to "run without stumbling to obtain your heavenly promises." The image of running communicates the intensity of our intentions and investment. The image of stumbling identifies the true nature of any pursuit, attitude or behavior that takes our focus off God and the track he has set before us.

A vital complement to this first theme is to learn to distinguish between temporary goods and lasting, eternal goods. The collects call us to attach ourselves fully to the latter and to use the former only, and insofar, as they aid our attaining the latter. "Grant us, Lord, not to be anxious about earthly things, but to love things heavenly; and even now, while we are placed among things that are passing away, to hold fast to those that shall endure."

We focus so easily on the needs of the moment that press on us from outside ourselves—the business of our jobs, housework, getting ready for school, preparing some meal, meeting this or that deadline. The "clouds of this mortal life" threaten to "hide from us the light of that love which is immortal." Under the weight of such demands, we grasp for the refreshments and painkillers that are also available in the moment, wearing for ourselves deep ruts that become the equivalent of instinct. Days, weeks, months, years easily pass without our truly attending to those things that shall endure. So many regrets uttered beside—or from—a deathbed are born of "not having had enough time," often a euphemism for having spent so *much* time so *poorly*. The collects train our hearts and minds to live each day in the pursuit of eternity, investing ourselves in love for God and love for one another.

Several of the collects hold up before us the goal of becoming more like Jesus and make this the focal point of our prayers: "Grant us so perfectly to know your Son Jesus Christ to be the way, the truth, and the life, that we may steadfastly follow his steps in the way that leads to eternal life." The way to attain God's promises and hold on to what is eternal is the way of following Jesus' example and teaching. Imitation of Christ is a focal lens for discipleship throughout the New Testament. Paul calls us to let Jesus' mindset be ours as well, looking out for what will accomplish God's good purposes for others rather than looking out for our own interests and advancement (see Phil 2:3-11), until we can say with Paul, "it is no longer I who live, but it is Christ who lives in me" (Gal 2:20). Giving ourselves away, Jesus promises, is the way to find ourselves for eternity (see Mk 8:34-35).

Christian discipleship means embodying Jesus. It means continuing Jesus' ministry by devoting ourselves to doing what we see him doing: reaching out to the outcast; restoring the penitent; tending the sick, disturbed and seekers with love and mercy; challenging unjust systems, both political and religious, that misrepresent God's intentions for human community. We do this, embracing self-denial and the hostile responses of those who remain committed to domination systems, with an eye on God's promise to us that those who participate in Christ's death will also share in Christ's resurrection (see Rom 6:5; Phil 3:10-11). The proverb that calls imitation "the highest form of flattery" is, in this case, well spoken. We honor Christ most when we seek to embody his heart, attitudes and agenda in our daily lives.

A fourth theme in the collects—one that will reappear throughout the "Prayers of the People"—concerns the unity of the church. We pray not only "that we may be devoted to God with our whole heart," but also to be "united to one another with pure affection." We cannot do one without the other. As we are "joined together in unity of spirit by the teaching" of the apostles and prophets, centered on Jesus the corner-stone, we become "a holy temple acceptable to God." Fissures between us threaten the whole building's integrity. Cracks also threaten our witness. Only as we are "gathered together in unity by God's Holy Spirit" do we have the capacity to "show forth God's power among all peoples."

This prayer is entirely in keeping with Jesus' own prayer on the eve of his passion and death, in which he identifies our love for and unity with one another as the sign to the world that God had indeed sent him. Praying for unity is particularly appropriate in connection with the celebration of Communion, the rite that enacts and nurtures our communion not only with God but also with each other—and if not with each other, then neither with God!

As our prayers and aspirations are shaped by these collects, our cherished divisions within the local and universal church are challenged (see 1 Cor 11:18-22; Gal 3:28; Rev 5:9-10). Where we are taught by our politicians and media to think of a certain population as "them,"

God reminds us of the Christians in the midst of that population, who always remain part of the "us" of God's church and reminds us of God's longing that we include every "them" in our love and care. The collects thus challenge us to contribute to the fulfilling of Jesus' own prayer —that we all may be one.

Most prevalently, the collects remind us of our dependence on God's help to live so as to hold fast to those things that shall endure, and the assurance that this help is always available to us. We humbly acknowledge that "in our weakness, we can do nothing good without you," and so we ask, "give us the help of your grace, that in keeping your commandments we may please you both in will and in deed." In collect after collect we pray, "Give us grace," reminding us that we make progress in newness of life not by our own watchfulness and efforts, but by the ever-present help of the God who wills and works in us what pleases him.

❀❀❀❀❀❀❀❀❀❀❀❀❀❀❀❀❀❀❀❀❀❀❀❀❀❀❀❀

PUTTING IT INTO PRACTICE

Use the five major themes of the collects as focal points for a time of prayer.

Hold before you some features of God's promises to you as a part of the people of God. (For example, see Ex 15:26; Ezek 36:25-27; Mt 11:28-29; 28:20; Jn 4:14; 8:12; Heb 13:5; Rev 21:3-5 or the Scripture passages used in the previous two exercises.)

1. Pray to receive what God promises, to enjoy what he longs to give you during this life and to have a foretaste of what he promises for the life of the world to come.

2. Ask God to reveal any ways in which you need to make more room in the midst of the pursuit of temporal goods and goals this day and, more generally, for the more open pursuit of "running to obtain [God's] promises" (BCP, 234) and those goods that shall endure.

3. Ask God to show you where in the past day you have followed in

Christ's steps and where you have walked in your own way. Pray for guidance and help to walk more fully in line with Jesus through the day ahead.

4. Pray for the unity of the church. Ask God to illumine those convictions, feelings and behaviors within yourself that contribute in some way to the ongoing divisions within the people of God. Ask God to reveal the root of these tendencies and to heal you of them.

5. Ask God for grace to hold on to all that you have received from him and to release all that he has shown you that holds you back from walking in newness of life. Ask for continual awareness of God's ever-present grace to empower you for what his holiness requires throughout the day ahead.

We often go to God in prayer, motivated by the needs of the moment as defined by the *temporal* challenges that press on us. While this is legitimate (see Phil 4:6; 1 Pet 5:7), a collect or other prayer can help us also to focus on what we need to seek from God from the perspective of *his* priorities in the midst of those challenges.

Select a collect from the BCP (211-36) for such meditation and prayer. I have found the following particularly helpful: First and Fourth Advent; Second, Fifth, Seventh and Eighth Epiphany; Fifth Lent; Easter Day (first collect); Second, Third, Fifth and Sixth Easter; Propers 4, 5, 9, 12, 19, 22, 23, 26.

- What needs or challenges does the collect identify? What priorities does it elevate?

- How does the collect illumine your needs in the moment?

- How does the collect open you up to what God wants to see happen in your life right now, apart from or in the midst of the urgent needs of the day seen from a temporal perspective?

Pray through your reflections, seeking what God wishes to give you, thanking him for guidance and help. Copy the collect that you used in the previous exercise on a small card that you can carry with you throughout the day. Pray the collect at various times, asking God for illumination into your situation and for guidance concerning your responses to it.

If you found the previous two exercises fruitful, you might wish to make them a regular part of your spiritual discipline either for a selected season of the church year or for a complete cycle of the church year, taking the collect for each particular Sunday into the rest of your week.

21

Prayers of the People

❋

Celebrations of the Eucharist are consistently accompanied by prayers offered on behalf of the following:

The Universal Church, its members, and its mission
The Nation and all in authority
The welfare of the world
The concerns of the local community
Those who suffer and those in any trouble
The departed. (BCP, 359)

These focal points for prayer align with scriptural instructions about, and instances of, intercession. The apostles ask their congregations to hold up the larger church and its mission before God in prayer. The author of 1 Timothy urges prayer on behalf of authorities, so that people will enjoy the peaceful conditions conducive to giving attention to spiritual growth and pious service (see 1 Tim 2:1-3). Jeremiah instructed the scattered people of God to pray for the welfare of the cities in which they found themselves (see Jer 29:7). James prescribes prayer on behalf of those members of each local congregation who are physically ill or "sin-sick" as a means of healing (see Jas 5:13-18).

The "Prayers of the People" admirably gather these many focal points so that we can pray in line with the breadth of Scripture's whole vision for prayer and not allow our prayer lives to be distorted by focusing only on some small part of this vision. We do not simply pray about what's on our minds, though there's certainly room to give attention to this. Instead, the "Prayers of the People" train us to consider the needs of church, nation, the world beyond our shores, as well as local community, and especially to attend to petitions on behalf of "those who suffer and those in any trouble" as we go before God in prayer (see Rom 15:30-32; Eph 6:18-20; 2 Thess 3:1), learning to expand the scope of our concern beyond *our own* to *God's own*. Worship leaders who practice extemporaneous prayer in congregational settings would do well to take this point to heart. Pastoral prayers in less liturgically oriented traditions too frequently remain entirely focused on the present congregation in the present moment, contributing to the congregation's inner-directed, self-centered focus rather than challenging them to expand their scope of concern beyond their walls.

What we pray for, we learn to long for, and what we long for, we will seek to nurture. James makes this point rather directly: "If a brother or sister is naked and lacks daily food, and one of you says to them, 'Go in peace; keep warm and eat your fill,' and yet you do not supply their bodily needs, what is the good of that?" (Jas 2:14-17). Pious wishes— "May you be warm, may you be fed"—are no substitute for pious action, but, if the wishes are genuine, they tend to lead to pious action. What we seek from God in prayer on behalf of others informs our own investment in making these things happen in the lives of others.

Anglican theologians are fond of the Latin motto *lex orandi, lex credendi*—roughly, "what we pray is what we believe." But we could extend this to read *lex orandi, lex credendi, lex vivendi*—"the rule of what is to be prayed is the rule of what is to be believed, and the rule of what is to be lived"—so that our prayers do not merely inform our believing, but also our living. Some prayers are entirely in God's hands to fulfill, but we can become the means by which he fulfills other petitions. Several of the forms of the "Prayers of the People" have the danger of remaining quite general. Forms two and four avoid this problem by inviting us to make specific petitions under each "category" of concern. If in our prayers we can see the specific faces, needs and challenges, the Spirit can prompt us more readily to specific acts of relief, outreach and witness.

The "Prayers of the People" can help the heart of God for those in need take shape in us more fully. If they are to have this effect, however, we will need to pray them more reflectively and more frequently than is possible in the context of the Sunday Eucharist. We would do well to pray them regularly during the week and to give God time after each petition to raise to our awareness ways in which we could offer ourselves as a means by which God graciously invades, confronts and relieves.

CREATION

The "Prayers of the People" invite us to encounter the environment surrounding us as "creation," the handiwork of a good and generous God rather than impersonal "resources" to be exploited for our own purposes. The natural world becomes a channel through which we recognize and enjoy God's kindness and generosity, as we see more and more of the character of the Creator through our experience of the magnificence and bounty of creation (see Rom 1:19-20). We call on God as the *giver* of increase, by which we confess that we cannot *manufacture* produce, but only work to provide the conditions for growth. We receive the physical environment as a gift with which we are entrusted, gathering its fruits with gratitude, care and modesty rather than greedily getting all we can out of it, like raiding the pantry of someone who has invited us to dinner.

We are also called to show our faithfulness toward the Giver through the responsible use of his gifts. Conscientious recycling, repairing before replacing and reusing rather than disposing are just a few of the steps that can be taken in this direction. The role the prayers assign to us is that of *stewards* of creation. The vision of stewardship, rather than ownership, fosters relationships and nurtures community through sharing and working together to ensure everyone's enjoyment of life's most basic blessings. Thus we ask God to guide us "that we may use earth's resources rightly in the service of others" (BCP, 388) because "the earth is the LORD's and all that is in it" (Ps 24:1), given by God for the benefit of all persons, not just the most aggressive or rapacious. Where there are still "victims of hunger, fear, injustice, and oppression," we have not yet arrived at "the just and proper use of your creation" (BCP, 392).

We are called to examine our own participation in the unjust and improper use of God's creation in our own practices, those of the corporations we support with our labors or investments, those of the governments and other systems of which we are a part. Here, as ever, prayer leads to self-examination, behavioral change and prophetic critique and witness, as we call people who remain co-opted by the world's domination systems to stop sacrificing relationship for profit, *shalom* for dividends. One of the important lessons an international student taught me had to do with looking carefully at the environmental practices of companies I supported through mutual funds and stock purchases, particularly environmental practices in their offshore facilities where regulation may be more relaxed. "Green" companies may not produce rapacious dividends, but, as an investment also in creation, may indeed give the best long-term return.

JUSTICE AND PEACE

A consistent feature of the "Prayers of the People" is the petition that God will direct *all* government toward justice and peace. We pray to a God who reaches out in love and longing for all people, not one with partisan loyalties who seeks the interests of one nation at the expense of others. In these prayers, we relinquish our single focus on "national security" and "preserving *our* way of life" in favor of allowing God to teach us how we may "honor one another and serve the common good" (BCP, 388). We cannot ourselves participate in nor countenance a government's pursuit of policies that seek to *use* another nation to advance our own interests. We ask God instead to work through all those in authority to "promote the dignity and freedom of every person" living under their authority and, through foreign relations that are guided by a growing "spirit of respect and forbearance," beyond their immediate sphere of authority (BCP, 390). In essence, our prayers seek the *common* good.

FAITHFULNESS TO OUR CALLING AS
A COMMUNITY OF DISCIPLES

Praying for the church naturally includes those in our midst who are sick, suffering or troubled. But the "Prayers of the People" focus our attention on the broader contours of what it means for us to live together as "church" and to be faithful to the calling with which God has entrusted us.

Our overarching prayer is that we will "show forth God's glory *in all that we do*" as God's people (BCP, 391, emphasis added). This becomes our frame of reference for all our words and deeds. Where we live in line with God's desires, we witness to the worthiness of this God to be served by human beings. When we allow his generosity, outreaching love and passion for justice and *shalom* to become manifest in our speaking and acting, we create opportunities for others to acknowledge his worthiness and goodness.

A primary means by which to accomplish this is—as the collects also emphasize—by seeking unity with one another in Christ. It is as we are "united in God's truth" and "live together in God's love" that we best "reveal God's glory in the world" (BCP, 388). In Jesus' own prayer for the harmony, love, cooperation and solidarity that he longs to see among his followers, he knew that such unity among his visible followers would proclaim to the world the unity of the Father and the Son, that is, would confirm that Jesus was, indeed, from God (see Jn 17:11, 21-23).

To pray for unity in Christ's church means that we ourselves must not contribute to the divisions within the church. When we harbor prejudice against our sisters and brothers who worship Christ as part of another denomination with its own distinctive polity, worship style or emphasis, we put our preferences and our comfortable traditions ahead of Jesus' desire that we exhibit love and unity among one another. When we honor one another's expressions of faithfulness to and love for Christ, we have the capacity to learn from the distinctive emphases and practices of our fellow Christians and to enrich their experience of God and walk of discipleship with our own as well. When we harbor scruples about communing with one another across denominational lines, we deny the spiritual reality of our unity in Christ that the Eucharist is meant both to enact and nurture. When we prefer to separate from members of our own denomination—or push an agenda to the point of precipitating separation—we injure the unity of the body of Christ for the sake of our own interests and rights.

The prayers also call us to recognize that the gospel we proclaim and the sacraments we enjoy are a sacred trust from God. The calling of "all bishops, priests, and deacons" is to be "faithful ministers of your Word and Sacraments" (BCP, 387). The apostolic witness is not presented here as a human invention to be altered in accordance with our whims, vanity or preferences. When the gospel challenges our worldview or our ethic, our first task is not to adapt the gospel to the times, but to question whether or not our worldview or ethic has become distorted, perhaps in service to one or another domination system whose interests are not served by the gospel in all its aspects, perhaps to facilitate our holding onto our untransformed affections and behaviors. We pray to be "filled with truth and love" (BCP, 389), for this is what makes the church the *church*, the restored reflection of the image of God, the voice of God calling to our world, the arms of God still reaching out. Scripture, the voices of Christians from centuries past, Christians from other lands who can speak to us from outside our Western worldview, and the voice of God still calling are all essential conversation partners as we seek to remain faithful to *God's* truth and witness to its healing, transforming power.

These prayers also lay on our hearts our own ongoing progress as the people of God toward newness of life. We pray for God's help to walk more fully in our baptismal covenant and to be delivered from hardness of heart toward other people, so that we may respond to them in a way that reflects Christ's heart for them. We pray that we will act from our new person toward those "whose lives are closely linked with ours" such that we "serve Christ in them, and love one another as he loves us" (BCP, 388). As we pray this petition, we are invited to examine what we want from our families and our closest networks of friends. Do we want to get them to do what we want, or do we want God to show us the opportunities to serve Christ in them or, to put it another way, to let Christ serve them through us? The "Prayers of the People" keep insisting that we make our faith real in these most familiar relationships.

We are also taught to facilitate the rekindling and new kindling of faith, both throughout the people of God and among those who have yet to identify themselves with God's people. We pray for the mission of the church, to bring the good news of God's love and his vision for wholeness in community effectively to all people. We are led to pray even "for our enemies and those who wish us harm" (BCP, 391) rather than, perhaps, our own wishes for them. At the same time, we pray "for all whom we have injured or offended" (BCP, 391), a reminder to us that we have often acted as enemies ourselves and share a common need for forgiveness.

As we pray these prayers alert to the stirring of God's Spirit within us, we cannot fail to invest ourselves in contributing to their fulfillment. We open up our homes and our own spiritual journeys to people who seek God, providing safe opportunities for their explorations. We advance mission as we tell those around us about some way in which God has set us free from an old wound or a besetting sin, or helped us think differently about our relationship to money, or to family, or to people across some humanly made dividing line, such that we have discovered a new dimension of wholeness and community. We find the strength and the courage to extend the hand of fellowship to our enemies, or do them a kindness, with the result that the hostility is slowly defused. As we pray, we are changed. And as we are changed, we contribute to the fulfillment of the prayer that encompasses all the others—that the church "be found without fault at the day of the coming" of our Lord Jesus Christ (BCP, 389).

THE DECEASED

In our baptismal covenant, we affirm "the communion of saints," the fellowship of all Christians living and dead, a connection forged in Christ that not even death can overcome. But how are we to live out this communion of saints? How are we to relate to the departed, particularly in prayer? Many Christians are uncomfortable with the idea of offering prayers for the departed, believing that a person's eternal destiny is sealed at death and that his or her state can no longer be affected by prayers. They read of the great gulf that divides the redeemed from the condemned immediately after death in Jesus' parable of the rich man and Lazarus (see Lk 16:19-31) or Paul's affirmation that judgment will be carried out on the basis of "what has been done in the body, whether good or evil" (2 Cor 5:10), and naturally conclude that our time "in the body" is decisive for our state beyond death. If the deceased are among the redeemed, they need no further prayers; if they are among the condemned, further prayers cannot help.

Others sense a greater degree of continuity between life here and life beyond death. These look at the perfection of the saints as a process that begins here, but continues on the other side of death, as we move from grace to grace and from glory to glory. For such people, our solidarity as the people of God transcends death to the point that we can still sue for God's mercy on behalf of those who have died and that our prayers on their behalf are as effective as our prayers for the living.

The forms of the "Prayers of the People" include a variety of prayers concerning and on behalf of the departed. These prayers reflect both our deep longings for ongoing connection with the saints who have crossed over to the distant shore and our uncertainty about the nature of that connection. The prayers offered in connection with rite one of the Eucharist, according to which we ask God to "grant them continual growth in thy love and service" (BCP, 330), are more in line with C. S. Lewis's vision of the afterlife. Form four is the most open in regard to how effective our prayers can be on behalf of the deceased: "We pray for *all* who have died, that they may have a place in your eternal kingdom" (BCP, 393). We express here our fervent wish that, in the wideness of God's mercy, all our departed will enjoy his favor beyond death, and none be excluded. This is especially poignant for me, since several family members lived and died committed to the Buddhist faith, explicitly having chosen *not* to know God as revealed in Christ. Theologically, I can only affirm Christ as the way to the Father. Nevertheless, the prayer expresses my longing for these souls, asking the God "who desires everyone to be saved and to come to the knowledge of the truth" (1 Tim 2:4) that, if it is possible, they may indeed "have a place in God's eternal kingdom."

The prayers in forms four and five are more reserved, seeking no special dispensation for the departed. Here we simply yield them up to God's mercy and the fulfillment of his will for them, as he decides, without presuming to name what that should be. We are reminded, however, that we cannot presume to know from their visible behavior what was in the hearts of the deceased, as we pray not only for those who have died "in the communion of your Church" but also for those "whose faith is known to you alone" to have "rest in that place where there is no pain or grief, but life eternal" (BCP, 391).

Other forms contribute to keeping our sense of the communion of saints vibrant by directing our desires toward sharing in the kingdom that God has prepared for all his saints. Our common destiny becomes a focal point that binds us together with those who already enjoy God's eternal presence. We pray that God would so help us live here that we will enter into that unbroken fellowship there.

The BCP thus reflects the range of the ambiguity of our theology and our wishes regarding those who precede us in death. Nevertheless, it consistently guides us to express our trust in God by entrusting to him the life beyond death—both our own and that of the deceased—accepting with humility the limitations on our knowledge and our power in the face of that "last enemy to be destroyed," death (1 Cor 15:26).

Several of the forms of the "Prayers of the People" commend to us the contemplation of the example of the departed, and all the saints, as a means by which to keep ourselves mindful of the communion of saints. The author of Hebrews certainly understood the power of this kind of reflection for reinvigorating and giving direction to our faithful living, invoking the departed heroes of faith as a "cloud of witnesses" that surrounded his congregation with their encouraging and guiding example. In this regard, the prayers invite us to remember those who stand out in that cloud of witnesses. I think of the rector who baptized me and invested himself in my early education in the faith. I think of my grandmother, who encouraged me to "search the Scriptures." I think of a Pentecostal campus minister and an Episcopalian organist who taught me about prayer in the Spirit and dared to offer brotherly critique when they discerned the old person on the rise in me. I think of my grandfather, who showed constant love in an attitude of servanthood. And the faces multiply, reminding me how much I have been "supported by this fellowship of love and prayer," and how much being "surrounded by their witness to [God's] power and mercy" assists me as I move forward in this journey of faith (BCP, 395).

As we "praise God for those in every generation in whom Christ has been honored" (BCP, 386), remembering the positive contributions that our forerunners in the faith have made by their example, their sacrifice or even their personal investment in our lives, we also pray "that we may have grace to glorify Christ in our day" (BCP, 386) living our lives in such a way that we, too, will become part of that cloud of witnesses to whom others may look for encouragement.

When all our prayers are done, the collects that conclude the "Prayers of the People" make us return to the essential lessons of prayer. We ask once more that God will help us to seek "only what accords with God's will" (BCP, 394), acknowledging frankly the limitations we face in prayer—not daring, or being sufficiently aware, to ask God for his best for us. The prayer of faith is not simply the prayer offered by the person who does not doubt that God will give him or her what he or she asks. It is the prayer offered when we trust that God will give what he knows to be best, even if that should be contrary to the prayer itself, and that he will open our eyes and direct our longings more and more toward the good gifts that he longs to give to us and work within us.

PUTTING IT INTO PRACTICE

Read through one or more forms of the "Prayers of the People." What picture do you get of the priorities of prayer from these various forms? How does the scope of these forms compare with the list you made of your own typical prayer concerns in an exercise suggested in chapter nine? How might you restructure your prayer life to make more room for any underrepresented concerns?

Use one of the forms for the "Prayers of the People" as a guide for a time of prayer and intercession. Forms two and four are especially well suited to this practice, first giving directions for prayer and then providing space to practice prayer in regard to specific areas of concern. The other forms can be used as well, taking each petition as a prayer prompt to guide more specific intercessions.

If you do not know how to pray in a certain area, remember that "the Spirit helps us in our weakness; for we do not know how to pray as we ought, but that very Spirit intercedes with sighs too deep for words," praying "for the saints according to the will of God" (Rom 8:26-27). In such times, practice asking the Spirit to pray within and through you.

Be alert to ways in which God's Spirit prompts you to act in response to the prayers you offer. How does praying change *you*, your behavior, your agenda for the day or week ahead?

22

The Lord's Prayer

❦

However varied Christian worship has become across denominations, almost all Christians know the Lord's Prayer and many pray it regularly, whether in their congregations or in their personal prayer lives. During an internship as a hospital chaplain, standing beside the beds (including the deathbeds) of patients from the whole spectrum of Christendom, I could always unite in prayer with these patients and their families using the Lord's Prayer. Indeed, when we pray this text, we unite our voices with saints from every Christian tradition in every age. And what better resource could we have for learning about asking such things as shall please God than the prayer that Jesus offered to his disciples as the model for their own (see Lk 11:1-4)?

The fact that we are sufficiently familiar with the Lord's Prayer to pray it from memory is a great asset, since we always have it on hand. But our familiarity can also prevent us from really listening to the prayer and allowing it to sink deep into our consciousness so as to shape our intentions and desires. Take some time to hear afresh what Jesus' prayer teaches us to seek from God and to show forth in our living.

OUR FATHER, WHO ART IN HEAVEN
What is your "God-image" as you pray? How do your understand your relationship with this God? Jesus wants us to see God as Father and to see ourselves as God's children. We are not slaves who must grovel before a master; we are not petitioners who stand afar off from a patron or king. We are brought near to God as members of his family and allowed intimate access to him. When we call God "Father," we

acknowledge that he is parenting us anew (see Heb 12:9), and we position ourselves to be shaped, corrected, disciplined and raised afresh by this most loving and nurturing of parents.

When we call God "Father," we do not assume that what is characteristically male is also characteristic of God, nor that the male human being is more fully created in the image of God than the female. We need to be cautious to look at what Jesus does affirm to be characteristic of God as "Father" and not extrapolate beyond this from our images of the masculine. Our images of God also need to be balanced by the feminine images used throughout the Scriptures to create a fuller picture of the character and heart of God. Moreover, to call God "Father" is not to attribute to him the hurtful and, in some cases, abusive behaviors of our own fathers, in whom the image of God was as distorted by their own brokenness as it is in ourselves. Jesus invites us to find in God the Father what we need in order to be nurtured well as children, into whose likeness we will mature by the working of his Spirit within us.

For Jesus, this is a father whose kindness and generosity toward God's children surpasses that of any earthly father (see Mt 7:9-11). This is a father who gives a loving, generous, joy-filled welcome to the wayward child, rather than a stiff lecture and a reluctant acceptance (see Lk 15:21-24). This is a not a father who sets us up for failure with impossibly high expectations, but a father who positions us to succeed in our coming to maturity as disciples and who will provide whatever it takes to help us get there: "Do not be afraid, little flock, for it is the Father's good pleasure to give you the kingdom" (Lk 12:32).

HALLOWED BE THY NAME

I heard one pastor suggest, attempting to modernize this petition, that we should pray, "Holy be your Name." But God's name is *already* holy. What we pray here is for more people in ever-widening circles to recognize and revere the holiness of God's name. While this prayer will ultimately be fulfilled when God judges the world and reveals his glory, it finds fulfillment now chiefly through the behavior of those who are identified as his people (see Rev 14:7; 15:4).

Where God's people fail to honor him by consistently doing what pleases him, those who look on, who know God only through his household, lose respect for God. Paul wrote concerning his fellow Jews in this regard, "You that boast in the law, do you dishonor God by breaking the law? For, as it is written, 'The name of God is slandered among the Gentiles because of you'" (Rom 2:23-24). By contrast, when people who associate themselves with God's name do what is good, generous, noble or otherwise reflective of his virtuous character, those who witness their behavior think more highly of the One in whose name and on whose behalf they do these things. Thus Jesus teaches, "Let your light shine before others, so that they may see your good works and give glory to your Father in heaven" (Mt 5:16; see also 1 Pet 2:12).

When we pray, then, that God's name be revered as the holy name that it is, we commit ourselves to speak and act so that we will give people no occasion to speak ill of our Lord, and every occasion to acknowledge that there is "something to this Jesus."

THY KINGDOM COME

Jesus, like John the Baptizer, proclaimed the coming of the kingdom of God, the anticipated age when God will establish justice and wholeness throughout human community. This was good news for all who found themselves hemmed in and pressed down by the military and economic practices of the day, but bad news for those who willingly participated in and profited from the same. God's kingdom would not come in quietly to coexist alongside those domination systems, but would put an end to every power that plunders and slaughters and calls it "government" or makes a desert and calls it "peace."

Praying for God's kingdom to come means giving up our own participation in—and, often, profit from—the systems that work against the enjoyment of God's justice and wholeness by *all* persons. We have to be willing to give up our larger share—our idolization of "more"—so that others can enjoy "some." In so doing, we will gain the greater privileges of finally experiencing true community without the divisions that allow one party to ascend at the expense or to the neglect of the other.

THY WILL BE DONE, ON EARTH AS IT IS IN HEAVEN

The Gospels give us a dramatic picture of what it means to wrestle with this petition when Jesus prays it a second time in the Garden of Gethsemane. Praying that God's will be done means putting God's purposes ahead of our own preferences, his desires ahead of our own agendas. But to call Jesus "Lord" without being willing to do this is meaningless (see Mt 7:21).

Jesus shared the apocalyptic worldview that envisioned everything in heaven—the angelic hosts, the stars in their courses, the progression of seasons—moving in tune with God's decree. It is the human sphere that is out of step with God, where he must reassert his leadership. This petition invites us to find our proper place as creatures in God's created cosmos, in the seeking and doing of the will of the One who made us for his good pleasure. How different from the prayers of "help me get my way," "make everything turn out the way I want it to" and "bless my projects" that we are so often disposed to offer! The more we are able to internalize this petition—"Thy will be done"—the more complete our journey to maturity in Christ.

GIVE US THIS DAY OUR DAILY BREAD

New Testament scholars debate whether the word *daily* in this petition means "today's" bread or our ration "for tomorrow." Either way you slice it, this remains a very modest petition in terms of asking God for a share of this world's goods. On the one hand, praying, "Give us this day our daily bread," keeps me mindful of the fact that the nourishment my family and I enjoy each day is a gift from God and is to be received with gratitude. But on the other hand, we are so far from being in danger of *not* getting meat, fruit, vegetables and snacks for the next *year*—let alone daily bread—that the petition seems almost quaint. At the same time, for so many, what a gift it would be to have bread *today!* What an unthinkable blessing it would be to be assured of its being supplied *tomorrow!*

As I pray this petition, I remember that I do not pray it alone. My sisters and brothers in Christ in the Sudan, in refugee camps throughout the world, in nations where confessing the faith means economic embargo, pray it as well. Their petitions convict me of my plenty. If they are part of the "us" for whom we pray, "Give us this day our daily bread," perhaps God has already answered their prayer in what we hold in our possession. The failure may not be in God's giving, but in our distribution of those gifts. Are our investments, our laying up of treasures on earth, the equivalent in God's sight of containers of food and supplies rotting in a warehouse while nearby populations die for want of food and medicine?

FORGIVE US OUR TRESPASSES, AS WE FORGIVE THOSE WHO TRESPASS AGAINST US

Where our traditional text of the Lord's Prayer generally follows the version in Matthew rather than the considerably shorter version in Luke, here Luke's influence is greater. Following Matthew 6:12, we would actually pray, "Forgive us our debts, as we also *have forgiven* our debtors," making our forgiveness of others prerequisite to praying. If we search out other texts in the Gospels about forgiveness, we find something of a circle of forgiveness being set in motion. God forgives us our offenses against his dignity. We, in response, forgive those who injure our sense of our honor and worth in one form or another. Because we are faithful to our implied obligation to imitate God's forgiving character, we dare to come again to him, asking forgiveness for our further offenses against him. In the parable of the unforgiving servant (see Mt 18:21-35), Jesus teaches that the requirement to forgive as we have been forgiven is simply a matter of mathematics. Our sins have cost God so much more than other people's sins against us have cost us, that we would offer God the greatest insult of all by holding onto our grudges against other human beings after expecting God to "get over" our affronts to him.

Forgiving is difficult. Sometimes it is difficult because we are rather prideful people. Where this is this case, we need to reread the parable of the unforgiving servant until we understand that, if God can forgive us our affronts against his honor, we can forgive other people. But sometimes it is difficult because we have been so deeply hurt, betrayed or demeaned. This, too, is not foreign to God, whom we betray whenever we choose self-gratification over pleasing him who gave us the gift of being. Just as God wants us to experience freedom from our *own* sins, so that we can move forward in our life with him, he also wants us to experience freedom from the sins of *others* against us, which are just as distorting and just as hobbling.

What God commands, God also enables. If we cannot pray this petition as people who have already forgiven "those who have trespassed against us," we can pray for God's help to come to the place where, having been so loved and healed by his Spirit, we can forgive and move forward in freedom.

LEAD US NOT INTO TEMPTATION, BUT DELIVER US FROM EVIL

This might seem like an odd petition. Is God really going to lead us into temptation? Isn't that more the role of Satan, traditionally seen as the one dangling an apple in front of Adam and Eve?

The word translated *temptation* also denotes testing. This sense is seen more clearly when Jesus rouses the sleepy disciples in Gethsemane and tells them to pray "that they come not into the time of *trial*" (Mt 26:41, emphasis added). In this petition, we pray to the God who knows us better than we know ourselves, who discerns our weaknesses from afar and who may exercise our faith so as to make it stronger and proven, but will not allow us to be tempted beyond our capacity. When we pray this petition, we ask of God, "Don't ever bring us where our faith will falter."

And this does not always mean places of adversity. Prosperity can be just as destructive to faith, if not more so. Attaining the financial goals or the move or the career shift that we want might bring us into places where the weakness of our flesh would finally overpower the steadfastness of our spirits. And so to pray, "Lead us not into temptation," is once more to pray to God to give to us what he knows to be best for us and to receive this in faith as the best answer to our prayers.

FOR THE KINGDOM, THE POWER AND THE GLORY ARE YOURS

As early as the last years of the first century, Christians were adding this doxology to the Lord's Prayer. It is a reminder, each time we pray this prayer, that nothing we have asked therein is beyond God's ability to provide. God's power assures us that, ultimately, his desires *shall* be accomplished. The kingdom whose coming we earnestly seek is already in God's hand, waiting to break in on the petty fiefdoms of our world's empires. God's glory outshines all the pretensions we see around us. It is because of the certainty of this declaration that giving away our lives for the sake of Christ and his good news means securing our lives for eternity.

❀❀❀❀❀❀❀❀❀❀❀❀❀❀❀❀❀❀❀❀❀❀❀❀❀❀

PUTTING IT INTO PRACTICE

Use the Lord's Prayer as an outline for reflection and prayer. Pause after each petition, and ask God to reveal to you how to live more fully in line with that petition in your specific circumstances. This might lead to self-examination and confession, a vision for how to approach particular situations with the aims of the Lord's Prayer in mind or the prompting of some new action on your part. Pray for grace and strength to walk in line with what God shows you.

Read through one of the many brief devotional commentaries on the Lord's Prayer, perhaps one of the following: James Mulholland, *Praying Like Jesus: The Lord's Prayer in a Culture of Prosperity* (San Francisco: HarperSanFrancisco, 2001); N. T. Wright, *The Lord and His Prayer* (Grand Rapids: Eerdmans, 1997); William H. Willimon and Stanley Hauerwas, *Lord Teach Us: The Lord's Prayer and the Christian Life* (Nashville:

Abingdon, 1996). Write down in your journal what points strike you
as relevant and what impressions, convictions or suggestions are laid on
your heart as you read. When you are done, pray through what you have
written down, asking God for insight into walking henceforth more
fully in line with Jesus' prayer.

23

Adoration

※

If we approach the Eucharist through the gates of confession, we draw closer to the courts of praise. Immediately after the "Collect for Purity," in which we ask God to clear our minds and hearts of all that is impure and distracting so that we can worthily magnify God's glorious name, the Book of Common Prayer gives us an opportunity to address God in worship with the *Gloria* ("Glory to God in the highest"), a hymn that Christians have used to praise the Trinity since at least the fifth century. Adoration is facilitated later in the service also in the "Offertory," which is first and foremost an act of worship, and in the preface to the Great Thanksgiving, in which we join "with angels and archangels and all the company of heaven" in the *Sanctus* ("Holy, holy, holy"). And, of course, hymns such as accompany the opening of the service often focus our hearts on adoration.

Adoration is thus a spiritual discipline that the BCP seeks to nurture just as fully as self-examination and confession, on the one hand, and intercessory prayer on the other. But it is frequently an overlooked or misunderstood discipline. Marva Dawn's book about worship, *A Royal Waste of Time*, captures in its title one of the basic reasons for this. Self-examination and confession are to the soul what diagnosis and treatment are to a cancerous body. We can understand the value of that. Prayer is a means of gaining access to God's resources to meet pressing needs. We can understand the value of that. But what, really, is the use of worship?

More vehement objections have been posed. Perhaps you have heard, as I have, the comment that "any God who demands worship doesn't deserve worship." Or, for those trying to hold together the image of

God as Parent with the idea of worship, the question arises, "What kind of father would want his children to bow down and grovel in front of him?" For some people, the idea of worship evokes an image of God as a power-crazed, egocentric tyrant.

But worship is not something God demands. It is something that his majesty and wonders cannot help but elicit. We are compelled to worship, not from without by a tyrannical God, but from within by our own deep awareness of something greater than ourselves on which our lives depend. When we worship, we sense some connection with this "something greater" that raises us up out of our own mortality and finiteness, answering the deep craving of our inmost selves, where God has placed the image of his own eternity (see Wis 2:23).

Worship, the adoration of the numinous, is one of the most basic instinctive drives in human beings. It is practiced among the remotest tribes. It is in evidence in ancient ritual sites and burial mounds. We *will* worship something. The trick is to worship the *right* something, that which is worthy of such a degree of acknowledgment and affirmation of value, such that it is also worthy of our devotion, our service, our investment of our limited time in this world.

Worship serves the very important purpose of opening us up to the Divine. Adoration involves acknowledging, and therefore becoming aware of and alert to, the Divine Other. It is a means by which we become present to God and become aware of his presence—a most fitting preparation for approaching Holy Communion. Worship is not an intellectual enterprise, in which we remind ourselves *about* God— although it may begin like that. It is a relational enterprise, through which we are ushered into a face-to-face encounter with God. In adoration, we take the time to be overwhelmed by the excellence, the beauty, the goodness, the majesty of God, the "Thou" to whom we speak and whom we encounter face-to-face in worship. And in that encounter we discover more fully that which gives meaning to the remainder of our time, that which makes it time well spent. In this and the following three chapters, we will explore the spiritual discipline of adoration, not merely as a ritual act, but as a lifestyle.

IN THE PRESENCE OF THE AWESOME

I'm not particularly what you would call a nature lover. Yet even I am awestruck by a sunrise or sunset, especially over the ocean, or the starry sky on a cold, clear winter's night. When I allow myself to drink in such sights, I am filled with awe, with an awareness of what is beyond myself, bigger than myself, which puts my self, my concerns, my complaints, my *self-centeredness* in perspective. As I marvel at the beauty and wideness of creation, I realize that *I* am not what is significant, and that is good! For then, at least for a while, I begin to find my true significance and cease to chase after my illusions.

That sense of awe in the face of the grandeur of *creation* positions me to enter into an even greater sense of awe at the greatness of the *Creator*. This is captured admirably in a familiar hymn:

Fair are the meadows,
fairer still the woodlands,
robed in the blooming garb of Spring;
Jesus is fairer,
Jesus is purer,
who makes the woeful heart to sing.
Fair is the sunshine,
fairer still the moonlight
and all the twinkling, starry host;
Jesus shines brighter,
Jesus shines purer
than all the angels heaven can boast.

Paul, well in line with his Jewish heritage, looks to the wonders of nature as the reflection of an even greater Wonder, namely God's own self. "What can be known about God" is spread out before us in God's skillfully crafted work: "Ever since the creation of the world his eternal power and divine nature, invisible though they are, have been understood and seen through the things he has made" (Rom 1:19-20). Or, in the words of the psalmist, "the heavens are telling the glory of God; and the firmament proclaims his handiwork" (Ps 19:1). Allowing myself to be lifted out of myself by the wonderful "otherness" of Nature moves me closer to seeing the wonderful "Otherness" of God.

The eucharistic liturgies remind us of this every time they direct us to recite the *Sanctus*, the "Holy, holy, holy," and to affirm, "Heaven and earth are full of your glory." We are continually encouraged to come alive more and more fully to the ways in which God's immeasurable greatness pervades the cosmos in which we live. To do so is to come alive to a deep, spiritual energy that transforms our lives in a mundane world.

The great cathedrals were built with a view to arousing the same experience of awe, and to the same end. The edifice, with its vaulted arches and tall, narrow spires, is orchestrated entirely to direct your attention upward at the same time that you are struck with the overwhelming massiveness of the place—a building representing the investment of the lives and combined skill of an entire labor force over centuries. It is a space that lifts you out of yourself into the communion of the thousands of people who labored to build it and ultimately lifts you closer to grasp the awesomeness of the Almighty, to whom the building is a testimony, of whose grandeur it is but a small reflection.

Losing ourselves in the worship of God, we find something ever so much more than ourselves. Knocked out of orbit around ourselves, we are brought into harmony with angels and archangels and all the company of heaven, who are rightly centered on the Creator, their orbits fixed on God in worship. We are tuned, as it were, to the music of the spheres, the involvement of all creation in adoration of its Maker, and we transcend, for a moment, our own finiteness.

This experience is reflected in the fact that portrayals of the life of the world to come, from John's Revelation to Dante's *Paradiso*, involve scenes of endless adoration. Worship is the business of heaven, when we stand perpetually in the presence of the Awesome and where no clouds of mortal thought and distractions of mortal life obscure that vision.

> I'll praise my maker while I've breath,
> and, when my voice is lost in death,
> praise shall employ my nobler powers.

My days of praise shall ne'er be past,
while life, and thought, and being last,
or immortality endures.

The writer of this hymn experiences adoration as that activity that transcends death and that assures him of his own transcendence of death as he looks forward to continuing in adoration for eternity. In this way, the practice of adoration offers a cure for the fear of death that so often drives us into compulsive and dysfunctional attempts to transcend our own mortality (for example, through achievement, through the acquisition and exercise of power or through the amassing of goods that give the illusion of permanence to our lives).

Worship is ultimately related to our sense of purpose and meaning, which is vital to our survival. Without purpose and meaning, we drop into depression. Our quest for this matrix of meaning fuels our impetus to find that object or those objects that are greater than ourselves, that can elevate us above our finitude, and we express our relationship to that object in worship. Ascribing worth to something at this level reflects back on *our own* worth. If what we worship with our lips and with our lives is truly *worth* the investment of the ever-draining sand of our lifetime, the passing of our lives becomes time well and meaningfully spent. If we worship what is not worthy, we doom ourselves to the kind of regret for which there is no cure—the regret of a life poorly spent, even wasted.

What is worth *my* devotion? What is worth the investment of my time in this limited span of life? The witness of the Scriptures and the saints of both synagogue and church speak with one voice in response: "You, O God, alone are worthy!" To say that God is "worthy to be praised" is to say, "You deserve to be acknowledged; your greatness and character, your works and your gifts deserve to be acclaimed and appreciated. *You* are a worthy compass point and target for my life." When we feed this core purpose through adoration, we can engage all other aspects of our life—marriage, relationships, work, entertainment—in right measure and fruitfully, since we are not distorting our engagement with any one of them by seeking our life's meaningfulness primarily in relationship to it.

No matter what your previous experiences of "worship" may predispose you to believe, such adoration is not boring. Worship often seems static. Whenever I read the book of Revelation in my early teens, I found myself impatient with the scenes of worship, especially the two-chapter-long liturgy of Revelation 4—5. I wanted to get to the "cool stuff," the plagues, the beasts—the *action*. But when we are engaged in worship as adoration, the experience is anything but static. It involves us in the heightened attentiveness to the other that we experience with another human being as we are falling in love, savoring the growing connection between two people. The movement may be slow to the observer, but the small, incremental steps the lovers take toward each other only increase their experience of shared energy and focus.

Like the space surrounding two lovers, the space of adoration has the beauty of another world. The psalmist frequently enters and speaks about the atmosphere of this other world:

Strength and beauty are in [God's] sanctuary. (Ps 96:6)
Worship the LORD in the beauty of holiness. (Ps 96:9, as quoted in BCP, 726)

The space of standing in awe before God has a character that awakens us to become our most fully alive. It is a place of radiance, a place of wonder. Sunrise, sunset and starry night sky all pale in comparison.

And, yes, adoration, like human love, can indeed lead us into emotional, unselfconscious self-expression. It took me some years in a charismatic Episcopal church before I could begin to allow the wonder of being in the presence of God to manifest itself in even a subtle bodily gesture. But just as the lover must reach out for the beloved, so the worshiper finds it irresistible to lift up a hand toward the God of her devotion. Some will always find such enthusiasm distasteful. Saul's daughter Michal despised even King David, her husband, for forgetting himself, as it were, in his ecstasy before God. But David was not the one in the wrong that time (2 Sam 6:14-23).

Of course, adoration does not require manufactured emotionalism. It does not mean faking a smile or ignoring our trials and pain. It does mean acknowledging who God is in the midst of them, the God whose goodness and wonders remain unchanging in the midst of our ever-changing feelings and fortunes. Job gives us our most extreme, but not unparalleled, example of this: "The LORD gave, and the LORD has taken away; blessed be the name of the LORD" (Job 1:21).

The eucharistic liturgies invite us to find ourselves more fully as we become "lost in wonder, love, and praise," to live out of our fuller purpose by living from a life centered on God. Through the regular practice of adoration, we move from knowing *about* this God to encountering and knowing this God as the most significant Other, in relationship with whom the rest of our life takes on its proper and most wholesome shape, whom to know is eternal life (see Jn 17:3).

PUTTING IT INTO PRACTICE

Find a place of retreat where you can unselfconsciously express yourself in adoration before God—perhaps an unoccupied sanctuary, a forest, some unfrequented part of a park or meadow, or the sofa in your living room if you have the place to yourself for a while.

Equip yourself with several hymns ("Holy, Holy, Holy," "Fairest Lord Jesus," "Praise, My Soul, the King of Heaven" are a few that come to mind), praise choruses ("Holy Lord, Most Holy Lord," "I Will Come and Bow Down" and "Bless the Lord, O My Soul" are just a few possibilities), canticles (for example, Canticles 13, 18, 19, 20 and 21 on pages 90-95 of the BCP), and psalms (Ps 145—150 are all well suited to this exercise), and have a Bible on hand. Use a number of these hymns and texts, speaking or singing them aloud, to enter into a time of adoration, focusing on the presence of the God whom you are addressing.

As you become more aware of God's presence, transition to using your own words in direct address to God, returning to the hymns and canticles as you feel led. Remember that your goal is not to ask for anything from

God, but just to enter his presence, acknowledge and appreciate his character and works, and see more of his wonder and beauty.

Repeat this exercise several times throughout the week, and make a short time of adoration a part of your regular devotional practice. Depending on your mood at the time, your comfort level and many other factors, the first few experiences may feel awkward or as if you're shouting at a closed door. Try not to become anxious or push too hard. The self-consciousness *will* yield to consciousness of God; the cloud *will* lift. Meditating on a text such as Isaiah 6:1-8 or Revelation 4—5 (especially with its inviting image of the "open door" in heaven) and then acclaiming the *Sanctus* (BCP, 362) or canticles 18 and 19 (BCP, 93-94) might help to open you up more to an awareness of your access to God and his immanence.

Idolatry, Then and Now

❉

There is, of course, a shadow side to this experience of awe. Just as we can look at creation or a great cathedral and be rapt in adoration of the Creator, we can look at other sights, feel awe and be swept away toward the worship of the illusions—the idols—in whose name those temples and shrines were erected. Idols are deceptive, but they are also seductive. We *long* for something greater than ourselves, since finding that "something greater" is directly connected with our finding purpose and a context for meaningfulness—if not for our whole lives, perhaps at least for a while. So we allow ourselves to be awed by the grand "cathedrals" built, and images erected, to the gods of this age. We are duped into a sense of awe and into an investment of our lives that is illusory, a counterfeit of true worship.

I have to admit, in this regard, that I am a sucker for architecture. I have frequently been struck by the grandeur of state capitol buildings and, even more, the monuments and other public buildings of the nation's capitol. And, of course, the nation is something vastly greater than myself. Nevertheless, the feeling of awe and illusion of permanence that these shrines are constructed to evoke can easily mask the impermanence and manufactured nature of our government and our nation, which will surely go the way of all governments and which must always be held accountable not to itself (the god Nation that one could easily slip into worshiping in these shrines), but to the God of the prophets, whose kingdom surpasses and succeeds every human empire. And who has not stood at the foot of the Empire State Building or, in its time, the World Trade Center without being struck by the awesomeness of what human beings could achieve, and the greatness of the god Business to whom these great cathedrals were erected, whose service was duly performed therein? Even upscale shopping malls or spacious hotel lobbies are designed specifically to lift their visitors' spirits and raise them a little bit outside of themselves, but this momentary exhilaration is a gift of the goddesses Consumerism and Luxury and an impetus to invest oneself in acquiring the wealth needed to belong to their congregations.

The world into which first Judaism and then Christianity were born was a world of "many gods and many lords" (see 1 Cor 8:5). Fundamental to conversion to either faith was a willingness to turn "from idols, to serve a living and true God" (1 Thess 1:9) and to allow one's encounter with this living God to reshape one's priorities, ambitions and behaviors—in short, to bring about newness of life.

What did these idols represent? Consider the familiar Greco-Roman pantheon, as an example. These gods are fairly transparent representations of facets of the social order on which that order depended. Many are explicitly connected with human pursuits and success in those pursuits. Ares (Mars) is the god of war, whose favor was courted by those who had a vested interest in the domination system of militarism. Hades (Pluto) was the giver of wealth (a side benefit of being god of the underworld was knowing where all the gold and silver was to be found). Hephaistos (Vulcan) represented skilled craftsmanship; Aphrodite (Venus), courtship and sex; Apollo and Athena (Minerva), knowledge, science and art; Poseidon (Neptune), safety in regard to sea travel, which was basic to trade and commerce. Others were the deified faces of natural processes on which human society was dependent, including Demeter (Ceres), who gave fecundity of crops, and Dionysus (Bacchus), who blessed the vine with fruit. Alongside these were idolatrous cults erected to represent human domination systems quite directly and unabashedly—the emperor cult, the cult of the goddess Roma Aeterna, personifications of virtues associated with imperial rule, such as Pax (peace) and Securitas (safety, "national security"). The cults of the Canaanites, Babylonians, Egyptians and others with which the people of the First Testament had to reckon were similarly structured.

As the Scriptures of both testaments commend the worship of God, so they warn against the worthlessness of such idols. The fundamental critique of idols is that they are lifeless and represent what will never be life giving: "They have mouths, but do not speak; eyes, but do not see" (Ps 115:5). Those who direct their lives toward what is lifeless will become like the things they worship—lifeless shells of beings, remade in the image of their gods rather than recovering the image of the living God. The Jewish authors of anti-idolatry polemics like Psalm 115 well understood that the idol was merely a representation for something larger and more abstract, but they also understood that there was an ironic appropriateness that a lifeless image should represent those facets of our existence which, when chosen as the "something greater" that will supposedly give our lives meaning and allow us to discover our created purpose, result in our spiritual deaths and the shipwreck of our lives.

Jesus didn't talk about idols much, probably because he moved almost entirely within a region where he and his audience would have encountered none (the Greek cities of Galilee, Decapolis and the coastal areas being the exceptions). But he does name one idol rather prominently: "You cannot serve God and wealth," or Mammon (Mt 6:24). Apparently that was an idol to which even the idol-rejecting monotheists could fall prey.

There was a man in my church—perhaps you knew him in yours as well—who tried to serve both. God was beautiful to him, especially in his youth. But as he moved into adulthood and had to deal with the realities of wages and bills, and had to reckon with the limitations placed on him and his young family by their finances, other images took the place of God. He saw images of the life of the wealthy, the homes they enjoyed, the trips they could take, the way they lived "bigger than life." Those images inspired awe, a feeling of looking at something that was able to lift him out of himself and place him where he would have a life worth living. He went to church, of course, and fit in what he could of the life of the church, but his heart was really set on this other vision.

So he worked, saved, invested, got the house, worked some more, invested some more, took the vacations, worked some more, but never came to that place of fullness. He looked up from his deathbed at the grown son and daughter he barely knew, at the wife he had forgotten in the day-to-day crusade, at the home he had acquired but never really lived in. He could *not* see the specters of the people who died of starvation and want while he stored up his wealth, the friends he never made and relationships he never nourished, the disciples he never mentored.

In the pursuit of his idol, he had missed life. Even as he chased the vision that he thought would expand his life and make it full, his life became smaller and smaller, narrower and narrower. He had become as something dead and lifeless, without eyes to see the people around him, without ears to hear their words of love, humor or spiritual guidance, without lips to speak the life-giving words of a father to his children or a husband to a wife, without hands to offer bread to the poor, invite them to share a meal and experience the kingdom of God together. He became like the lifeless thing he worshiped.

We become like what we worship. We conform our lives to what we believe will please our God, whether that is the living God of Jesus Christ or the god of commerce, the god of power, the god of pleasure and the rest of our society's pantheon.

> Jesus calls us from the worship
> of the vain world's golden store,
> from each idol that would keep us,
> saying, "Christian, love me more!"

The call of such a lover is the invitation into a relationship that leaves no room for regret at the close of life.

※※※※※※※※※※※※※※※※※※※※※※※※※※※※※

PUTTING IT INTO PRACTICE

Gather a number of small clay pots, a marker and a hammer. If you are more artistically inclined, you might wish to bake modeling clay into a number of small figurines instead.

Spend some time in God's presence, asking him to reveal the idols in your life. Where have you been placing value and in relation to what have you been seeking meaningfulness inappropriately? From what dried-out cisterns have you been looking for life-giving water?

Name the idols that God raises to your consciousness. Write the names of these idols down, each on one of the pots or figurines.

When you are ready to renounce them—and that might not be all at once and all right now—smash the pot or figurine bearing the name of that idol. After each act of renunciation, recite the *Shema:* "The LORD is our God, the LORD alone. You shall love the LORD your God with *all* your heart, and with *all* your soul, and with *all* your might" (Deut 6:4-5, emphasis added).

25

What Gift Shall We Bring?

❈

It would be easy to miss the offertory while reading through the Book of Common Prayer, as it is mentioned only in the rubrics, the italicized directions most readers tend to pass over. Of course, within the liturgy itself, it is impossible to miss the offertory, as it is common practice for ushers to draw your attention to it by planting a large plate in front of your face. This part of the service is not, however, just about dropping money into the collection or "paying your dues to belong," as one parishioner remarked. Passing the plates is part of a larger liturgical process of gathering the whole congregation's offering and bringing it forward to the altar in a symbolic act of presenting it to the Lord as an act of worship and adoration.

A text from the Psalms frequently serves as a prelude to the offertory: "Ascribe to the LORD the glory due his name; bring an offering, and come into his courts" (Ps 96:8). The offerings we give constitute one manifestation of our giving honor to God, alongside singing hymns of praise and other acts more commonly associated with adoration. Again the analogy with courtship seems apt. I can remember with what care I chose flowers or a dress or a certain opal ring for my wife while we were dating and with what delight I gave these things to her as tokens of the esteem in which I held her and the love that was growing between us. We honor another with speech, with song, with actions and also with gifts.

The offertory, then, is an act of adoration. It stands in a long tradition of relating to God or to the gods through gift-giving, even as human relationships are often created, nurtured and maintained through gift-giving. There were two principal motives behind giving gifts to the gods in the ancient world. One was *do ut des*, "I give, so that you may give." Offerings were inducements to the gods. By giving what we could as humans, it was hoped that the gods would give what they could as gods, what humans could not acquire for themselves, for example, a safe journey, a fruitful harvest, healing from a disease. The other motive expressed the mirror image of this: "I give *because* you have given." This was the prominent strain in Israelite religion and early Christianity, and is certainly the way the BCP directs us to make our offerings and to relate to our possessions as a whole.

> You are worthy, our Lord and God, to receive glory and honor and power, for you have created all things, and by your will they existed and were created. (Rev 4:11)

> Yours, O LORD, are the greatness, the power, the glory, the victory, and the majesty; for all that is in heaven and on earth is yours; yours is the kingdom, O LORD, and you are exalted as head above all. (I Chron 29:11)

These two offertory sentences come from fuller scriptural scenes of adoration. One of the truths about God that we acknowledge in adoration is that, as the Creator of all that is, seen and unseen, he is the real owner of all that is, seen and unseen. As Paul would ask, "What do you have that you did not receive? And if you received it, why do you boast as if it were not a gift?" (I Cor 4:7).

This way of thinking poses a strong challenge to our ideas about ownership, about earning a living, about the fundamental conviction about what is "mine." At the same time, it drives the necessary wedge between us and our property that makes it possible to put relationships and community ahead of private ownership through lending, giving and sharing, and to love our neighbor as ourselves through spending what we have to relieve their needs as we would our own (see I Jn 3:16-18). Our act of giving to God some portion of what we have received is an act of adoration that puts our money where our mouths are. We give as a testimony that God has given, that we experience his generosity throughout the week, in all that we earn, spend and enjoy.

But we give more than money in this act. Liturgical theologian Leonel Mitchell writes of the offertory that it "expresses symbolically and ritually the self-offering of the people of God." We're not just writing God a check. We are offering some portion of the fruits of "our life and labor to the Lord" (BCP, 377). We are offering the time and energy it took to raise that money. We are offering the tasks we performed in order to earn that money. As the tithe represented the whole of the produce of the land, acknowledging that all—even the strength and opportunity to sow and reap—came from God, belonged to him and was graciously given by him, so the offertory becomes a symbol of our offering our whole lives to him, the "living sacrifice" that is our "spiritual worship" (Rom 12:1). Our offering immediately precedes the Great Thanksgiving: it is a facet of our offering of our selves to God in connection with and in response to Christ's offering of himself for us.

So much of the discipline of adoration simply has to do with awareness, specifically our awareness of God and the God-centered, God-ward orientation of our lives. The offertory invites us to take this awareness with us into the places where we labor throughout the week and into the places where we enjoy the fruits of our labor, mindful that even these activities are gifts from God and reminders of his presence and care.

❋❋❋❋❋❋❋❋❋❋❋❋❋❋❋❋❋❋❋❋❋❋❋❋❋❋❋

PUTTING IT INTO PRACTICE

Think about how much money you will give to God this week or month in the offering and other charitable contributions, and approximately what percentage of your workweek that represents. Each day, identify that block of time (say, the hour immediately following a morning break or lunch) that will be spent earning the money you will contribute, and offer that time and all your activity within it intentionally and consciously to God as an act of adoration.

Throughout the day, engage in brief acts of thanksgiving to God and brief acts of offering yourself to God. For example, thank him for the gift of life for a new day, and offer yourself and all you will do that day to him. Receive each meal with gratitude as a gift from God, and offer your renewed strength to him. Thank God for the strength and opportunity to work, to care for family, to engage in whatever the day's tasks are, and offer yourself and your engagement to him as a response to his gifts.

26

Through the Open Door

❦

The book of Revelation is a marvelous text for exploring the spirituality of liturgy. Scenes of adoration and other liturgical acts fill its pages, as well as pronouncements of blessing and invitations to come into God's presence. Sadly, the popular use of Revelation to play "pin the tail on the Antichrist" and to try to convince everyone that the countdown for "the last seven years" starts this coming Tuesday has made it the last book of the Bible many sane Christians want to read.

Before the first and fullest scene of adoration, John looks up "and there in heaven a door stood open!" (Rev 4:1). He hears words of invitation to "come up here," and, caught up in the Holy Spirit, he finds himself in the presence of God and Jesus, the Lamb. This is popularly read as a text about some end-time "rapture" in which the faithful are taken up to heaven so as to avoid a period of serious persecution and testing. But it is a text about "rapture" of a completely different kind—the rapture we experience as we enter into God's presence through adoration.

What John "hears" on the other side of this open door is a hymn of praise that is a form of the *Sanctus* as it is sung in the Great Thanksgiving: "Holy, holy, holy, the Lord God Almighty, who was and is and is to come" (Rev 4:8). The praise song of the strange angelic order John calls the "four living creatures" echoes the hymn heard by the earlier Israelite prophet, Isaiah, in his famous experience of standing in the presence of God, from which our *Sanctus* is taken verbatim: "Seraphs were in attendance above him. . . . And one called to another and said: 'Holy, holy, holy is the LORD of hosts; the whole earth is full of his glory'" (Is 6:2-3).

As the *Sanctus* opens us up to the activity on the other side of the "open door," the liturgical acts that precede the singing of this hymn (called collectively the *Sursum Corda,* "Lift up your hearts") provide a path by which to enter through that door. This path begins with the celebrant's simple wish, "The Lord be with you," a wish that the people reciprocate, saying, "And also with you." It directs our desires toward God's presence, toward allowing the promise of Jesus' name—"God with us"—to be realized in our lives. The celebrant bids us take a second step forward into God's presence: "Lift up your hearts" (BCP, 361).

This calls for an internal act on our part to accompany the words we speak in response. As we affirm that we do, indeed, "lift them up to the Lord," we come out of ourselves and set our attention and intentions above what occupies us within, above what we see around us and toward the God who meets us at this altar and in this sharing of bread and wine. The words invite us to do so with an attitude of hope and expectation, with hearts lifted, the opposite of being cast down in our hearts, looking to him from whom our help comes in this moment. "To you, O LORD, I lift up my soul" (Ps 25:1). We elevate our selves in an offering of adoration, even as the bread and wine will be elevated as the focal point of our offering of ourselves in conjunction—in communion—with Jesus' "full, perfect, and sufficient sacrifice" (BCP, 334).

The celebrant bids us "give thanks to the Lord our God," and, whatever our mood at the moment, we affirm that it is indeed "right to give him thanks and praise" (BCP, 361). We are invited in this moment to be mindful of God's benefits, perhaps *in,* perhaps *despite* whatever circumstances now engage us. Whether all is going well or all is going miserably, there are certain ways in which we have been graced by God. When we keep our hearts fixed on what God has given, we discover a place of centering, a source of wholeness. We find an anchor in the midst of this life's changes and the resulting emotional turmoil, as awareness of God's gifts and gratitude to him stabilizes our hearts. Though not thankful *for* adverse circumstances, we can be thankful *within* them, remembering God's gracious interventions. The Great Thanksgiving unfolds to help remind us, whatever our present circumstances, of what

God has done for us in creation and in our redemption, and therefore what cause we have to be glad, to be grateful, to be lifted above our circumstances by the ways in which he has already invaded our lives and circumstances—and stands poised to do so again in the sacrament.

In this space of thanksgiving, we grow in our awareness of God's presence through our awareness of his interventions on our behalf, both as individuals and as part of the collective, his people. We have been given the gift of life itself by God's good pleasure (see Rev 4:11). Even the simplest pleasure of feeling the sunshine, breathing the cold, crisp air of January or petting a dog is a gift from God. We have been bought back for God from our debt-slavery to sin, selfishness, systems of domination and Satan, and have been given the possibility of a whole new life in the kingdom of God and the dignity of serving as his priests, mediators here of his presence and favor (see Rev 5:9-10). We have been made clean to stand before God and receive his commission, his gift of purpose for our lives (see Is 6:6-8). Our current circumstances, joyful or adverse, are opened up to God's creative involvement more fully as we give ourselves over to gratitude to him for who he is, as well as what he has done.

The prelude to the *Sanctus* opens up the vaults of our awareness to the activity of angels in worship around God's throne, to that other realm that puts this present world in its proper perspective when the horizons are merged.

> Rank on rank the host of heaven
> spreads its vanguard on the way,
> as the Light of Light descendeth
> from the realms of endless day,
> that the powers of hell may vanish
> as the darkness clears away.

By the time we sing the *Sanctus*, the roof where we have gathered is blown off to reveal the swirling ranks of angels in festal gathering around God, and we discover afresh the true center of the cosmos and the true center of our lives—the One seated on the throne. We find our rightful place, and our wholeness, in adoration. As creatures, we need this element of adoration in our lives to be *complete*. As God's created daughters and sons, we are not in touch with our genuine selves or with our true place in the world, apart from being in touch with our Creator in adoration.

The eucharistic liturgy thus gives us a pattern that might be helpful for entering into God's presence in adoration at any time. We begin with the desire, the prayer, for God's presence that focuses our attention and directs our intentions. We make a liturgical act of lifting up our hearts—our thoughts, our feelings, everything we are in that moment—to God in an offering of ourselves, which at the same time opens up all that we are to him and invites him to respond by receiving this offering. We make ourselves mindful of all God has done on our behalf, speak our thanksgivings to him and move from there fully into adoration of him for who he is.

The *Sanctus* does not simply invite us to join in the heavenly adoration of God. It is an invitation into the *perpetual* adoration of God that characterizes the beings who live in the full presence of God. Those who are closest to God worship him *all the time:* "Day and night without ceasing they sing, 'Holy, holy, holy, the Lord God the Almighty'" (Rev 4:8).

This is also the life of those who are closest to God on this side of the open door. Adoration pervaded the daily life of the psalmists, whose mouths were "filled with your praise, and with your glory all day long" (Ps 71:8), who paused "seven times a day" to "praise you for your righteous ordinances" (Ps 119:164). This last quotation is an important verse for the development in the Medieval period of a particular form of monastic spirituality that involved praying the "Hours," worship services held at roughly three-hour intervals throughout the day and night. The practice of praying the Hours, in turn, eventually gave rise to the more modest Anglican practice of the Daily Office, the cycle of daily times of prayer—particularly morning and evening prayer—designed to fill our mouths and minds with God's glory all day long.

The psalmists carried adoration into their nights as well: "My soul is satisfied as with a rich feast, and my mouth praises you with joyful lips when I think of you on my bed, and meditate on you in the watches of the night" (Ps 63:5-7). Being given to sleeplessness, I try to keep this verse ever in mind, so that, even if I don't get the refreshment of a full night's sleep, I might be refreshed in a different way by praise of and conversation with the God to whom the night is as day.

Those who worship continually grow closer to God, just as couples who continually spend time together grow more intimate. One could look at the practice of praying the Hours and say (rightly), "That's fine for monastics!" Even the full cycle of the Daily Office would strain the schedule of most people (though there are not many better things we could do as a family than pray through a condensed form of Morning Prayer before going in our different directions for the day and a form of Evening Prayer when we reunite). However, the practice of adoration, even "seven times a day" praising God "for [his] righteous ordinances," can be built into anyone's schedule, since it does not require a specific duration—just a specific attention and intention.

The picture the Hebrew Scriptures paint of David is that of a person who kept the adoration of God in the forefront of his mind. Even during his years as the CEO of Israel, he wasn't too busy to continue in worship throughout the day and into the night watches. Indeed, he was too busy *not* to do so! For David, "a man after God's own heart," adoration was not something extra to fit into a crowded schedule. He had cultivated a genuine thirst for worshiping God, born of the deep satisfaction that came from adoration, from drinking in the presence and awesomeness of the divine Other like a lover the presence of the beloved.

Yet adoration is not escapism. It is not about becoming so heavenly minded that one is no earthly good. There are some choruses that, on first blush, might suggest this, and even encourage this. One promises that, as we "turn our eyes upon Jesus," the "things of earth will grow strangely dim." But it is not the case that adoration of God blurs or diminishes our perception of the world around us. Rather, it allows us to see "the things of earth" as they *are* and not as they pretend to be through the propaganda of our culture's domination systems and not as we magnify or distort them through our own warped leanings and longings.

The practice of adoration allowed John to witness and to join in the scenes of adoration of God and the Lamb in Revelation. This, in turn, positioned him to view the world of western Asia Minor under Roman rule quite differently than the "official" portraits of life under Roman domination, which depicted Rome as a beneficent goddess bringing order and economic prosperity to the world. Adoration of God contributed to his being able to penetrate the veil of imperial propaganda and to see the emperors and Roman domination from an entirely different perspective, without the lenses that Empire wanted to keep over his eyes and the eyes of his fellow subjects. Adoration of God meant liberation from the webs of lies spun by the powers and principalities, empowering John to name the crimes of Empire for what they were—violence in the service of domination, pillaging the provinces and client kingdoms in the service of the elite's conspicuous consumption, suppression of dissent and critique through marginalization and martyrdom. Adoration contributed to freeing John and, through him, the churches of Asia Minor, to discern the response of faithfulness to Jesus Christ in such a setting, rather than follow the path of cooperation and collusion suggested by other voices around— and among—them.

The psalmist acclaimed of God that "in your light we see light" (Ps 36:9). Through adoration, we see more of God. But we also come to see our world far more clearly, seeing it in the light of God.

PUTTING IT INTO PRACTICE

Make brief offerings of time and attention to God, inviting him to make you continually aware of his presence and splendor, throughout the day as your commitments permit.

Equip yourself with a number of short acts of adoration that you can easily pull out and use. Here are some suggestions:

Psalm 108:1-5 (morning)
the *Gloria* (morning)
Psalm 113 (midday)

the *Phos hilaron* ("O Gracious Light," BCP, 118; sunset)
Psalm 134 (night)
Psalm 92:1-5; Psalm 96:1-6; Psalm 111 (any time)
Canticles 13, 18—21; Psalms 145—150 (any time)

Type up and print off a number of these in small, business-card-sized blocks of text, and use them as starting points to addressing God in adoration also in your own words.

Reflect in the evening: How did these acts of adoration alter your experience of the day and your perceptions of its priorities and business?

If your schedule and temperament permit, you might consider trying the preceding exercise in conjunction with a predetermined set of "hours." One possible scenario would be to offer these acts of adoration in conjunction with a brief time of prayer (1) upon rising; (2) just before going in to work, school or setting about the day's activities; (3) mid-morning; (4) lunchtime; (5) mid-afternoon; (6) just before leaving work or welcoming family home from work or school; (7) sunset; (8) just before retiring to sleep. Consider locating places where you can be more expressive in your devotions than, say, at your desk at work.

Compose a psalm of adoration. What have you known about and seen in God that deserves to be acknowledged and appreciated? What has God done in the world around you, in the lives of the people and communities close to you and in your own life that deserves to be acknowledged and appreciated? Don't worry about making the idiom sound "biblical"; just write what you've experienced, seen and come to value about God. Now sing your psalm to the Lord!

27

Shaped by the Story
of God's Self-Giving

When we want to get to know people, inevitably we ask them to tell us their story. By knowing where they came from and what brought them to this place where they are now, sitting across from us at a dinner table or walking beside us along a canal or perhaps even sitting on the other side of a desk at an interview, we believe we will get to know who they are and even divine where they will go from here and whether or not we want them to go with us. When someone prompts us, "so tell me about yourself," we often talk about our *selves* by selecting elements of our *stories* that we think will give a fitting picture of our *selves*. In this and the following chapters, we will explore the story into which God invites us and how this story gives shape and direction to our lives.

The ancient Israelites understood the importance of story as the vehicle for knowing God and what to expect from him. The most important episode of this story, celebrated yearly in the Passover, was the exodus from Egypt. This story defined them as a people and defined God as the God of deliverance and justice. It was a story that became the story of every Israelite, as generation after generation made the profession "*We* were slaves in Egypt, but the LORD heard our voice."

The Israelites would keep coming back to this story to remember who they were, no matter how far they had come from being slaves in Egypt. Much later, after centuries of being settled in the land of Canaan, they would have to come back to this starting point. When the Babylonian armies conquered Jerusalem and deported a large segment of the Judean population to Babylon, the exodus story became a focal point for hope. Surely the God of that story would create a new exodus for the people God had brought so far! This, in turn, became a source of strength to resist joining in the worship of idols and otherwise blending in with the Gentiles around them, erasing their story and its witness to the one God.

The greatest danger facing the Hebrews as they entered the land was not the Canaanites. It was the danger of forgetting this story once they were sitting comfortably in the land, enjoying its fruits, as they began to think to themselves, "My power and the might of my own hand have gotten me this wealth" (Deut 8:17; see also Deut 8:11-20). If they lost sight of the larger story of God's redemptive actions on their behalf, the Israelites would begin living out another story, a distorted story—the story of the self-made person. This would, in turn, lead them to respond to one another, to their wealth and to God in ways that would violate and eventually break apart the *shalom* of the people of God. They would regard their wealth as the result of their own efforts, not given as God's gift. They would therefore not honor God with the proper offerings and would not release debts and act to relieve one another's needs, since they had lost sight that they were only stewards of *his* wealth. Forgetting the story would mean forgetting how to respond to what they saw around them in the present moment. Their ultimate fate would be to perish "like the nations" that God drove out to make a home for Israel (Deut 8:20).

The story we carry in our minds gives us our sense of identity, direction and purpose. It tells us where we came from, where we're going and the shape of how we get there. Sometimes we carry around with us a personal story that binds us, limits us, holds us down.

This was certainly the case for Barbara, who was subjected to repeated sexual abuse at the hands of her uncle and cousin, an episode in her personal story that overwhelmed other plot lines. As a result, as she continued to live out her life from that story, her sense of identity was always marred with images of being dirty, defiled and shamed. Her image of God was of a parent who either did not know or did not care enough to intervene. Her relationships tended to be with men who would make her relive that story, rather than introduce new, transforming plots.

Karen's story constrained her life in different ways. She was born a part of the fourth generation of an immigrant family that had arrived in abject poverty and had succeeded in climbing one rung up the ladder with each passing generation. Having heard the stories of her family from her childhood, the plot line continued to drive her corporate-climbing life. She attained success beyond the hopes of her parents and beyond the imagining of her grandparents, but never listened to the yearnings within for family, for relationships, for those good things that even her great-grandparents had enjoyed.

Even more insidious was the effect of America's larger story on Bill's vision. After two decades as a successful entrepreneur, Bill moved to take a position teaching in a school of business at a regional university. Several international families attended the church that he joined, and many business people came from other countries to study in the program. But Bill had drunk in too uncritically the story of his country and its legitimation of its increasing, almost paternalistic role as international policeman and regulator, and he lived out this story in his relationships with the non-American students and families he engaged. While he shared his expertise with them, he never sought to learn from their insights—with the result that the other students in the class never benefited from them either. He was happy to see them coming to church, but never inquired about the practice of Christianity in their home countries or their insights into American (or *Americanized*) Christianity with a view to deepening his understanding of the gospel's vision and demands.

The lives of Barbara, Karen and Bill were limited and constrained by some facet of their own story, their family's story or their nation's story. But God has always been in the business of inviting us into *his* story, a story that opens new doors in dead ends and in which we take on roles and possibilities that would never be ours if we lived only within our personal story. The Israelite theologians who framed the Pentateuch and the Israelite poets who composed the psalms understood the importance of story and of keeping each individual's story thoroughly integrated with God's redemptive story. When the proclamation of the gospel of Jesus the Messiah went out from Israel, it went out in the form

of a story about God's new redemptive acts in Jesus and the people God
was calling anew. The BCP continues to invite us to know ourselves and
live more and more fully from that story of redemption. God's story
provides a larger interpretative frame for all our stories, opening up our
stories to the larger narrative possibilities within the frame of, and living
in response to, God's story.

Reading and reflecting on Scripture is, of course, the practice by means
of which we most fully encounter this story and engage it with a view to
reinterpreting the many stories that define our identities and lives (personal
story, family story, ethnic and national story). The eucharistic liturgies reflect a clear awareness of the place of Scripture in this formational process,
dedicating the first half of the worship service largely to reading and engaging the Word of God. After all, how can we learn to love what God
commands, unless we know what those commandments are? How can we
learn to desire what God has promised, unless we are exposed continually
to those promises, to the vision of life that those promises entail?

We have already explored at length how Scripture feeds the practices
of self-examination and confession. We have seen how it shapes our
praying and orders our living in light of the story of God redeeming us
in Jesus, calling us to die to our life apart from God. We have noted
how it calls us daily to welcome into us the Holy Spirit to enable us to
walk in newness of life. In the following two chapters we will look at
the summary of the fuller scriptural story as it is communicated to us
through the regular elements of the liturgy: the Nicene Creed, which
defines the contours of that story, and the Eucharistic Prayers, in which
we hear again the great acts of God for which we give thanks together in
each celebration of Holy Communion.

PUTTING IT INTO PRACTICE

Take a few moments to center your thoughts on God and become
aware of his presence. Spend some time thinking about your story and,

perhaps, the story of your family. Ask God's Spirit to guide you to features of your story, or even episodes, that are significant for who you are now, how you live now, what priorities you embrace and live out, and the like, and go where you sense the Spirit directing. If possible, write down your story in your journal.

Where do you discern the need for healing from God, perhaps from wounds arising from a specific episode or episodes, perhaps from general trends and drives in your overall story? Open up to God about these facets of your story and listen for his leading.

What is God's role in the story you have recollected and written down? How do your stories intersect?

28

The Nicene Creed

When we were baptized, we became part of the larger story of a community of faith, a story passed on in summary form in the Nicene Creed (see appendix B). The creed gives us our foundational story line, which in turn gives us our identity, our sense of direction and our orientation to the world—if we allow it! Like the confession of sin, the creed uses *we* forms. It is an affirmation of our commitment to a story that we received from a community of faith that has struggled to live in line with this story across the millennia. Ours is not a private faith, nor is the story one that we are free to alter to suit our liking. Indeed, the Nicene Creed exists largely as a result of the church's working out the nonnegotiable contours of the story of God's interventions in God's world in response to some independent thinkers—who would come to be known as "heretics"—whose innovations were viewed as unhelpful tampering with that story. The early church leaders who wrestled with the formulation of the creed did so not only out of a desire to get the story and the characters straight. They also did so out of a knowledge that the story we tell about God is the starting point for living out our lives before him and in line with him.

The creed is often divided into three "articles" of faith, each focusing on the work of one person of the Trinity. But these divisions could equally well be considered acts within the great drama of God's story, a term that will also help us see the creed not simply as a statement of beliefs, but rather as an overall plot summary, as it were, of the epic of God's interactions with us. The first act opens the drama with creation, as God fashions heaven, earth and all that is—both the world we can see and the world we cannot see. Already in this first statement the creed is reacting against earlier distortions of the story, particularly Gnosticism. Gnostics believed that the material world, including our bodies, was inherently evil. Rather than ascribe the creation of this inferior world of matter to the highest God, they told the story of a demiurge, a lower god, who was actually responsible for creation. Their version of the story continued to nourish a devaluing of life in the body and life in creation.

Against these distortions, the church continued to maintain that creation is good, and it is *God's*. God's majesty and beauty could be known through their reflection in creation, and the world and all that is in it is to be valued, cared for as the possession of Another, and redeemed. This story also affects our relationship to our bodies and the bodies of others. We are to care for the bodies of other people as part of God's good creation, tending their needs. At the same time, our bodies are sanctified by God's indwelling Spirit. They are suitable to be offered to God as living sacrifices by using them always in a way that honors him and advances his interests in this world. Far from being a tomb in which the soul is imprisoned, our bodies are the seeds of our eternal bodies (see I Cor 15:42-44).

This was a challenging story for Barbara, whom we met in the previous chapter, to engage. In so many ways she had been alienated from her own body by the abuse she had suffered. But it became part of her healing process to accept that it was the perpetrators who were evil, ugly and defiled—and not her body, which was part of God's good creation, which he had sanctified and cleansed with his Spirit and which God would recreate anew for eternity. She did not have to live a stranger to her own body, nor allow other men like her uncle to continue to treat it like a worthless shell, to do with as they pleased. God's story helped bring reconciliation within herself.

The first act of God's story reminds us of our ultimate dependence on him. We do not live out this article of the creed as long as we try to fit God into our concerns in the visible world, to attend to everything else first and then, if there's time leftover after we've attended to the "real" business of life, think about religion. God is more real than all else, since he is the cause of all else. The story told within the creed directs us to build our whole life on the foundation of God, even as "all things, seen and unseen," depend on that foundation. We are reminded each time we recite the creed that the invisible God is the more solid foundation than the visible world that is "too much with us." This is ultimately the foundation for faithful action in this world.

Hebrews 11 contains the famous litany of the heroes of faith, but before directing our attention even to Abel and Enoch, the author says, "By faith we understand that the worlds were prepared by the word of God, so that what is seen was made from things that are not visible" (Heb 11:3). At first this might seem like a strangely disembodied sentence about faith in a chapter where faith is otherwise demonstrated not by belief but by the embodied action of real people. Nevertheless, it is foundational to all the rest. Throughout the chapter we find that people of faith build their lives around the central reality of the God who stood behind and beyond this temporary, material world. They ordered their lives around God's Word to them: "Build an ark. . . . Leave your homeland. . . . Go, tell Pharaoh." To build our lives first and foremost on God and God's word to us is to build on the solid rock, the rock on which everything else, seen and unseen, depends. Any other foundation is secondary—even though we often act as if just the opposite were true.

The second act focuses on the story of Jesus, though perhaps more than a third of this act is taken up with statements about the Son's precise relationship with the Father. It was vitally important to the framers of the creed to affirm that "God was in Christ" (see 2 Cor 5:19, my translation), that Jesus' story begins ultimately before the story of creation itself. Because God was in Christ, we know that we can see God reflected in him. We know that Christ's self-giving is not done merely to appease an angry God, like a child giving himself to the wrath of an abusive father to spare some third person (often, the mother). Rather, we see in Christ's death a self-giving act of that self-same God for us—the revelation that "God *is* love" (I Jn 4:8, emphasis added).

The story told in the second act focuses on Jesus' incarnation, passion, death, resurrection and coming again. The creed is very similar here to

Paul's summary of the plot line of the story of Jesus,

> who, though he was in the form of God, did not regard equality
> with God as something to be exploited, but emptied himself, taking
> the form of a slave, being born in human likeness. And being found
> in human form, he humbled himself and became obedient to the
> point of death—even death on a cross. Therefore God also highly
> exalted him and gave him the name that is above every name, so
> that at the name of Jesus every knee should bend, in heaven and on
> earth and under the earth, and every tongue should confess that
> Jesus Christ is Lord, to the glory of God the Father. (Phil 2:6-11)

Many theologians have criticized the framers of the creed, and Paul as
their forerunner, for putting so much emphasis on the death and resurrection of Jesus (a small, though climactic part of the gospel story) and taking
almost all emphasis off his life and ministry. They accuse Paul of reinventing
Christianity, making it a "Christ cult" rather than a group of disciples imitating their teacher's way of life and practicing his teachings. Much recent
discussion about the "historical Jesus" has sought to do just the opposite,
placing more emphasis on Jesus' manner of life, looking at his death as the
unfortunate but inevitable end, and cutting the story short there.

But, once more, the framers of the creed (like Paul himself) formulated
the story in such a way that certain effects will follow in our lives, as we
live like people who believe. When Paul recited the "Christ Hymn" (see
above), he did so with a view to exploring its spiritual formation implications for his friends in Philippi. The story of Jesus' self-giving, refusing
to grasp and exploit the privileges and position he enjoyed and putting
the interests of others ahead of his own, was the story Paul hoped would
take shape in the lives of Syntyche, Euodia and others, who seem to have
been getting swept up in defending their status and having their "say"
in the congregation: "Do nothing from selfish ambition or conceit, but
in humility regard others as better than yourselves. Let each of you look
not to your own interests, but to the interests of others" (Phil 2:3-4).

Far from replacing the teachings of Jesus with the mystery cult of a
dying and rising god, the creed preserves the story that assures us that

this man's teachings and self-giving example are indeed the way of life that pleases God and triumphs over death. It is the story that assures us, in the end, that living in line with what Jesus taught—looking out for the interests of others, or serving rather than being served, or giving away one's life in order to find it—is not, in fact, "missing out" on what life has to offer, but rather the path to discovering all that *God* has to offer (see Mk 8:34-35; 10:45). It is the path that leads to exaltation with Christ and everlasting life with God, when we encounter Jesus coming a second time, not in humility, but in power and great glory.

How important it was for Karen, that driven daughter of an immigrant family, that she listened to and reflected deeply on this story, allowing it to challenge the story she was living. While her family's struggle to establish itself on solid financial ground had bequeathed to her many virtues—she had never lacked diligence, drive or determination—it had also oriented her toward all of life in a way that was diametrically opposed to Jesus' orientation. As she pulled back from her over-investment of herself at work, doing all the "extras" that it would take to get that next promotion, she found the space she needed to refresh herself in relationship with God and other people. In turn, she found the inner fullness that her career-climbing had never given her, a fullness that allowed her to "empty herself" as she spent more time mentoring younger women in her corporation and in her church's senior-high youth group, providing a more balanced model of achievement, self-care and service.

The third act begins by focusing our attention on the story of the Holy Spirit's engagement with God's creation and creatures. Regarding the Spirit as an afterthought, a sort of postscript to the story, is a danger that faces many churches. Belief in the Father and the Son is only part of our faith. It happens to be the part to which we may give most attention, but it is not the whole story of who God is in himself, nor who God wishes to be among us—not only the Creator and Savior, but also the God who breathes himself into us, among us and through us into the world.

The Spirit "*proceeds* from the Father and the Son." Throughout the story of God's interventions, the Spirit is moving out from the Father and the Son, going forth from God into his creation. The Spirit hovers over the shapeless waters to bring forth creation (see Gen 1:2). Generation after generation, the Spirit enters into pious souls to make them friends of God (see Wis 7:27). The Spirit is continually being poured out over God's people, the church, to make God's presence vividly known, God's word unmistakably heard and God's power present to accomplish God's purposes (see Acts 2:1-4; Gal 4:6-7; Rev 2:7). The Spirit proceeds from the Father and the Son to dwell within each of us and among us as a Christian community (see 1 Cor 3:16; 6:19). The Holy Spirit is the soul, as it were, of the body of Christ, of which we are all cells or parts, breathing life and direction and desire into the whole.

In proceeding from the Father and the Son to live in us and in our midst, the Spirit transforms our Christian faith from a religion into a relationship. It is a relationship in which we keep inviting the Spirit that we confess to have come on us at baptism to fill us anew, to keep connecting us to God the Father and God the Son, following the injunction to *"keep being filled* with Spirit" (see Eph 5:18). The context of this quotation is especially interesting: "Do not get drunk with wine, for that is debauchery; but be filled with the Spirit, as you sing psalms and hymns and spiritual songs among yourselves."

Are you feeling empty? Don't keep turning to your inferior strategies for numbing your pain or comforting yourself, whether alcohol or shopping or emotional eating or hours of TV or workaholism or whatever. God's story tells us that he is continually sending forth the Spirit, making his fullness available to us in our emptiness, so that we may receive continually from his Spirit, which is the path to abundant life.

This relationship with God through the Holy Spirit marks the fulfillment of God's promise to Abraham and the purpose of Jesus' death on our behalf: Christ died "so *that we might receive the promise of the Spirit* through faith" (Gal 3:13-14, emphasis added). It is the gift that empowers us for and guides us into newness of life as we learn to walk in line with the Spirit (see Gal 5:16-25), the "Lord" and "giver of life."

In the church in which I grew up, people always acknowledged the Spirit to have been given in baptism and present in our lives as believers.

But the Spirit was expected to be present more or less like the fourth player in the card game Bridge—as the "dummy," the "silent one," the player who doesn't lead from her hand herself, but whose cards are placed in the hands of her partner to use as the partner sees fit.

But the Spirit is not the *silent* one. The Spirit is the *eloquent* one. Another important element in the Spirit's story highlighted by its presence in the creed is that "he has spoken through the prophets" of the Old and New Testaments. And the Spirit continues to speak out to every believer, bearing the living voice of the living Christ (see Jn 14:26; 16:13). The Spirit continues to speak out to the churches, communicating Jesus' encouragement, diagnosis and instruction for recovering the right way. "Let anyone who has an ear listen to what the Spirit says to the churches" (Rev 2:7; also Rev 2:11, 17, 29; 3:6, 13, 22). He continues to speak through those whom he empowers for witness, with the gifts of wisdom, knowledge and prophetic utterance (see I Cor 12:4-11), just as he filled and moved Elizabeth, Zechariah and Stephen (see Lk 1:41, 67; Acts 7:55-56).

To hear the Spirit's voice, we must learn to listen to the church in all its wideness. The Spirit empowers the speech of prophets and grants words of wisdom and discernment not only to Christians like ourselves, but also to our sisters and brothers across the globe, across ethnic lines, across the lines between "us" and "them" drawn by governments, across denominational lines, across gender lines. Only if we cultivate an ear attentive to what the sister in Christ from Iraq or the brother in Christ from Mexico has to say to us will we discern "what the Spirit says to the churches."

Bill, trained to speak—but not to listen—to those from beyond his borders, finally connected the story of the Spirit speaking through the prophets with his confession of belief in "one holy, catholic and apostolic Church." He began to understand that the internationals around him had insight where he and many of his fellow American Christians had blind spots. As he listened more carefully, he heard the voice of the risen Lord speaking timely diagnosis where he had tamed the gospel, or blocked out elements of it altogether, to make too much room for the business practices and ethos of competition he had learned from corporate America and now was passing on in his classroom.

❋❋❋❋❋❋❋❋❋❋❋❋❋❋❋❋❋❋❋❋❋❋❋❋❋❋❋❋❋❋❋❋

PUTTING IT INTO PRACTICE

Think about a person whose demeanor and actions genuinely reflect some aspect of the story of God's redemptive acts—perhaps a person in whose presence people come alive to the wonder of creation, or a person who consistently puts the interests of others ahead of his or her own, or a person in whose presence you sense the presence of God and who has spoken words of the Spirit to you. How has it affected you to know this person? How has your story changed—and how might it change even more—by virtue of this person's interaction and example?

Where do you find *yourself* living most in line with God's story? What would it look like if you sharpened this congruence even further? Is that a step in your discipleship God is calling you now to take?

Return to the space of awareness of God and to the story that you have written down in your journal. Where do you find your story pushing you to think, desire or go in directions that are at variance with God's story? For example, how do you think about and treat your body and the bodies of other human beings? Do you do so in ways that reflect their creation and redemption by God or in ways that suggest a lower estimation of them? If there is a discrepancy, where does it come from in your story?

Reflect on the remaining statements of the creed and the explorations above, particularly where they challenge you or provoke a strong response. Where you find yourself living at variance with what we confess about God's story (and its implications for our lives as people who believe that story), spend some time in conversation with God (and others) about those issues, exploring them and listening for his direction.

29

The Great Thanksgiving

❦

The BCP offers a variety of eucharistic prayers, including two of great antiquity. Eucharistic Prayer B is based on the eucharistic prayer preserved by Hippolytus, dating back to the early third century, while Eucharistic Prayer D is based on St. Basil's revised Communion liturgy, dating from the late fourth century. Each of these prayers reinforces the basic story line of the Nicene Creed. In almost every one, there is the common pattern of creation, fall, redemption, while the details are fleshed out with different emphases. The congregation that regularly uses the spectrum of eucharistic prayers will be exposed to the following composite story.

As in the creed, the story begins with God's gracious creation of all that is. Sometimes this is broken up into two acts: the creation of heaven and earth, and the creation of people in God's image (BCP, 341, 370). The creed does not draw attention to the latter detail, but it is a crucial point for our identity. However marred we are by our own sin and by the sins of others perpetrated on us, the image of God remains at the core of our being, and our redemption consists in allowing the Spirit of God to restore that image within us. The many ways in which Scripture, the prayers and the liturgy guide us toward the imitation of Christ all contribute to this end. In this great story, the image of God once imprinted on humankind and lost is fully restored and visible once again in Jesus, with the result that, as we walk more and more closely after his example and teaching, we find the image of God recovering its proper shape within us as well.

This story of Jesus and its relevance for our story is fleshed out during the course of the liturgical year in the "proper prefaces." A proper preface is a brief paragraph interjected into the opening moments of the Great Thanksgiving, recalling seasonally suitable elements of Jesus' narrative. Almost all of the prefaces for the major liturgical festivals and seasons from Advent through Pentecost call attention to some specific benefit we have received from God through an episode in the story of his Son. They call our attention to ways in which we participate in each phase of Christ's journey—how our story is shaped by his. Christ's incarnation—his taking on flesh—enables us to become children of God.

Christ's epiphany—the manifestation of his glory to the nations— merges with the shining of God's light into our hearts as well. Christ's victory over every temptation is our empowerment to share in that victory over temptation day by day with the help of his sustaining grace. Christ's passion and death is our deliverance from death. His resurrection is our hope of eternal life in him. His ascension signals his preparation of a place for us, who will yet go where he has gone. These represent yet another way in which we are called to live out Christ's story in our own, and let his shape our own, with the promise that "the way of the cross" will be "none other than the way of life and peace" (BCP, 99).

This was very much what Karen discovered as she began taking the courageous steps back from her career-climbing path, the path down which the momentum of generations impelled her, and created spaces in which to lay down her life to nurture others. Looking at the liquid capital and the equity she had amassed relatively quickly, she began to wonder if some measure of downward mobility would open up her life even more to the fullness of life that Jesus promised those who would follow him. Still single herself, she sold her small condo in the city (with its still sizeable mortgage) and bought a larger house virtually outright in a less costly location an hour's train ride from her office. Working together with some members of her church, she converted part of the house into two small studio apartments where victims of domestic violence and abuse could take shelter, as these needs became known to the church. Every woman, every child, who came through her door confirmed that she had made the right move.

God commissioned humanity to serve as caretakers of his creation (see BCP, 373), a perpetual reminder to us of our proper relationship to the world, its resources and its inhabitants, and a constant challenge to our exploitive practices and our tendency to use earth's resources, including its wealth, without due concern for God's purposes and for the need of all earth's people. Rather than accept our role in God's creation, we rebelled and fell into sin. The story of the Fall dramatizes our awareness that we do not live now as God intended. We ourselves do not walk in line with God's justice and *shalom*, and we suffer the ravages of the injustice and brokenness compounded by millennia of human sin. The story of the Fall both confirms that this is not the "best of all possible worlds" and diagnoses precisely why this is the case, calling us to pursue the paths that make for *shalom*, even though contrary (even ridiculous) to the wisdom of the world (see 1 Cor 1:18-31).

In the face of our rebellion, our inability to walk faithfully in our relationship with God, God's commitment to us never falters (BCP, 373). God reveals his character in his merciful dealings with Israel, in his speaking through the prophets, persistently calling us back to himself (BCP, 370, 373), and finally in giving Christ to be born into this creation to redeem it, speaking again in the Word-Made-Flesh. God is indeed the Father who stands at the entrance gate of his estate, outside the comfort of his own home, waiting and watching for the wayward child. God is indeed the Lover who never loses hope of wooing back the wayward beloved, nor slackens in commitment to do the same.

Christ's suffering and death "for our redemption" (BCP, 334, 341), by which he "destroyed death, and made the whole creation new" (BCP, 374), is the ultimate display of God's love for us and self-investment in us. As Barbara continued to struggle with questions of self-worth in her process of recovery, she found it helpful to reflect on how much she was worth to God. Informed by the story of redemption, she could ask God this question and see, in response, Jesus answering, "This much," as he stretched out his hands and died *for her*. This message healthfully challenged and eventually overcame the earlier answers she had received to her question of her worth from her uncle and cousins, which was, "you are worth what we can get out of you, what we can take from you, this and nothing more."

The story merges with ours now in several ways. Christ makes a new people "by water and the Spirit" (BCP, 371), a people among whom we now stand as we gather around the Communion rail. Bill was transformed as this facet of the story came to life for him at one Eucharist. It was the Sunday closest to All Saints' Day. As Bill stood at the Communion rail, waiting to receive, he looked around at the faces. About half of them were Anglo American. There were two African American families, a family from India, a young Hispanic couple and a Korean woman with her daughter and son-in-law. He realized that he was seeing a reflection of the passage from Revelation read earlier in the service: "I looked, and there was a great multitude that no one could count, from every nation, from all tribes and peoples and languages, standing before the throne and before the Lamb, robed in white, with palm branches in their hands" (Rev 7:9).

Part of that multitude now stood around that altar. They had *all* stepped out from their nations to come forward as the people of God, in which were no Jews or Greeks, no Scythians or barbarians. That was the moment it dawned on him that he was not here as an American to help enlighten the foreigners who came into his country. Rather, he stood there as one member in a great, white-robed army, whose nationalities signified only the posts to which they had been assigned as witnesses to Jesus, to whose voice they all had equal access through the one Spirit. It was a revelation that humbled Bill, but also liberated him to relate to his international sisters and brothers in Christ with far greater immediacy, attentiveness and, ultimately, benefit to his own understanding of Christ's challenge to him as a Christian in the United States.

Christ also pours out his Holy Spirit on his church "to complete his work in the world" (BCP, 374). Our coming together as a community of believers and our commitment to walk in the Spirit represent the direct continuation of the story of God's acts of redemption. This part of the story speaks to our own quest for purpose and meaning, which are not to be found in the pursuit of our own agendas or attainment of our own career and personal goals as shaped by the values of the competitive, consumerist society around us. We have been bought back for God and equipped with the Spirit's guidance and gifts to continue—each one of us individually and all of us cooperatively—the agenda announced by Jesus in his ministry and to advance the goals to which he will hold the world accountable at his coming in power and great glory. This is what it means when we pray, "Sanctify us also" (BCP, 363). It is to pray, "Set us apart for your own use and your special purposes in this world. Even as this bread and wine have been set apart from all ordinary food to be Christ's Body and Blood given for us, set us apart to be Christ's Body, given for the world."

The story also merges with ours in the act of celebrating Communion. The eucharistic prayers of Rite I observe that, as part of his story, Jesus himself commanded this perpetual remembrance of his self-giving act (BCP, 334, 341), which connects us immediately with his story as we gather around the table in fulfillment of his command. And the focal point of the story told by the eucharistic prayers is none other than Christ's actions and words serving the bread and the wine to his disciples on the night before he died. The words of institution are the most consistent element of the prayers and the episode of the story told consistently with the greatest detail, down to verbatim speech and minute details of action. As the broad sweep of God's story of redemption slows down and takes sharp focus here, we are compelled to give it our close attention—indeed, compelled to enter into that scene. From one camera angle, it is Jesus who extends his arms to offer bread and wine; from another, it is we ourselves who reach out to receive it: "Faith still receives the cup as from Thy hand."

The sacrament of Communion occurs in the blending of the horizons of these stories, giving us a place to return to again and again to be touched by Jesus in the fullness of his love for us as he extends his arms to us and gives himself to us without reservation. Poet Jaroslav Vajda skillfully captures how this rite positions us for immediacy in our encounter with God in this moment of Jesus' offering himself to all his disciples:

> Now the silence
> Now the peace
> Now the empty hands uplifted . . .
> Now the Father's arms in welcome . . .
> Now the heart forgiven leaping
> Now the Spirit's visitation
> Now the Son's epiphany
> Now the Father's blessing
> Now
> Now
> Now

As time seems to stand still when two lovers come fully alive and alert to one another in the moment, so we are invited to experience the "now" of the moment of Communion in the words of institution and the reception of the bread and wine "as from Thy hand."

The time of receiving is potentially a time of special awareness of the presence of the Lord, a time to be savored as we linger in prayer and contemplation. The time that it takes for the whole congregation to commune is a fine opportunity for this, and celebrants might well extend that time to allow parishioners to take full advantage of this invasion of grace. Thomas à Kempis advises, "No less vigilance is required after Communion than devout preparation beforehand. . . . Remain in some quiet place, and savor the presence of God."

Eucharistic spirituality brings us back to this place "as often as you drink" the wine and eat the bread, making the story of Jesus offering himself to us and for us the focal story to which we respond. In so doing, it fuels our imitation of Christ—our embodiment of Jesus—even as we take the bread and wine into ourselves. We experience anew Jesus' love for us and so learn more deeply each time we attend to Communion (not simply *attend* Communion) how to love one another *as Christ loved us.* We see afresh the costliness of our having been forgiven and know better how far we must go to forgive one another as Christ forgave us. We witness the spirit in which Jesus laid down his life for us, his connection with us as he did so, and we experience the effects of being so loved and cared for by him, so that we know better how to lay down our lives for one another.

Karen had discovered this in her journey, as she did not merely provide a service to battered women, but provided a listening ear, a supportive presence and companionship when they felt most alone. Though it took a long time, Barbara, too, came to the place where she was able to forgive as Jesus forgave, and in the process she found release from the hold her relatives' sin had had on her for decades.

Holy Communion makes us return again and again, week after week, to meditation on the Passion, the place where these values and virtues are displayed before us, not only for our imitation, bur also for our embodiment anew as we receive Christ's life into our lives more and more, as Christ keeps taking on our flesh, until we are what we eat and can say with Paul, "It is no longer I who live, but it is Christ who lives in me" (Gal 2:20).

✻✻✻✻✻✻✻✻✻✻✻✻✻✻✻✻✻✻✻✻✻✻✻✻✻✻✻✻✻✻

PUTTING IT INTO PRACTICE

Think about the stories of Barbara, Karen and Bill as these have unfolded over the last three chapters. Can you identify one or two ways in which participation in Holy Communion has changed your self-perception, your perception of others or your perception of God? If you were to add your own before-and-after story alongside their testimonies, what would it be?

What part of who you are needs to be touched more fully by Jesus' self-giving love? What in your life needs to be shaped more fully after the pattern of his self-giving love? Is it in what you believe about yourself, what day-to-day priorities drive your life, what perceptions of others shape your relationships and openness to others?

Ask the Holy Spirit to guide you to select one or two of the particulars you have identified, and pray for transformation in these areas. Write about these areas in your journal, and return to these entries as you continue to pray and as you discover ways in which God is working to heal and change you.

30

Send Us Out

※

We need more of Jesus. That is what drives us again and again to the Communion rail. We need to experience again his love, to be assured of our acceptance by God, to be nourished by an encounter with him. But we do not come only for our own spiritual benefit, important and prerequisite as that is. We are reminded of this by the prayer "Deliver us from the presumption of coming to this Table for solace only, and not for strength; for pardon only, and not for renewal" (BCP, 372). The encounter with the holy One evokes change in the lives of those who partake. Tongues that have sung, "Holy," must now be kept from deceit, eyes seeing Christ's love must remain full of hope. Our speech and our affections cannot now return to the practices and desires of the old person. The body and blood of Christ are the food and drink that fuel the life of the new person.

But the implications of receiving that bread and wine from Jesus' hands are far greater even than this. The story of God's redemptive acts must continue as we leave the altar to give ourselves "to complete Christ's work in the world" in the power of the Spirit that he continually breathes into us (BCP, 374). Having received the spiritual favors—the graces— of Holy Communion, we are bound to respond with grace, that is, with due gratitude, living now no longer for ourselves, but for him who gave his life for us (see 2 Cor 5:15). As Christ has offered himself on our behalf, so we are called to respond by giving ourselves to God for the sake of Christ's ongoing mission. Paul called this "living sacrifice" the appropriate response to God's generosity shown in Christ (Rom 12:1).

The more we keep Christ's act of self-giving love before us, and indeed receive that love in the moment of Communion, the more our own desires and thoughts and wishes can be directed toward him in response.

Our response continues the story of Jesus' self-giving. Without that response, we break off the story prematurely. Eucharist involves taking Christ into ourselves and then taking Christ out into the world as we respond more and more to his self-giving by giving up our life to *his* service. Thus in the prayers of thanksgiving after receiving the sacrament, we pray:

> Send us out to do the work you have given us to do, to love and serve you as faithful witnesses of Christ Jesus our Lord. (BCP, 366)

> Send us now into the world in peace, and grant us strength and courage to love and serve you with gladness and singleness of heart. (BCP, 365)

Here is the point at which many disciples falter in their spiritual journey. We can well understand why, because chances are each one of us still struggles with the fundamental call of Jesus—to die to ourselves, to give away what remains of our lives, to say no to many of our hopes and desires for ourselves so that we can be free to say yes to God. But we still hear the promise of the one who reaches out to us with bread and wine, offering us his life and love to fill our vacuum: "If you try to hang onto your life, it will slip away through your fingers; if you offer it to those around you to complete my work in them, you will find genuine life and keep it forever" (Mark 8:35, freely adapted).

Stephen looked ahead to a promising career teaching the Hebrew Scriptures at a seminary. He had prepared for this career out of a commitment to the church, hoping to help students integrate biblical studies with their future ministry more fully than had been his experience in seminary. Over the first few years, the demands of course preparation and being sufficiently active in research and publication to be retained and promoted fairly well swamped his vision for his work. In its place grew ambition to teach at a more visible school, which he nourished by greater involvement in the guild of scholarship. Finally, he had to ask himself whom he was really serving. Was it God or his own ambitions, interests and, to some extent, vanity?

The Spirit worked on him over the course of several years, teaching him anew how to give himself to Christ's service. He began to spend more time mentoring students in his office and keeping in touch with graduates serving churches, serving as a resource person for them as they continued to wrestle with their vision for ministry or encountered some particular challenge. He wrote more for the church and less for the academy, bringing his expertise in biblical studies to bear on issues of spiritual formation and challenging questions his denomination was wrestling with. Giving up himself to Christ's service meant not writing the kinds of articles and monographs that would get him noticed by a first-tier school, but accepting God's call to stay where he was, where he had the freedom to do what God had laid on his heart.

Jesus fills us with more and more of himself in the Eucharist to free us from being quite so full of ourselves in the rest of life. Jesus' food was to do the will of the One who sent him and to complete his work, and that was fullness of life for him (see Jn 4:34). Holy Communion brings us, perhaps, to the ultimate step of faith: will we make it our food, as well, to live our lives searching out and doing what *God* has for us to do day after day, year after year? Whenever we come to the altar, the revelation of Jesus' love for us expressed in his death *for us* positions us to say yes to God again.

One of the eucharistic prayers includes the petition "that we may . . . serve you in unity, constancy, and peace" (BCP, 363). Unity, constancy and peace are certainly core values for Christian community and discipleship. As we gather around the table with one another, each one receiving the life of the same Lord, each one growing in the awareness of how the love of Jesus reaches out to all around the altar, we grow toward the unity that is everywhere urged on us as the undivided body of Christ. Constancy is an especially valuable gift offered by regular participation in this rite. As Jesus' giving of himself for us and to us becomes the constant touchstone from which we live our lives, we become more and more constant in our response to give ourselves for him and to him.

Frequent Communion heals our deadly double-mindedness, now responding to Christ's gracious self-giving on our behalf, now responding to our self-serving desires and the agendas, urged on us by all the sources of our unwholeness. And that single-mindedness is, at last, peace—the peace of being fully committed to one thing, the peace of walking in line with our confession and hope, the peace of not limping between two opinions. Frequent Communion is, in this way, the means by which we are sustained on the way toward fulfilling, and indeed are empowered to fulfill, our baptismal vows.

Giving ourselves to Christ's service, at the cost of serving our own plans for ourselves, whatever their source and whatever their merit, is the response of faith and the cost of discipleship. But the gospel remains good news. It is about giving away our lives so that we can secure them for eternity, even as we look to the end of the story in the midst of our Communion prayers: "And at the last day, bring us with all your saints into the joy of your eternal kingdom" (BCP, 363). Giving up ourselves to Christ's service is all about loving what God commands and desiring what he promises, a love that will not turn sour and a desire that will not be frustrated. The collective testimony of the saints who have gone before is that Jesus did not lie about the way to let life slip away and the way to find life and keep it forever. As C. S. Lewis expressed it in his *Surprised by Joy*, "Aim at heaven and you will get earth thrown in. Aim at earth and you get neither."

PUTTING IT INTO PRACTICE

Through hymns, Scripture and liturgy we hear the call to give ourselves wholly to God and to his service. But we are not always ready to do so, at least not in every area of our lives.

Ask the Holy Spirit to help you answer these questions: What part of my self, my life, my hopes am I not prepared to give to God? What do I want to hold on to? The answer could involve something you want out of a relationship, some goals you have regarding career or achievement, anything that you would use to complete this sentence: "I'll give myself to your service, just so long as . . ."

Write down in your journal the things that come to you during this time of reflection. Pray to God to show you why you are vesting these things with such importance and to reveal any brokenness within you standing behind these attachments. Write down anything you are shown, and continue to pray about these areas as the Spirit directs.

Invite the Holy Spirit to guide you as you reflect on how you have spent your time during the past few days and how you anticipate spending the coming day or days. Where do you see yourself giving up yourself to God's service in the way you spend your time or the way you determine and set your goals? Ask God to make you sensitive to the Spirit's promptings as you move throughout the coming day, and see what opportunities God opens up for witness and service that you might not anticipate. In your journal, write down what you sensed and what transpired. (This is an exercise that might profitably be repeated regularly.)

PART THREE

Christian Marriage

Partnership for a New Life

Marriage Made in Heaven

❋

Donna Jean and I approached our wedding service with a great deal of intentionality. I was in my last year of seminary and a church organist who had already played for dozens of weddings. She was a director of Christian education and youth. The church service was very important to us, and we thought with care about the selection of the hymns and Scripture readings and about including the celebration of Communion for the whole congregation. Nevertheless, we were both so starry-eyed and emotionally involved during the actual service that our experience was, for all our preparation, still quite a blur. However, each wedding we have attended (or for which I have played) continues to hold before us our own marriage covenant. We are given fresh opportunities again and again to view our own marriage—both its promises and challenges!—through the lens of this covenant and the vows we undertook many years before.

The rite of marriage is, indeed, crafted not just for its one-time effect on a couple, but also for its ongoing effect on all those who attend, both married and single. At each wedding, the celebrant prays also for the many married couples in attendance: "Grant that all married persons who have witnessed these vows may find their lives strengthened and their loyalty confirmed" (BCP, 430). At each wedding, the whole assembly promises to "do all in [their] power to uphold these two persons in their marriage," reminding us that the success of individual marriages depends on the support and, often, timely counsel and intervention of other Christian disciples, whether married or single.

Participating in each wedding ceremony is an invitation not only to share in the joy of the couple but also to remember God's vision for marriage, to explore the health of our own marriages and to invite the Spirit afresh into them so as to live the life of the new person in our most intimate human relationships more fully and to love as we are loved by Jesus.

MADE FOR EACH OTHER

The celebration opens with the statement that "the bond and covenant of marriage was established by God in creation" (BCP, 423). Marriage is not merely a social convention, a convenient arrangement for procreation and the transference of property across generational lines. It was God's idea, inherent in the process of creation itself. Adam's solitude as the only human specimen in the midst of creation is the first thing that God saw was "not good" in the cosmos he made (Gen 2:18). The creation of Eve and the joining together of the first couple perfected God's work. The complementarity of man and woman is inherent in creation: "You have created us male and female in your image" (BCP, 425). This complementarity and interrelationship is part of the image of God imprinted on humanity. It is not Adam as male human being that reflects God's image, but Adam as humanity, male and female in intimate relationship, that reflects the image of God. The need for a partner, for companionship, for relationship is an important aspect of this image of God, whom we confess to be Three-in-One, the Entity within which companionship exists eternally.

The stories of Genesis talk about husband and wife as helpers and partners, charged above all with giving themselves to each other as a primary source of help and emotional support, with exercising guardianship over creation in partnership together and with extending human community through childbearing and nurture. What distinguishes this from other relationships within community is the special degree of intimacy between husband and wife that makes them "one flesh," figuratively depicted in the creation of Eve from Adam's rib, so that he should not be complete without her.

Marriage is also the sphere in which Scripture foresees the power of erotic love—a force that makes all creation come more alive for those who experience it and an undeniable part of what brings us to marriage—finding full expression. This is especially evident in Song of Solomon, a portion of which stands among the options for the Old Testament reading to be used during the wedding service (Song 2:10-13; 8:6-7). But we are also cautioned to weigh our motivations carefully. A reading from Tobit—one of the few texts from an apocryphal book "sanctioned" to be read at a public worship service—depicts Tobias and Sarah praying on their wedding night. In his prayer, Tobias affirms that he takes Sarah to be his wife "not because of lust, but in sincerity" (Tob 8:7). They are not driven to marriage by passion alone, but by a shared commitment to the larger purposes of marriage. Since erotic desire waxes and wanes, it cannot be the driving impulse of marriage.

Part of that larger purpose involves being "a helper and support" to one another, as Tobias also affirms in his prayer (Tob 8:6; see Gen 2:18). How are spouses called to help or to provide support? A prayer spoken over the couple gives some specific suggestions: "Give them wisdom and devotion in the ordering of their common life, that each may be to the other a strength in need, a counselor in perplexity, a comfort in sorrow, and a companion in joy" (BCP, 429). Part of the wisdom involved in the ordering of our common lives is the protection of time for one another, so that needs and challenges can be expressed and strength and counsel shared. Part of the devotion required involves dying to self in regard to what we want for ourselves out of our marriage and in regard to our own interests when they are threatened by our spouse, so that we can be fully available to the other.

Of course, marriage is the primary context for the raising of children. The celebrant prays over the couple: "Bestow on them, if it is your will, the gift and heritage of children, and the grace to bring them up to know you, to love you, and to serve you" (BCP, 429). The prayer does not take for granted that every couple ought to bear children or that marriage is in any way incomplete without child bearing. On the contrary, the couple without children of their own are free to invest themselves in many more children, in more specialized ways or in times of special need. But if a couple does bear children, the prayer reminds them that the purpose of raising children is not to perpetuate the species, nor to find fulfillment in the role of being a parent, nor to provide for care and comfort in their old age. It is, rather, about making disciples, working together as a couple to make sure each child comes to a vibrant trust in God, commitment to Christ and thirst for the Spirit.

Husband and wife are helpmates not only in the day-to-day responsibilities of this life and the more challenging trials that interrupt that routine. They share a common goal—obtaining "those eternal joys prepared for all who love you" (BCP, 432). Their union has in view from the outset helping each partner arrive at the eternal joys of the marriage supper of the Lamb, presenting no obstacle to the same. By fixing our eyes on that ultimate goal, the intimacy of the marriage relationship can become a valuable resource for helping each other discern God's call and direction, deal with sinful attitudes and behaviors and find renewed strength for progress in discipleship.

The story of the archetypal marriage ends with the striking detail that "the man and his wife were both naked, and were not ashamed" (Gen 2:25), a level of openness and vulnerability that is lost after the disobedience and fragmenting of relationships in Genesis 3. Nevertheless, this image speaks to another quality of God's intentions for the marital relationship, namely, transparency and comfort with being transparent to one another. This quality can be progressively recovered as both partners work to create an atmosphere of trust and safety by loving one another with the constancy of God and out of Christ's love, on which each continues to feed. This trust emerges as each partner adopts the point of view that each is given to the other to help him or her recover the image of God, not to condemn, despise or devalue the other for the lingering distortions of that image.

❋❋❋❋❋❋❋❋❋❋❋❋❋❋❋❋❋❋❋❋❋❋❋❋❋❋❋❋❋

PUTTING IT INTO PRACTICE

For married persons

Make a list of the purposes and goals for marriage as reflected in this section. Discuss the list with your spouse, if he or she is willing. How would you prioritize these purposes in terms of their importance to you? How would your spouse?

Take it to the next level with your spouse. How do you fulfill these purposes for one another and with one another? Think of examples of when you've both done some well and when you've not done some so well. Which of these gifts could you offer more fully, and how?

For singles

Make a list of the purposes and goals for marriage as reflected in this section. To what extent and in what ways do they overlap with God's purposes for human community, especially Christian community? How have you found support and partnership among this community? How have you contributed to it?

Think about conversations you have had recently with friends about their spouses or marriages. In what ways do you detect God's purposes for marriage being fulfilled in their lives? What signs have you observed that your friends may need refocusing?

32

Made to Reflect God's Love
for His People

※

The marriage vows that we have so often heard, perhaps even recited ourselves, emphasize the importance of the constancy of love and favor in the midst of changing circumstances. Indeed, this constancy is *mandated* in the wedding rite. The celebrant asks for each party's commitment to "love . . . in sickness and in health; and, forsaking all others, [to] be faithful . . . as long as you both shall live" (BCP, 424) and does not proceed without assent. Husband and wife are called—and promise to make it their constant aim—to reflect the constancy of God's love for the other.

In one of the readings from the Old Testament recommended for wedding services, we hear about the need for fidelity, for absolute and exclusive commitment to one another: "Set me as a seal upon your heart, as a seal upon your arm; for love is strong as death, passion fierce as the grave. . . . Many waters cannot quench love, neither can floods drown it" (Song 8:6-7). What the translators render here more benignly as *passion* could equally well, if not better, be rendered *jealousy*. It is a call for absolute loyalty between husband and wife, loyalty of the kind that God displayed toward Israel—and expected *from* Israel.

Throughout Scripture, marriage is the metaphor of choice when talking about the relationship between God and his people. The common theme unifying the many uses of this image, particularly in the Hebrew Scriptures, is the insistence that, despite Israel's flirting with other gods or forming "adulterous" compacts with one or another neighboring nation, God refuses to desert his wife utterly. God remains faithful, committed and invested in the relationship and works ever toward the ultimate restoration of Israel, his spouse. The relationship between husband and wife in its constancy and exclusivity seeks to mirror God's absolute commitment to his people.

Susanna once shared with me that her husband's love and constancy made God's love and constancy credible to her. She told me that if her husband, whom she could see, were inconstant that would seriously hurt her ability to trust in the love of the God she could not see. While there are obvious dangers here in terms of her own spiritual stability, her perception cuts to the heart of what is at stake in the vows we make in marriage, and it raises an important red flag for spouses to consider. What is my witness to the constancy of God's love in this marriage? I would quickly add that this is not sufficient reason to remain in a house where there is danger to your person, physical or psychological. But it is something to consider as we examine our motives, bearing and behavior toward a spouse.

In the New Testament, the metaphor of marriage is further applied to the relationship between Christ and the church. Paul seeks to present his congregations "as a chaste virgin to Christ" (2 Cor 11:2-3). John the Seer portrays the consummation of God's redemptive acts as a "marriage supper" between Christ and the church and the New Jerusalem "as a bride adorned for her husband" (Rev 19:6-9; 21:2). The BCP keeps this connection before our eyes throughout the service. Marriage is indeed to represent "the mystery of the union between Christ and his Church" (BCP, 423). The love of wife and husband provides "an image of the heavenly Jerusalem, adorned as a bride for her bridegroom, your Son Jesus Christ our Lord; who loves her and gave himself for her, that he might make the whole creation new" (BCP, 381).

Among New Testament writings, Ephesians is perhaps the most explicit about marriage as a model for Christ's relationship with the church and uses this relationship, in turn, as a model to be imitated within the marriage of husband and wife. To husbands, the author writes, "Love your wives, just as Christ loved the church and gave

himself up for her. . . . In the same way, husbands should love their
wives as they do their own bodies. . . . No one ever hates his own body,
but he nourishes and tenderly cares for it, just as Christ does for the
church" (Eph 5:25, 28-29). To wives he writes, "Be subject to your
husbands as you are to the Lord. . . . Just as the church is subject to
Christ, so also wives ought to be, in everything, to their husbands"
(Eph 5:22, 24). Christ's love for the church, which includes his love
for any particular husband and wife, is the model to which husbands
are to look as they live together with their wives. The church's calling to serve Christ's purposes and complete his work in the world, a
calling that involves any particular husband and wife, is the model to
which wives are to look.

Stopping there, of course, would fall short of the complete vision the
author spins for the Christian life in general and for Christian marriage
in particular. Many readers *have* stopped precisely there, resulting in the
use of this text to support imbalances of power and the subjugation of
women to men. These words to Christian couples are all prefaced with
the general rule "Be subject to one another out of reverence for Christ"
(Eph 5:21). This overarching statement governs *all* Christian relations
within the household. Husbands and wives are both included in the
call to seek not after their own interests, but the interests of the other
(see Phil 2:3-4), and to seek to honor the other more than themselves.
Husbands and wives are both included in the call to relinquish self-will
and the grasping at authority over other people, in favor of serving (see
Mark 10:41-45).

If husbands are called to practice submission to wives just as wives
are called to mirror the church's deference to its Lord, wives are also
called to exhibit the costly love toward their husbands that Christ showed
to the church. Ephesians 5:2 is the rule according to which *all* Christians
are to walk: "Live in love, as Christ loved us and gave himself up for us."
Husbands and wives are therefore both called to reflect the heart of both
Christ and the church (at its best) in their relationship to one another
and in their response as a couple to the larger community. For either one
to look only to the role of the corresponding gender in the metaphor of

Christ's union with the church is to miss the whole picture.

In the prayers recited over the couple, the celebrant asks that God will "make their life together a sign of Christ's love to this sinful and broken world, that unity may overcome estrangement, forgiveness heal guilt, and joy conquer despair" (BCP, 429). This came true in the marriage of one couple I know in a rather dramatic way. Linda had come to that point at which many find themselves in their early forties. She was no longer fulfilled in her relationship with Martin; she had lost sight of herself for too long in her responsibilities as a mother. She did what so many of us do, thinking that something new and fresh would breathe new life into her. Her affair with one of Martin's colleagues became a source of great satisfaction to her, and she moved out of the house to live with Greg. As this became known, a woman in the congregation she attended came alongside her and helped her look long and hard at the root issues that had led to the affair in the first place and also at the pain she was bringing to her two daughters and her husband. Finally, she and Martin agreed to go to counseling together. While it was extremely difficult for both of them, they also shared with one another like they had not done since their courtship.

It took months to heal the pain, months more to restore the vitality that had been lost in their marriage in the years of focusing on work and child raising. But it was a vibrant "sign of Christ's love to this broken world," a witness that unity may indeed "overcome estrangement" and "forgiveness heal guilt." Martin modeled Christ's forgiveness and steadfastness in a manner reminiscent of Hosea's modeling of God's love for his straying people. Linda modeled Christ's commitment in the face of an unsatisfying relationship, as marriage to the church surely has been for Christ many a time and for long seasons.

Because the love of man and woman is so powerful, it is a force that often opens us up to fathom more fully the love of God for us. If we allow the Spirit to speak to us through our experiences of marriage or of observing married couples, we can often learn much about God's passion for his people. This, in turn, can position us to respond more healthfully to our own spouse or to offer help to our sisters and brothers experiencing difficulties in their relationships, with the result that the love of God and the love of Christ will indeed be reflected more fully.

Lori had been having serious difficulties in her marriage to Daniel. She felt taken for granted. She was angry with Daniel for not investing more of himself in her interests, interests that they had once shared. She resented the fact that he sought his own satisfaction in ways that robbed her of finding satisfaction in their relationship (top of the list would include his spending most of the few precious hours in which they were not both working in front of the television, watching sports, paying no attention to her or to the kinds of activities that would nourish their relationship). For two years, she had fought the urge to find a more satisfying relationship, but she had come to the end of her self-restraint. Fortunately for Lori, she had an active prayer life and no problems expressing herself to God. She found herself walking alone under the stars one night, talking to Jesus about her situation and the temptations to which she was about to succumb.

"You were fortunate to have died before you got married," she found herself saying. "You never had to face the pain of seeing the relationship that once gave you life and boundless joy wither into a pathetic shadow of a marriage that sucks the very life out of your soul." The voice that came back to her was clear, as if it had been spoken into her ear. "I have been married for nearly two thousand years. Do I get everything I want from my bride? Does she respond to my love and my investment of myself in the relationship like I deserve? Does she never take me for granted, or do what pleases herself in direct opposition to what would please me? But I love her still. I love *you* still."

That night, Lori experienced no more satisfaction from her marriage than before her walk. But she understood in a new way how it reflected the union of Christ with the church—which is not always a good reflection—and how she herself was a face of the bride whom Jesus continued to love through all her times of putting herself above him, all her times of spending her time in empty distractions rather than nurturing her relationship with him. Discovering this, she felt the constancy of Jesus' love more fully, and she became more fully able to think about how to reflect that in her own marriage.

❀❀❀❀❀❀❀❀❀❀❀❀❀❀❀❀❀❀❀❀❀❀❀❀❀

PUTTING IT INTO PRACTICE

Make another list, this time of the characteristics of God's relationship with Israel and Christ's with the church that are held up as exemplary for Christian marriage.

In what ways are you positively reflecting the love and loyalty of God, the other-centeredness, selfless love of Christ and the submissiveness of the church in your bearing and behaviors toward your spouse? In what ways is your spouse doing this toward you? Where is there cause here for celebration, and where is there room for reflecting these characteristics more completely and healthfully?

Marriage is not the only context in which unfailing loyalty is demonstrated and God's love and commitment reflected. Moreover, all disciples are called to reflect the love of Christ and the attitude of mutual submission in their relationships with one another. In what ways have you exhibited—or failed to exhibit—these traits in these other relationships? How have you found assurance of the love of God through the loyalty and love offered to you in these relationships?

Single or married, male or female, we are all brought together in God's love as the bride of Christ. The metaphor of marriage invites us to explore several dimensions of this *spiritual* marriage in conversation with our Redeemer-Spouse. Center yourself in the Spirit and spend some time in prayer:

• Ask Christ to reveal to you how you have delighted him as his bride, "what he sees in you," as it were.

• Ask Christ to identify some behavior or attitude of yours that causes him pain or disappointment; repent and seek his help to grow more pleasing to him in that area.

- Allow Christ to reassure you with the sense of his constant love and
  unfailing loyalty, shown most clearly in his willingness to give his life
  to create this relationship with *you*.

33

Made Within Community,
Made for Mission

❉

The bride and groom are not the only people to take vows on a wedding day. After hearing the couple declare their commitment to one another, the celebrant asks, "Will all of you who witness these promises do all in your power to uphold these two persons in their marriage?" (BCP, 425). I've never actually heard anyone respond no, but still have seen entire congregations stand by at a distance as marriages dissolved. If we took this promise with equal seriousness as the promises made by the couple, husbands and wives would find it less burdensome fulfilling their marriage vows.

This vow sets marriage within the context of Christian community—indeed, the same community that takes a similar vow at each baptism, promising "to do all" in their power "to support these persons in their life in Christ" (BCP, 303). Just as the individual's growth in discipleship depends on the investment, the support, at times even the correction of other members of the community of faith, so it is with the couple's growth toward reflecting the love of Christ and the response of the church in their union with each other and in their outreach to the world.

For Linda and Martin, the couple who had recovered from an affair (and the disappointment that had led to it), the failure of their church to live out their promise would have spelled divorce and deep wounding. Rather than pass by on the other side, a sister in Christ took the risk of engaging Linda, gently leading her to examine her choices with greater circumspection and in light of the calling of the baptismal life. It wasn't enough for this community of faith, however, simply to have Linda conform to her marriage vows as to a straightjacket. Over the year that followed, two different Christian couples, who had themselves worked through some rocky times, came alongside Martin and Linda. Rather than avoid the issues that were evident to all, they used the awkwardness of the situation to offer support, help, a place for openness and vulnerability.

Having hit bottom in their relationship, Linda and Martin gratefully received the companionship and support as they sought to rebuild their marriage. One of the husbands helped Martin look at his own overinvestment of himself in his work and the issues behind that. As he learned more about how these couples shared their lives, he realized how much he had denied himself and Linda by becoming content to coexist. They celebrated breakthroughs together, encouraged each other when they seemed to be taking a step backward, prayed for one another and kept inviting the Holy Spirit to breathe new life into the relationship.

That sister and those two couples did all in their power to uphold Martin and Linda in their marriage. In this case, the solution for marital problems was not for the couple to get more involved in church, as I've often heard, but for the church to get more involved in the couple. As their relationship took on new life, Linda and Martin were able to provide other couples the same kind of support they had received in their crisis year, from open and honest sharing and exploration to simple but important services like watching another couple's children to give them time alone together.

For marriages to flourish, couples need the support of Christian friends both in times of crisis and in ordinary time. For such support to exist, Christian friends—and especially couples—need consistently to reach out in love and concern to married persons. The prayers spoken over the bride and groom ask God to make each new marriage a vehicle for outreach, a vessel filled with God's love and care so that *others* may drink as well. The celebrant prays over the couple that they will create together a home that "may be a haven of blessing and peace," not just for each other and their children, but for others as well. The couples that surrounded Linda and Michael offered such a haven, inviting them both figuratively and literally into their homes, into their circles of love and care, empowering unity to "overcome estrangement, forgiveness heal guilt, and joy conquer despair."

Another petition prayed over each new couple is the following: "Give them such fulfillment of their mutual affection that they may reach out in love and concern for others" (BCP, 429). Marriage finds its ultimate fulfillment as husband and wife join in shared mission to others, both within the Christian community and beyond. The "fulfillment of their mutual affection" is not an end in itself, but becomes a means and resource for contributing to the completion of Christ's work in the world. Where the focus of the couple remains on self-gratification or even in achieving couple-centered goals (for example, certain professional or financial goals, a new house or the like), the inward focus brings eventual stagnation.

Keith and Valerie were both on the fast track in their professions and still managed to keep the vibrancy of their relationship alive through spending their few off hours well together in activities that each enjoyed or just spending time talking over long walks in the late evening or sitting outside with friends over a bottle of wine and candlelight. During one of those conversations with another successful couple, they discovered that all four of them had, in some way, been empowered to succeed because someone had invested himself or herself in them in a life-changing way during their youth. Keith had terribly low self-esteem as a teenager after his father left the family, until a certain chemistry teacher made a special point of investing in him and holding up a mirror with a different reflection. Valerie was raised by a very conservative family that took for granted that her destiny was to settle down, raise children and do the housework. Were it not for a woman in her church who took an interest in her and invited her to a summer apprenticeship at her office during high school, she never would have discovered many of her own gifts and graces.

Over the next few days, Keith and Valerie discerned that God was calling them now, from their places of strength, to offer similar gifts. The diocese had a ministry with at-risk youths, and they began to volunteer there together for several hours each week, tutoring high school students and leading outings together. Through their corporate connections, they were both often able to get complimentary tickets to plays and sporting events. They taught teenagers to dream about their future and to find the necessary discipline to get there. They helped them see more in themselves than their circumstances made possible. Their marriage, too, became a "haven of blessing and peace" for many young people, who would look back on their encounter with Keith and Valerie as the turning point in their lives.

PUTTING IT INTO PRACTICE

Reflect on one or two specific occasions when a Christian couple reached out to you and provided support, a "safe haven," timely counsel or whatever was needed at the time. What did their willingness to include you in their home and relationship mean to you and your journey? In what ways have you opened up your home (whether you are married or single) to provide such help along another person's journey?

If your marriage is strong and you know of a couple in your parish experiencing difficulties, consider how you might embrace them more fully with your friendship and offer your home as a place to share, explore and seek perspective and support for their marriage. If you are experiencing difficulties, consider asking another couple in your parish for such support. Your pastor might have some ideas about whom to ask.

Consider teaming up with another couple and starting a marriage support group in your church or parish, if one does not already exist. Use the material in this section, if you wish, to present the group's goals and philosophy to the congregation. Your pastor, Christian education director or local Christian bookstore can help you locate resources to get started leading such a group productively.

Together with your spouse, compile a list of the outreach and support ministries of your congregation and other local churches, as well as out-reach ministries sponsored by your diocese or denomination. Add any relief or support needs of which you are aware that perhaps are not adequately addressed by existing ministries. Discuss together which draw out your interest and passion for ministry, try out a few, and discern together which one or two would best fit your strengths *as a couple* for long-term involvement.

34

Bringing the "New Person"
to the Marriage

❋

The marriage covenant is built on the baptismal covenant. Living the baptismal life is foundational to and included in the vision for the marriage relationship nurtured by the Book of Common Prayer. Our commitment to die to our old selves and walk in newness of life undergirds Christian marriage. It is the bedrock for fulfilling our vows to love, honor and provide the support needed by the other. Similarly, the marriage covenant takes place within the context of the Eucharist, which is often celebrated in connection with the marriage service in the Anglican Communion. Marriage is sustained by ongoing participation in the Eucharist, the spiritual disciplines it fosters and the constant nourishment of the love of Jesus that the sacrament is intended to provide. In this chapter we will look more closely at the connections between marriage and the sacramental life, exploring how couples can learn to walk together in that newness of life into which each is invited in baptism.

The epistle lessons appointed to be read at the wedding ceremony are largely visions for the baptismal life, originally written not to address husband and wife in particular, but rather addressing whole Christian communities—couples, singles and families. By inviting us to encounter these texts within the marriage ceremony, the liturgy for weddings reminds us that the kinds of attitudes and behaviors we are to embody toward one another as disciples in general, such as we explored in the section on baptism, also need to be embodied specifically within the Christian marriage relationship. Walking in newness of life, or clothing ourselves with the new person, applies as we engage our spouse no less than when we interact with any other Christian sister or brother.

Christian marriage, indeed, has a dual basis. The author of I Peter captures this clearly in his instructions to Christian husbands: "Live considerately together with your wives as with a more fragile vessel, paying honor also as to fellow heirs of the gift of life in order that your prayers may not be hindered" (I Pet 3:7, my translation). On the one hand, the Christian couple are husband and wife—roles that inherit a certain body of expectations, limitations and so forth. That is seen here in the author's adoption of the cultural expectations that the woman will be "weaker" in constitution, as well as the Greco-Roman ethical instruction that this "weakness" called for consideration on the part of the husband rather than exploitation.

But they are also, and ultimately, "fellow heirs of the gift of life," or, in other words, brother and sister together in the family of God. This role brings a quite different set of expectations and goals for the relationship. It is a role, moreover, not limited by traditional views of what husbands and wives should be like, what they should do for one another and what the power dynamics of their relationship ought to be. Since we confess this second identity to be the one that continues forever, and indeed the only facet of the marital bond that survives death, it follows that we would do well to regard it as the fundamental basis for marriage that cannot be trumped by the other, more limited set of roles.

Seeing her husband from this "second identity" brought saving grace to Diane's marriage. Diane knew that Andrew was wrestling with being attracted to other women. Quite understandably, she found this threatening and demoralizing. She wanted to ignore it, deny it, resent Andrew for it. One evening, Diane looked at Andrew not as a husband who was causing her pain, but as a fellow disciple who was struggling with living out his own commitment to the baptismal life. In her role as a sister in Christ and as one who was better poised than anyone else to offer support to him, she gave him the gift of being a "strength in need" and a "counselor in perplexity."

It took great courage on Diane's part to invite this, gently confronting Andrew with the behaviors she had observed and creating a safe space for him to open up about what was behind it all. She died to self in terms of her feelings as a wife, in order that she might give the gift of being what the marriage ceremony envisions for a Christian wife or a husband. It took great courage on Andrew's part, as well, to trust her with his struggles, to reveal his shame and to receive from her the partnership he needed. She discovered new ways to give him the support he needed from her. He discovered that he could trust her commitment to him as a brother in Christ. In turn, he was able to overcome his temptations and walk in line with his baptismal and marriage covenants. Their relationship deepened thereafter, as they each shared their struggles with discipleship more and more, and they became for one another deep, spiritual friends as well as husband and wife.

The baptismal life is all about dying to our old self and walking in newness of life. This includes dying to many expectations we might have for marriage and dying to our desire for many things we might want to get out of our marriage. Only then are we really free to fulfill not only our vows to "love, comfort, honor, and keep" (BCP, 424), but our calling to love our wife or husband with the love that flows through us from the Lord. Only then are we really free to *give*. The New Testament lessons appointed for weddings reinforce this point consistently:

Love one another as I have loved you. (Jn 15:12)

Live in love, as Christ loved us and gave himself up for us. (Eph 5:2)

Forgive each other; just as the Lord has forgiven you. (Col 3:13)

We may work very hard at exhibiting this kind of love outside marriage, but then treat the marriage relationship differently. We often think and act as if our marriage should run on the basis of romantic love, friendly affections and reciprocal satisfaction. And when, in the course of the changes and chances of life, that love and those affections wane, we fail to reach for the love of Christ as a resource to sustain and renew our relationship with our spouse.

But it is precisely where we are most intimate that we most need to draw on the love of Christ and to exhibit Christlike love. Where we are most intimate, we are most vulnerable; where we are most vulnerable, we are most defensive; where we are most defensive, we can least afford to be generous. For this reason, the BCP directs us in the midst of the marriage ceremony to readings that teach us to keep looking to God's unfailing supply of love and healing, so that we can dare to be generous even in the face of our vulnerability to our spouses. Being filled with God's fullness, strengthened through the Holy Spirit and embraced by the love of Christ (see Eph 3:14-19)—here is the well out of which to keep drawing the water that sustains a marriage and that allows each partner to be for the other the strength in need, the comfort in perplexity and the companion with which God seeks to grace the other in the gift of marriage.

Eucharistic spirituality is therefore an essential foundation for the marriage covenant. As we keep looking to Christ to fulfill our core longings and to invest himself fully in us through his Spirit, we are freed to respond to our partner with the fullness that Christ imparts and not out of the degree of fullness or emptiness we have in our relationship with our partner.

Rick felt very discouraged at the direction his marriage to Helena had been taking in the years since the birth of their third child. Helena had long since stopped showing any interest in growing intellectually or spiritually. She "let herself go" physically. She retreated to the coping mechanisms of television, magazines and food. For some time, Rick allowed his disappointment—and his feeling of being cheated out of enjoying the interesting and beautiful woman he married—to seethe. He started having lunch with a colleague at work whom he also knew from his church. He began to open up to Don about the struggles he was having. Because of their church connection, they began to explore the connections between their faith and Rick's situation. They began using part of their time together to pray; they attended a midweek Eucharist together after work on Wednesdays.

As Rick positioned himself to experience more of Jesus' love for him and to seek his sustaining strength, he was given the necessary distance to approach Helena as a sister in Christ rather than as a disappointing wife. As they began to talk more and lay a foundation of trust, Helena began to share about her own deep disappointment with her life, her frustrations with herself as a mother, her anger with God for not helping her in the ways that she asked. This opened up a way for Rick to offer her the kind of support she needed from him but had not been getting, to give her a venue for working through her anger toward God and, eventually, to help her discern a calling that would be more suited to her gifts and graces than being a stay-at-home mom. With Don's help, Rick was able to draw on the love and life of Christ sufficiently to "lay down his life"—at least in the form of his expectations and disappointments—for Helena. This, in turn, allowed the love of Christ and power of the Holy Spirit to enter the situation. Walking in the "way of the cross" within marriage proved itself again to be "the way of life" there as in the rest of our relationships and engagements with this world (see the "Blessing of the Marriage," BCP, 430).

My wife and I chose Colossians 3:12-17 as the epistle text for our wedding. Read in the context of the marriage service, it challenges us to make our Christian walk "real" by bringing it also into the home. The governing metaphor throughout the paragraph—how we should "clothe" ourselves—is particularly apt in this regard. We tend to dress up to go out. But what are we going to wear around the house? Paul has some excellent wardrobe suggestions: "compassion, kindness, humility, meekness, and patience," as well as the practice of mutual forgiveness and, above all, love. The latter is especially important. Because a couple is so close, so deeply involved in one another's day-to-day lives, they also have the most opportunity to hurt one another.

One way to make the vision for Christian relationships expressed by this passage real in our marriage is to practice self-examination, confession and forgiveness in our relationship with our spouses. We grow in compassion toward one another as we seek to examine our words and behaviors from the other's point of view. We grow in humility toward one another as we voluntarily suggest our faults or give our spouse permission to name them. We grow in meekness and patience toward one another as we realize both how much we cause hurt and how willing our partner is to forgive. It is no wonder that the liturgy specifically recommends this practice, asking God to make it a regular part of the couple's life together: "Give them grace, when they hurt each other, to recognize and acknowledge their fault, and to seek each other's forgiveness and yours" (BCP 429).

Loving is easy when our desires are being satisfied, but not so easy when we are disappointed in our marriages. But the baptismal life is the life of dying—dying to all within us that prevents us from loving as Christ loved, serving as Christ served, forgiving as Christ forgave. The good news of the Christian life remains that what God commands, God empowers.

***

PUTTING IT INTO PRACTICE

Think about your expectations for your relationship with your spouse. What do you want out of your marriage? What are you getting? What are you not getting?

In regard to the latter, how are your expectations—and your responses to finding them frustrated—affecting your feelings, words and actions toward your spouse?

Which expectations or desires do you need to die to in order to be free to love your spouse in the ways envisioned in the marriage rites and the Scriptures? Pray about these issues, and ask Jesus to keep filling your places of emptiness and disappointment with his love and fullness.

Ask your spouse to share one or two things he or she most needs from you that he or she is not receiving. Talk about why this is important and what it might look like. Brainstorm about a few things you might do this week to give your spouse this gift.

Talk with your spouse about how to make space in your relationship and in your day to name the sharp edges that cause pain or discouragement in your marriage and to exchange forgiveness directly and regularly.

Bringing the new person into the marriage is just one context for bringing our new person into all our relationships, whether we are married or single. Where are you experiencing tension in relationships with other people? Read Colossians 3:5-17. In what ways might this tension be maintained or exacerbated as a result of your living out of the old person in regard to the other? Listen in prayer to how God would challenge you to nurture reconciliation and restore partnership by bringing more of the new person to that relationship.

35

Bringing God to the Marriage

❋

A billboard on a highway not far from our home reads, in the familiar white lettering against a black background,

Loved the wedding. Invite me to the marriage.
—God

It is not enough to come to God's house for the ceremony if we don't also continue to bring him into our homes thereafter. In the passage from the book of Tobit that is offered as a possible Old Testament reading for the wedding service, the newlyweds bring adoration and prayer into the bedroom—even on the honeymoon night—offering a vision for how a husband and wife come together before God and invite him into their most intimate spaces.

One of the suggested Gospel readings speaks of building one's house on the solid foundation of Jesus' teachings rather than the shifting sands of conventional wisdom (see Mt 7:21, 24-27). Once again, even though the saying was originally meant to apply to any and all disciples, the image of building a house is especially suited to the task that faces a husband and a wife as a couple, who seek to build a *home* in shared commitment to embody the words of Jesus in all that concerns the shared life of the household. The reading from Colossians 3, explored in the previous chapter, further reinforces this, inviting us to bring the words of Scripture and the words of new songs and prayers we sing to God into our homes and marriages.

Using these texts to address husband and wife in particular nurtures the expectation that they will not only read and listen to the voice of the

Spirit speaking through Scripture on their own, but also will practice this discipline together so that they can discern together how to "build their home" on a foundation to which they are both committed.

Rob and Cheryl had often disagreed about finances. Cheryl wanted to save as much as possible for the future needs of the family; Rob wanted to enjoy more of the fruits of their labor in the here and now. Both were struck one particular Sunday morning by the priest's sermon on a text from Luke's Gospel dealing with one of Jesus' parables about our relationship to wealth. As it was the story of the *foolish* rich man who wanted to build bigger barns to save more, it seemed to play into Rob's hand (though clearly the point of the parable was not to go out and get more expensive toys instead!). At any rate, it sparked their conversation. They decided to spend some time each evening that their schedules permitted reading together through Luke's Gospel, especially talking together about passages relevant to money.

As they conversed and prayed, they found that they had reached a harmonious agreement on this topic that had been a source of contention. They would save less *and* spend less on things they didn't really need. Instead, they would set aside a certain sum each month to use for outreach and relief. They would inquire after any needs known to the parish or to a local relief agency, and shop together for groceries and clothing or whatever else might have been a pressing need for some family. A few months after Hurricane Katrina devastated New Orleans and the surrounding areas, they were able to use several months' "mad money" to drive into an area that had been struck hard, with their car full of supplies that they'd learned were most needed. Money became a means by which Rob and Cheryl discovered a common passion for mission and still a source of great enjoyment as they discovered more of the deep, abiding joy of Christ in their marriage.

Another of the prayers offered in the wedding service on behalf of the couple asks God to "grant that their wills may be so knit together in your will, and their spirits in your Spirit, that they may grow in love and peace with you and one another all the days of their life" (BCP, 429). Rob and Cheryl found this prayer partially fulfilled in their lives in regard to the one issue of money. They remained in tune with God, seeking the Spirit's leading for how to reach out in love and care. But once the Spirit of God is invited into one area of life so fully, it is so hard to keep it contained! Their growth in God-centeredness continued to spill out into other areas of their lives as well. As each was drawn closer to God and toward his leading, they moved closer and closer to each other as well. As their God-centeredness shaped their lives more and more as a couple, they became more joyfully and firmly united through a shared purpose, a shared process of discernment and shared execution of the plans that emerged from their prayer together.

Entering into times of adoration together as a couple, praying together as a couple, disclosing what one believes one is hearing from God's Spirit—all of these things involve taking the risk of greater openness to one another. As we practice these disciplines as a couple, however, and allow ourselves to be transparent to God in each other's presence, we become more and more comfortable being transparent to one another. Our level of trust with our spouse increases, our level of intimacy deepens. Indeed, it offers the hope that a couple may learn once again to be "naked and not ashamed" (Gen 2:25) in the presence of God and each other.

PUTTING IT INTO PRACTICE

Use the forms for "Daily Devotions for Individuals and Families" (BCP, 136-40) as a vehicle for worshiping and praying together with your spouse (and, if applicable, children). If you are single, these forms are equally appropriate for use with members of your family of origin or a circle of friends.

As your comfort level with the practice of praying together grows, expand the forms for "Daily Devotions," making room for more freedom. Here are a few suggestions:

• After the opening psalm, make a space for you and your spouse (or, if

single, the other members of your praying circle) to express spontane-
ous praise and thanksgiving.

- At the place appointed for Scripture readings, work through a short
  epistle one paragraph at a time during each time of devotions. Discern
  together its word of challenge or encouragement to you in your situation as a couple or family.

- During the time for prayer, pray about living out this word you have
  discerned, about concerns it raises and about any other needs known
  to each of you.

Together with your spouse, select a small group devotional or Bible
study resource to use as a basis for Scripture reading, conversation and
prayer together. If there is a particular area in which you are seeking
guidance together or having disagreements, perhaps a relevant topical
guide would be most fruitful. A pastor, Christian education director,
spiritual director or staff at a local Christian bookstore can help you
find an appropriate resource.

God desires to enter into and work through all our relationships. Are
there other people—a coworker or a friend, perhaps—with whom God
is prompting you to open up more fully this dimension of spiritual partnership by praying together, engaging in acts of outreach or service together and otherwise supporting one another's deepening discipleship?

PART FOUR

Christian Burial

The Gate of Eternal Life

36

Facing Death As a
People of Hope

Talking about death is difficult. Many of us try to push our own mortality from our consciousness and insulate ourselves from the awareness of death. Our society conspires in this avoidance by moving away from the expectation that people will die at home with their families to the assumption that they will die in the more peripheral spaces of hospitals, hospices and nursing homes. Even the cosmeticians at funeral homes try to make the corpse appear as lifelike as possible, so that we will not see death as it is. Many people who have lost a spouse find themselves to some extent excluded from their former circle of friends, who are uncomfortable around the grieving and adjust with difficulty to relating to the widow or widower as an individual. The absence of the deceased partner remains a perpetual reminder of death's intrusive reality.

Death is the elephant in the living room that we try not to notice, let alone invite center stage. But Christian faith refuses to cooperate in this conspiracy of silence. Indeed, death is at the center of our proclamation—the death of Jesus, and the way this death has transformed all deaths. Our tradition makes us face our fears about death instead of repressing them. Our Scriptures bring the topic out in the open, so that it can no longer possess us in secret and control us subconsciously. Christ died to "free those who all their lives were held in slavery by the fear of death" (Heb 2:15). One of the great gifts of our Christian faith, then, is that it enables us to look honestly and courageously at our own deaths, so that we can live more authentic lives, free of the distortions that come from repressing our own mortality and free of the regrets that inevitably follow when death shatters our illusions.

In this section, we will explore what spiritual counsel the rites for Christian Burial and the associated pastoral offices of Ministration to the Sick and Ministration at the Time of Death offer us for facing death square on as people whom Jesus rescues from this fear of death. In the first three chapters, we will explore what the liturgy offers as we gather to grieve the death of a loved one. In the remaining chapters, we will explore how those liturgies position us, as we walk away from that grave, to live the remainder of our own lives.

A prayer offered on behalf of the bereaved asks God to help them encounter the days to come "not sorrowing as those without hope" (BCP, 505). The prayer is inspired by Paul's words to the believers in Thessalonica, who had been caught off guard by the natural deaths of some of their congregation (see I Thess 4:13). Paul seeks to offer them hope in the midst of their grieving by reminding those disciples of Jesus' power over death, assuring them that, at Christ's return, both the faithful who are alive and the faithful who have died will be united together in the life of the resurrection. The dead are not lost to Christ, nor are they lost to the people who love them.

Grief remains a natural and necessary response to death. It is not Paul's intent that Christians keep a stiff upper lip or grin and bear it, as if the death of a loved one were not deeply painful and disorienting. He desires, however, to offer the consolation of tempering grief with the knowledge about death and the life beyond death imparted by faith in Jesus Christ and the illumination of the Holy Spirit.

The rites surrounding death consistently bear witness that death is a going forth, not a cessation of existence. At the time of death, the minister issues the charge, "Depart, O Christian soul, out of this world" (BCP, 464). One of my more vivid memories from serving as a hospital chaplain involves speaking these words at the bedside of a woman who had been severely injured in a motor vehicle accident. I was struck by the profound finality of sending her, as it were, from all that was familiar to her in this life and from all whom she loved and who loved her. But I was also struck that I was not sending her into the void. She had a journey to make that day and a destination beyond the grave: "May your rest this day be in peace, and your dwelling place in the Paradise of God" (BCP, 464).

These liturgies help us visualize this place beyond death and, more importantly, to see in our minds the ongoing existence and experiences of the departed. We see figures, known to us only through Scripture and tradition, greeting our loved ones in person: "Into paradise may the angels lead thee; and at thy coming may the martyrs receive thee, and bring thee into the holy city Jerusalem." We are invited to picture them hearing Jesus' words of invitation, "Come, you blessed of my Father," gazing upon Jesus "face to face," tasting "the blessedness of perfect rest." The departed even raise their voices afresh, as their "heart and soul now ring out in joy to you, O Lord, the living God, and the God of those who live." As the scenes fade, we are invited to imagine for our loved ones continued growth in discipleship, in that same journey that has occupied them on this side of death, beyond death still ever "increasing in knowledge and love of thee," going "from strength to strength in the life of perfect service."

No book of the Bible is more visual—or daring in terms of visualizing what cannot be seen!—than the book of Revelation, and the services of burial judiciously harness its power to help us "see" the ongoing life of the departed (and, therefore, our own as well). We catch a glimpse of the church triumphant, having emerged from "the great ordeal," the contest of this life with all its challenges to faithfulness. The view from the other side of the contest of this life is one of serenity and celebration, as angels and saints sing for joy to the God whose presence they now enjoy, and as God shelters each person from any further suffering or hardship. The vision culminates in the intimate scene of God wiping away with his own hand every tear from the eyes of those who have borne the rigors and hardships of the contest of faith and have overcome. Such scenes communicate the conviction that runs throughout the liturgies: "For your faithful people, O Lord, life is changed, not ended" (BCP,

382). Our loved ones may be parted from us, but they are not lost. Their existence, their individuality, their experience continues.

These rites and their associated Scriptures offer a further assurance: not only do our loved ones continue to exist, but they also continue to be loved and cared for. Some of the psalms speak of the grave as an absolute end to human experience, including our remembrance of God (see Ps 6:4-5; 88:3-5, 10-12). One of the greatest horrors about death for these authors seems to be that it puts people beyond the reach of God's help. If God does not restore health or bring help before death, is there anything he can do for the person after death?

This view of God's reach was too small for the author of Psalm 139. Lost in the wonder and praise of God, he declares that God's presence and power extend even to the grave: "If I climb up to heaven, thou art there; if I go down to hell, thou art there also" (BCP, 475; see Ps 139:8). Our loved ones may be cut off from our presence, but they are not cut off from God's presence. There is Someone on the other side to whom we give our loved ones, who will continue to love and care for those who have moved beyond the reach of *our* love and care. And so we liturgically enact our handing over of our loved one to Jesus again and again during the course of the services from the time of death to the burial itself.

As we attend to "letting go" on this side of the great divide, we also earnestly seek a safe arrival on the other side for our departed. We ask Jesus to "receive *him* into the arms of thy mercy" (BCP, 481) and to "acknowledge . . . a sheep of your own fold, a lamb of your own flock, a sinner of your own redeeming" (BCP, 465). The liturgies thus help us to sense that the departed has passed securely from our hands and care to the arms of Jesus.

The second assurance, then, that can help us to grieve—and even to approach our own deaths—as people who have hope is that the faithful find a place of belonging after death. Beyond death, we are received by the Savior who loves us and redeemed us. We are safe in the love of God, as Paul, in another epistle reading suggested for use at funerals, attests. Death cannot cut us off from God's love for us in Christ—not the departed and not those who are left to mourn (see Rom 8:38-39).

Just as we belong to God throughout life, we belong to God in death. The departed may be removed from our watchful care, but not from Christ's. Beyond death, "the Lamb at the center of the throne will be their shepherd" (Rev 7:17).

A third source of assurance is the affirmation of the resurrection of the body. The departed's physicality itself is not lost, no matter how the body has been ravaged by time, disease or violent death (and irrespective of the manner of disposal, whether burying or cremation). Paul uses the familiar metaphor of planting seeds in the expectation of the shooting forth of new life. We "sow" the physical body in death, planting it in the ground as the seed of new life. As in the world of plants, what we get out of the ground is ever so much more spectacular than the seed we plant: "What is sown is perishable, what is raised is imperishable. . . . It is sown in weakness, it is raised in power. It is sown a physical body, it is raised a spiritual body (1 Cor 15:36, 42-44). The liturgical act of committing the body to the elements, whether by burial or scattering, is performed as the act of sowing a seed in the expectation of the harvest of resurrection.

Finally, these liturgies assure us that our relationships with the departed live on. The rites hold up the "communion of saints" again and again as a vitally important source of consolation and hope. The relationship is not truly lost or ended at death, even though the separation or absence will be keenly felt. God, "who has knit together the elect in one communion and fellowship" (BCP, 480), does not desire the love we have received and extended to one another to end. Rather, our loving here is but the beginning—in many ways, the apprenticeship—of the love that will continue between disciples forever. Holding the communion of saints in our hearts as a means by which God keeps us connected with our loved ones who precede us can, in turn, help us to maintain our forward movement in our walk of discipleship, as we look to the time when, "by God's call, we are reunited with those who have gone before" (BCP, 493).

We are accustomed to thinking about death as absence—our loved one's absence from our lives, the deceased's absence from the relationships and activities that defined his or her life and continue without him or her. But as more and more of those people who are significant to us cross to the other side, the more we understand that life is also absence. We begin to understand life to signify *our* absence not only from our loved ones, but also from the full presence of God, from the relationships and activities around God's throne and throughout the eternal realm.

Paul wrote, "We know that while we are at home in the body we are away from the Lord" (2 Cor 5:6). Our departed are not absent from us. We are absent from them, and we are separated from our true home, to which Jesus has gone to prepare a place for us (see Jn 14:1-6). This becomes another impetus to invest ourselves in the baptismal life, the life of dying to self and walking in the new person, whose life is the seed of eternal life. Quite the opposite of trying to put our departed loved ones from our minds, keeping our love for them strong can become a reminder that much that is dear to us is already to be found in God's kingdom, so that our hearts may be more surely fixed—and our energies and attention more sharply focused—where our treasure, ultimately, will be found.

PUTTING IT INTO PRACTICE

When you think about heaven, what images come to mind? What activities do you envision there? Read Revelation 21:22—22:5. In John's vision, what is characteristic of the life of God's kingdom? How does this differ from our experience of life now?

Think about a loved one from whom you have been parted by death. What have you found helpful in the process of coming to terms with this change? How, or when, do you still feel connected with him or her? How does that affect you?

37

In the Shelter of the Most High

❈

Death is disorienting. It threatens all that we hold dear. The removal of a loved one can so change our experience of day-to-day activities—waking up to an empty bed, making two cups of coffee when you only drink one yourself—that we are buffeted again and again by the changes in our lives. We even feel alienated from the God who could have done more, who could have spared us this grief, but didn't. The Book of Common Prayer reminds us, however, that death does not alienate us from our faith. Or, to put it another way, even these intensely alienating experiences are held within our faith.

The liturgies of death and burial provide empowering assurances about the continuing experience of, and our ongoing relationship with, those who have died. But, when assailed by grief, we are profoundly in need not merely of convictions, but also of presence. As we gather in the shadow of death, whether mourning or dying ourselves, the liturgies also position us to experience God's comforting presence, for only he is truly able to help us in the face of this trial. The congregation's prayer for those who mourn is that they will encounter God and find his goodness and strength sufficient to bear them through the storms of grief. Such an encounter with God in the midst of grief or anxiety about one's own death can effect more healing and comfort than all the words from human lips.

The psalms appointed for funerals also remind us, when grief threatens to extinguish our hope, to raise our eyes to God and to cry out to him for help. When tears have become our "food day and night," it would be easy to drown and lose ourselves in this pool of sorrow. But the psalms, like the prayers offered throughout the rites, draw our gaze toward God. They urge us to lift up our eyes and look for God's help. They help us to express our thirst for God and to cry out to him to show his face. They position us to wait for the Lord in the expectation that what is now unbearable will become bearable, and that, unthinkable as it might be in the moment, there will again come a time when we will sing praises to God instead of laments.

References to the story of Jesus visiting Martha and Mary in their grief infuse the burial rite. In this story, Martha and Mary both greet Jesus with the words "Lord, if you had been here, my brother would not have died" (Jn 11:21, 32). The sisters are really saying, as I have said after several funerals, "You could have kept this from happening!" Our anger with God for refusing to intervene in the creeping progress of death is something with which our spiritual mothers in this story also wrestled. The Scriptures make room and give permission for these feelings. They invite us to speak to God out of the depths of our feelings, rather than in safe platitudes.

In the same story, we see Jesus coming to be present with Martha and Mary in their grief, both to accept their rebukes—which are also statements of faith, in a roundabout way—and to offer his assurance that new life is his to give and that he *will* give it. Jesus witnesses Mary's grief and the grief of those around her and begins to weep himself, even though he is about to call Lazarus out from the grave. Jesus does not stand aloof from us in our pain. Our grief touches Jesus' heart. He weeps with us at our sorrow. He loves our loved ones as we do. In the conviction that Jesus Christ is the same yesterday, today and forever, the liturgy connects what we see in the story of Lazarus with our story:

> Lord, you consoled Martha and Mary in their distress; draw near to us who mourn for N., and dry the tears of those who weep.
> You wept at the grave of Lazarus, your friend; comfort us in our sorrow.

You raised the dead to life; give to our brother (sister) eternal life. (BCP, 497)

The darkness between Good Friday and Easter morning is another such space in our tradition where our disorientation, our hopelessness, our pain finds a sympathetic resonance. The disciples who had walked with Jesus for several years now suffer grief, confusion and uncertainty about what they have believed. Will Jesus' words prove true? Or are the crushing realities of death the final word? For what must have seemed an eternity, they themselves lacked the resolution that finally came in Jesus' resurrection: "We *had* hoped that he was the one" (Lk 24:21). When our grief is strongest and we cannot find consolation from the assurance of the resurrection, we are still not alienated from our spiritual heritage, but can find in it a meaningful frame of reference and a hope that, just as the disciples eventually came to see that Jesus' words proved true, so will we.

With the psalmists, then, we are invited to bring our grief, our uncertainty, even our anger to God and to learn to take shelter there in his presence, or at least in the place of waiting for God and looking for him. With Mary and Martha we are invited to find Jesus coming to stand beside us in our grief, even if at first it seems he has come too late. The rites and the Scriptures are united in their word to us: you will find God standing with you in your distress. There is no darkness so dark that God, for whom "night is as clear as day," cannot find you (BCP, 475; translation of Ps 139:11).

Psalm 23 is perhaps the most universally read text at funerals. As I discovered during my hospital chaplaincy, it is also the most commonly requested passage of Scripture at the bedside of those who are ill or among families who are facing difficult decisions about end-of-life issues. This is not merely because it is so familiar, but because of its powerful evocation of a sense of God's presence, walking with us, preparing the road ahead of us, leading us for good and not ill. "Yea, though I walk through the valley of the shadow of death, I will fear no evil; for thou art with me; thy rod and thy staff comfort me" (BCP, 476; Ps 23:4). God's presence remains with us, even in the places where death confronts and overwhelms. God is not like our neighbors or friends, who often withdraw from walking with us through that valley on account of their own unresolved fears about mortality. We can lean on his love in the face of grief and of our own mortality, knowing that he stands by us in the valley of the shadow of death *and* shepherds us on the other side (see again Rev 7:17).

The burial rites are intended to be experienced in the context of the Eucharist, which is offered to the bereaved as "a comfort in affliction" (BCP, 482). It is particularly in its aspect as "appetizer" that this comfort is communicated. The Eucharist connects us with the realities beyond death as "a foretaste of your heavenly banquet" and "a pledge of our inheritance in a kingdom where there is no death, neither sorrow nor crying, but the fullness of joy with all your saints" (BCP, 498). Moreover, this rite becomes a point of fellowship with him or her as well. The celebrant prays in regard to the departed, "*He* was nourished with your Body and Blood; grant *him* a place at the table in your heavenly kingdom" (BCP, 497). In the Eucharist, we still have table fellowship, as it were, with those who now feast at the messianic banquet, of which the Eucharist is a foretaste. It becomes a tangible assurance, every time we go forward to receive, that God will reunite those whose relationships are now disrupted by death.

PUTTING IT INTO PRACTICE

Think about the time following the death of someone you loved. How did you feel about God? What did you express to God? In retrospect, how did God make his presence and love known to you in your grief?

Visit someone in your parish or church who has been recently separated from a loved one by death. Go without an agenda except to listen, to be present and to provide Christian companionship. You might take some flowers or some such symbol of care that will outlast your visit.

38

Growing Through Grief

❧

We rarely grow in times of happiness and enjoyment at the same rate as we do in times when our faith and our endurance are challenged. In addition to helping us grow in our consciousness of the continuing life of the realm beyond death and in our openness to the God who is present for us in our most painful distresses, the rites surrounding death and dying point us in several other growth-inducing directions as we move forward from grief to life again.

First, the prayers offered during the services for burial put an especially strong and repeated emphasis on the example of the departed saints. These prayers invite us not only to reflect on the examples of the departed admiringly, but also to try to embody their virtues more and more fully, so that we might more surely arrive where they have gone ahead of us. The Roman emperor Marcus Aurelius, who is more famous for his philosophical writings than for his rule, began his *Meditations* by reflecting on what he learned from deceased family members, whose goodness and strengths still lived on with him. His parents, grandparents and other relatives and teachers had such a formative impact on him that they were not truly absent.

My maternal grandfather was a quiet man who rarely used words to teach or to express himself. But he was a very thoughtful man who expressed himself in acts of kindness meticulously performed. For example, on many an afternoon he would prepare a plate of fruit, cheese and bread for my grandmother, mother and myself as a midday snack. He would cut all the fruit in sections and arrange them in patterns on the plate, interspersed with cubes of bread and cheese. Completely unnecessary, but it was in that "above and beyond" that he said "I love you." Similarly, he would spend long blocks of time with me as a child, taking me to explore forests or streams or to a quarry to collect rocks. It is with him that I feel most connected when I create some dinner for my own family or take care to spend hours with my own sons, so that they will also sense the same love that is more than words.

Imitating what we observed in our loved ones that was noble, generous, uplifting and helpful is one more facet of living out the communion of saints. Their lives continue to affect us, and we continue to feel their presence and often even their strength, insofar as we see the imprint of their lives on ours. Following their example is a way to walk on the other side of grief in a way that adds their strengths to our own and helps us to become more than we could on our own.

A lesson from 2 Corinthians read in connection with ministration to the sick directs us to another way in which we grow through these marginal times of illness, grief and confronting our own death. Paul discloses that he values his own experiences of hardship and suffering as opportunities to discover the resources of God's comfort, encouragement and healing, so that he can, in turn, share these with others (see 2 Cor 1:3-7). Paul's example empowers us to suffer no longer as victims, but rather to engage these experiences as opportunities to grow in sympathy for others in their times of distress and to discover what resources for patience, strength and healing God offers to us so that we can, in turn, offer them to others.

When Susan was diagnosed with breast cancer in her late forties, it had progressed to the point that she was in great danger of succumbing. The road to remission was difficult and uncertain, and she had to wrestle at several points with the possibility that she would die, leaving behind her husband and their three teenagers. But she did pull through and was granted a new lease on life. In the decade that followed, Susan used her experience—and her now intimate knowledge of the biology of breast cancer, of coping with living with the sentence of death associated with many cancers and of working through the psychological struggles with mastectomy associated with this particular cancer—to help other women in their struggle. From promoting awareness and early diagnosis to leading support groups to visiting the bedsides of women who were succumbing, she gave the gift of sharing the strength and extending the sympathy she had gained as one who had been there. She distinguished herself in this ministry until she died during a recurrence of the cancer twenty years later.

Paul's mindset can be applied to the experience of bereavement as well. Marvin felt the absence of his wife of thirty years so deeply that he despaired of life. This was compounded by the fact that she had died, by all reasonable estimates, twenty years before her time. He had, however, the constant support of several friends from the choir and from his own children, which finally convinced him that he was not alone. One of his closest friends, who had been similarly widowed, encouraged him to pray through his feelings. Marvin replied that he didn't feel much like praying. "Not that kind of praying. Let God have it! Tell him what you're feeling. If you're angry, let him know it, and why. If you're miserable, pour it all out to him." He tried it. At first it felt good just to give vent to his feelings. But, after a while, he no longer felt as though he were beating against iron gates with his words. He began to feel God's presence in the midst of his pain and feelings of being cheated, and it was a comforting presence, a restoring presence.

After he began to rebuild his life, Marvin decided that he would offer to others in their grief what his friend had offered to him, to offer the gift of letting his wounds remain visible so that others could find healing as he had. As Jesus shared in our flesh and blood in order to better sympathize with us and connect us to God's transforming power more fully, Marvin used his own flesh-and-blood experiences to learn deeper sympathy for others and to help them find their way back to God's embrace (see Heb 2:14-15; 4:15).

❈❈❈❈❈❈❈❈❈❈❈❈❈❈❈❈❈❈❈❈❈❈❈❈❈❈

PUTTING IT INTO PRACTICE

Think about loved ones—family or otherwise—who have died. What

did your time with them teach you about how to live? How have you embodied the gifts of their examples in your own life, such that part of them remains present with you?

Reflect again on a period when you had to wrestle with the grief of bereavement. What were your spiritual and personal struggles? What did you discover about God and about your faith during that period? Allowing that everyone's experience of grief is unique and deeply personal, how might your struggles and discoveries help you offer support to those who are more recently bereaved?

Reminders of Our Mortality

❧

Renaissance paintings of saints and scholars often show a skull sitting on the desk. Looking straight in the face of one's mortality, these paintings suggested, was an essential part of learning wisdom. The tradition linking mindfulness of mortality with wisdom and authenticity is much older, of course. When a Roman was elevated to the rank of emperor, the proverb *Memento mori* ("Bear in mind that you will die") was spoken in his ear as a check to ultimate power. And, of course, the Hebrew psalmist asked of God, "So teach us to number our days, that we may apply our hearts unto wisdom" (BCP, 473; Ps 90:12). Pausing from the endless stream of day-to-day concerns and squaring off with mortality gives us the opportunity to think about how we are spending our lives and, perhaps, to shape our lives more wisely now so that we will arrive at its conclusion with fewer regrets.

Few of us are likely to have a skull on our shelves or at our office. But life provides other opportunities for us to learn the same lessons. For about a decade, I suffered from acute migraines. At their worst, they would lay me out for two days, unable to move my head because of the pain and unable to find a way to lie that would allow me to escape the pain. I came to refer to these migraines as "reminders of my mortality." Although this began as a joke, it came to shape how I experienced them. They taught me many of the lessons that looking at one's own mortality can teach.

The Book of Common Prayer treats sickness as a kind of skull on our tables. The rites of ministration to the sick have much to teach us about living as people who are prepared to die. The minister prays that the unwelcome weakness that comes with so much illness would become the context for growth: "Sanctify, O Lord, the sickness of your servant, that the sense of *his* weakness may add strength to *his* faith" (BCP, 460). The first thing I gained from my migraines was a renewed awareness of my limitations. They reminded me when I was trying to do too much without properly attending to the needs of my body. They prevented me from being too sure of what I would be able to get done in any given week, making me learn the humility of adding "God willing" to the plans I proposed for myself (see Jas 4:13-16). They forced me to acknowledge my frailty and my dependence on other people and on God, a dependence I would tend to deny or suppress in seasons of strength. Such awareness, which teaches us not to put too much faith in our own strength, is essential to growing in faith toward God.

A side effect of this fresh awareness of dependence is the tendency to do some serious soul searching. There is an almost knee-jerk reflex when bad things happen. "What did I do to deserve this?" We ask this question because the most difficult thing for human beings is to suffer without knowing why. We also ask it because, when the awareness of our limitations and our dependency on God dawns on us anew, we want to be sure that there's nothing between us and God, no offense that prevents us from being assured of his favor and help in our time of need.

The BCP fosters this self-examination and confession of sin, even going so far as to include prayers that the experience of illness itself would fuel these disciplines. The same "sense of weakness" that nourishes greater dependence on God should also "add . . . seriousness to *his* repentance" (BCP, 460). Two readings from the New Testament recommended for the service of Ministration to the Sick link illness and the need for forgiveness of sins quite directly. In Matthew, we hear of Jesus first forgiving the sins of the paralytic and only then telling him to get up and walk away (see Mt 9:2-8). Similarly, James connects confession of sin and healing, advising the sick person to call for the elders of the church, to "confess your sins to one another, and pray for one another, so that you may be healed" (Jas 5:14-16).

These practices may seem to reinforce an understanding of sickness and suffering as a punishment for sin. We need to be theologically sound here, however. Even though our overall susceptibility to disease and death is understood as a consequence of sin (see Gen 3:17-19; Rom 5:12), a particular experience of disease is not to be easily identified as the result of particular sins. The story of Job and of the man born blind in John 9 both prevent us from making quick equations on that score. However, being confronted by our limitations and understanding afresh how fully dependent we are on God provides us with a good opportunity to examine our spiritual and moral frailty in the midst of seeking his help for our physical frailty.

Experiencing another person's funeral also serves as a good, hard look at the skull on our table. And, as in the rites provided for the sick, the burial liturgy also makes space for us to pray for the rightness of our own walk and for the forgiveness of our sins. As we think there about the end of life and our only hope for transcending death, our thoughts are rightly directed toward confirming our walk in that newness of life that pleases the One who has the keys of death and hell:

> Grant to us who are still in our pilgrimage . . . that thy Holy Spirit may lead us in holiness and righteousness all our days. Grant to thy faithful people pardon and peace, that we may be cleansed from all our sins, and serve thee with a quiet mind. (BCP, 481)

These brief encounters with our own mortality can have a profound and healthful effect on our living, providing the impetus for us to refocus our priorities on what is truly, in the *end,* important.

Don's stressful occupation, compounded by the significant debt he and his wife had incurred trying to afford the lifestyle that suited an executive in industry, eventually brought him to the emergency room with an ulcerous, perforated colon. It was touch and go with him for several weeks due to sepsis and other complications. As he gradually recovered over two long months in the hospital, he realized that what he had really feared losing was not his ability to keep spending his time and energy at work and not the beautiful home he and his wife had purchased and decorated, but the enjoyment of watching his daughter and son mature and being present for them through the challenges and joys of life.

Don and his wife shared some intimate conversations about what each of them really valued and how to shape their lives around these priorities. They sold their house and bought outright a smaller one in a much more affordable neighborhood. This enabled Don to scale back his responsibilities (and pay) at work and to give far more of his time and energy to his teenage children. Together, they were no longer living for illusions of what was valuable, but for the things that were really valuable, really worth spending one's life on.

For Katherine, the revelation came rather less dramatically. In the space of six months, she found herself attending four funerals. First, her mother had succumbed after a long battle with congestive heart failure. Then she accompanied her son to the funerals of two schoolmates killed in an automobile accident. Later that year she went to the funeral of a coworker who died suddenly, and in the prime of life, of an undetected, congenital heart defect. Attending these services made her look long and hard at her own life. What was she investing it in? Would her work produce fruit that really mattered? Or would her career in corporate law amount to nothing more than an honorable mention in her own eulogy, as it had in her coworker's?

She began to open up to her husband and one of her close friends about her doubts, and to discern God's guidance. After about a year of searching, she found a position where she could use her expertise in law more directly to benefit families in need of advocacy. The cut in pay was considerable, but the reward of investing her life in other people, of forming close relationships with many of these families and of knowing that many lives would be changed for the better for her having been alive more than compensated for this. We hear again the words of the psalmist, woven into funeral services for centuries, which became true in Katherine's life: "So teach us to number our days, that we may apply our hearts unto wisdom" (Ps 90:12, as recited in the BCP, 473).

✳✳✳✳✳✳✳✳✳✳✳✳✳✳✳✳✳✳✳✳✳✳✳✳✳✳✳✳✳✳✳

PUTTING IT INTO PRACTICE

Reflect on some particularly memorable experience of being ill, injured or otherwise laid up. What were your thoughts and feelings? What new awareness did you take away from it?

What experiences have served or continue to serve as a skull on your desk? How have you responded to these experiences? In what ways have they pushed you to look more to God and to your relationship with him?

Make a list of what is most important to you in your life. How well does your list reflect the two greatest commandments, as Jesus summarized the law (see Mk 12:28-31)? Where do God and seeking the good of other people figure into this list?

Now think about how you spend your time in a given week. How closely do your investments of your most precious resource mirror your priorities? What would your weekly schedule say was most important to you?

If you notice significant discrepancies, use this as a resource for further reflection, conversation with trusted friends and family, and prayer.

40

Some Dead Ends

❋

Not everyone has such salutary responses to looking at the skull on the desk. Our awareness of our own mortality can lead us into some very unwholesome and unholy paths if it is not coupled with a firm conviction of "the resurrection of the body and the life everlasting." Without this hope, our gaze is bent backward on this life, resulting in serious distortions. Looking at death as a brick wall into which we slam at the end of existence, we can easily succumb to the mindset that, if this life is all we can really count on, then we had better enjoy life to the full. Death becomes a mirror, showing us nothing but the world around us, focusing our attention and energies on what we can get out of life while we have breath.

We are no longer motivated by virtue. The good of the other is no longer the primary guiding value. Instead, we are seduced into an ethic of satisfying our own desires and even preying on others to do it. Wherever profit is valued above the well-being of people, wherever self-gratification is valued above consideration of how to meet another's needs, wherever people silence those who threaten their illusions about themselves, the power of death is working to distort human life. Without the hope of immortality, we become less than human, merely the craftiest of animals.

Justin stood at a crossroads in his relationship with his wife. The path of following in the way of Christ was clear: give her the support, love and space she needed to feel valued and safe in the relationship, irrespective of whether or not he would ever derive the satisfaction that he craved from their marriage. But he was also keenly aware that years were passing by, that there would be fewer and fewer left to enjoy with someone else were he to try to start over. His experience of time slipping away was a symptom of the larger problem hobbling his ability to walk in newness of life: death was still more of a wall than the "gate of eternal life" (BCP, 493). As a result, Justin found himself becoming more demanding in his relationship, more protective of his own interests in his decision-making. This is one pervasive way in which death can enslave us, keeping us from walking in the broad and open spaces of children of God who know that they have eternal life and so can be very generous with *this* life.

Death can take us captive through another angle as well, one in which we invest inordinate amounts of emotional and physical energy suppressing the awareness of our own mortality and trying to transcend our own deaths. The pharaohs of early Egypt sought to do this through the erection of great pyramids, which would preserve their lives, their wealth and their prestige for eternity—notably, at the expense of countless lives of their subjects.

The pyramid complex survives in many forms among us. A repressed fear of death lies behind many an attempt to climb closer to the top of the hierarchical pyramids of the corporate and political arenas. The same lies behind many an attempt to amass wealth, to acquire large homes and to accumulate possessions. The "stuff" we pile around us serves as a kind of insulation that we hope will keep death at bay. Of course, death can enslave us as we try simply to escape from it in the moment—moment after moment after moment—through substance abuse, sexual stimulation and a wide variety of other "painkillers."

Colleen would tell you she didn't think about death much at all. Instead, she thought about "living" and "making something of herself." At the age of forty, she had already made associate director in research and development at a major pharmaceutical company, with over twenty research publications to her name. She was renovating a house in a bedroom community outside New York City and was still able to add steadily to her investment portfolio.

The fact that Colleen would describe her success with phrases like "I'm here to stay" might begin to tip us off that, at the root, what motivates her is not a passion for developing new drugs nor a value system that suggests rising to the top and owning the best house in West Orange was really all that important to her. Rather, it was her way of combating her awareness that she, like all of us, was but "a mist that appears for a little while and then vanishes" (Jas 4:14). It was an attempt to do an end run around death and achieve some kind of permanence. The fact that it is all illusory does not matter. That is what is so insidious about the fear of death and its ability to take over our lives when we try to repress it or combat it on our own. In the end, death would shatter Colleen's illusion. It would show at last the futility of all her attempts at making a life for herself and taunt her with the regrets of the tastes of authentic life she passed over in her quest.

Death is not a stream we can cross on our own. Embracing this fact does not leave us helpless. Instead, it opens us up to the power and gift of the God who is our only help in the face of death. The BCP invites the person who is ill to pray, "O God, the source of all health: So fill my heart with faith in your love, that with calm expectancy I may make room for your power to possess me, and gracefully accept your healing" (BCP, 461). We pray the same, on a larger scale, in regard to death: for faith now to live as people who have nothing to fear in death, so that we may make room in our lives for God's Holy Spirit to lead us into the life that endures forever.

By itself, awareness of mortality is not sufficient to bring wisdom. By itself, it often leads to folly of the worst kind. While the Scriptures and the liturgy invite us to learn from the skull on our desk, they insist that we do so with another eye on the resurrected life that God has prepared for all who love him and walk in his ways through life and through death.

PUTTING IT INTO PRACTICE

Think about Justin's dilemma. Are you afraid of not getting to enjoy something you want to have for yourself before you die? Or, from another angle, is there something you're working very hard at getting for yourself, so you can enjoy it before you're no longer able? How is this impulse to "gather ye rosebuds while ye may" affecting your responsiveness to God and your ability to give of yourself as he would have you?

Think about Colleen's obsession and about your own engagement with career, pursuit of achievement and other drives. To what extent are you trying to transcend your own mortality and thus allowing yourself to be enslaved by the fear of death? What is the cost of these pursuits in terms of relationships you are not tending, interests and passions you are not feeding, and the like?

41

Smashing Down the Wall

❋

Is death the final word in our story, or is there a sequel? The burial rites answer *the* fundamental question of our existence with their solemn but hope-filled pronouncement: "even at the grave we make our song: Alleluia, alleluia, alleluia." These liturgies impress on us above all else that death is *not* a wall into which we slam at the end of life, but a threshold over which we pass. They help us to find the "faith to see in death the gate of eternal life" (BCP, 493). Through prayers and Scriptures, they lift the thick pall of death and allow us to see the continuity between who we are and what we have loved here and there, on the far side of death, provided we have loved the right objects, namely, God, one another and the people whom God sends our way to be touched through us with his love. For the faithful, "life is changed, not ended" (BCP, 382).

While this funerary "Alleluia" reminds us in general of the praise that we give God throughout life and even at its end, it rings with the more sonorous overtones of Easter's triumphant "Alleluia," the confession of our hope in the resurrection as we step into the waters from this nearer shore. Just as baptism found its fullest meaning when set in the context of Easter Vigil, highlighting our participation through baptism in the death and resurrection of Jesus, so also "the liturgy for the dead is an Easter liturgy. It finds all meaning in the resurrection. Because Jesus was raised from the dead, we too shall be raised" (BCP, 507).

To those who look at the grave as a dead end from which no one returns and whose lives are thereby distorted, Paul proclaims, "Christ has been raised from the dead, the first fruits of those who have died"

(I Cor 15:20). Someone *has* come back from the grave—not just to live the kind of life we live, but to show the kind of life we will have on the other side of death. The good news in Paul's gospel is not that Jesus' resurrection is unique, but that it is the first of many, the "first fruits" of a great harvest. The Easter message is not just that Jesus was raised from the dead, but that he is the firstborn of many sisters and brothers whom God would also raise from the dead. Christ's resurrection turned the tomb into a womb. It may swell now as its burden grows with each new death, but at the time of deliverance, new life will burst forth as the dead, whom we "entrust" to the earth and to the deep, are brought forth by God to live anew (see Rev 20:13).

Paul's point in I Corinthians 15 is that you can't believe in the resurrection of Jesus without also believing in your own. The confession that Jesus rose again "on the third day" must be uttered in connection with our confession in the general "resurrection of the dead," ourselves included (BCP, 496). And if you truly believe in your own resurrection, death will no longer act as a fun-house mirror, bending your gaze back on this life, distorting your vision and your priorities. Rather, death becomes a door, an open gate with the door knocked off its hinges, through which we peer to glimpse vistas of our life together with God forever.

A popular subject of religious art in the centuries prior to the Enlightenment was the "Harrowing of Hell," depicting Jesus leading out from Hades a procession of those who had died in righteousness prior to his crucifixion, with the gates of hell broken off their frames. These paintings depicted the unseen triumph of Easter between the cross and the empty tomb, the victory over death won by Jesus for all: "Christ is risen from the dead, trampling down death by death, and giving life to those in the tomb" (BCP, 483). One of the parting sentences read at funerals leaves the congregation with their minds fixed on this assurance: "He that raised up Jesus from the dead will also give life to our mortal bodies by his Spirit that dwelleth in us" (BCP, 485; reciting Rom 8:11). The Spirit, who brings the new life—the baptismal life—to light within us, is the pledge of our own resurrection, which we carry with us in sharper focus as we return to our lives.

How does this belief change life? The promise of our own resurrection has the power to free us from the snares by which death can enslave us. It can redirect us from the dead end of believing that we have to get all we want out of this life, no matter what the cost to ourselves or others and no matter how it compromises our commitment to walk in newness of life. It can liberate us from the house of bondage of our own Egypt as we slave away to erect our own pyramids, our attempts to insulate ourselves against death and oblivion, like the rich fool who thought to secure his future by building bigger barns rather than giving his surplus to those in need (see Lk 12:15-21).

This is a critical aspect of the freedom for which Christ set us free, walking boldly into death and into Hades like he owned the place and walking out from the grave to prove that he did. By focusing our minds on the eternity before us, which is God's gift to the faithful, the burial rites of the BCP position us to step more and more fully into this freedom from death's power to distort our thinking, valuing and striving, and to keep us subservient to those systems and powers that hold the power of death.

※※※※※※※※※※※※※※※※※※※※※※※※※※※※

PUTTING IT INTO PRACTICE

With what degree of certainty do you "look for the resurrection of the dead and the life of the world to come" (BCP, 359) or "believe in the resurrection of the body and the life everlasting" (BCP, 496)? What reservations do you have, if any, about this part of the creed? When, if ever, have you felt assured of eternity, and what were you doing?

Envision, for a moment, dying (the circumstances of how you get there don't much matter). Envision, after entering that final sleep of this mortal life, feeling the breath of God afresh on your face, seeing the brightness of the return of Christ, sensing the exhilaration of being caught up to meet him and being reunited with all whom you have loved and with him whom you have served. Imagine the satisfaction of hearing Christ say to you, "Well done, good and faithful servant," and seeing that affirmation in his eyes ever after. Imagine the joy that day, a day that will never end. Pray for God's Holy Spirit to illumine and direct your self-examination.

If you were absolutely assured of this future, how would you live differently? What pressures would you feel lightened? What drives would you feel diminished? What sorrows would be abated? How would this, in turn, affect your relationships with other people, from those closest to you to the stranger you observe in need? You might wish to write down any insights that you deem significant and return to them.

42

Living Like You'll
Live Forever

❃

At the beginning of our spiritual journey, baptism made eternity our objective. Eucharist sustains us on that journey, giving us tastes of the experience of Christ's love and presence, directing our gaze ever forward to the time when we shall stand in his unveiled presence and bask in that love. Entrance into the full presence of God for eternity is the goal of our discipleship, when sacrament gives way to substance, promise to possession.

If we are to live for eternity, however, we need to live *now* for eternity. John Donne, seventeenth-century poet and Anglican priest, said that "upon every minute of this life depend millions of years in the next, and I shall be glorified eternally or eternally lost for my good or ill use of God's grace offered me this hour." Such a thought might arouse some degree of anxiety. But when we push past that, we realize that it also gives profound significance to each moment. Our choices and actions here really matter. In these final chapters, we will explore how having the "faith to see in death the gate of eternal life" (BCP, 493) empowers us to live out our baptismal covenant and to embrace the life of dying with Christ so as to share also in his resurrection.

The burial service points us back to baptism, the beginning of our spiritual journey, as the context for looking at that journey's end: "Grant that all who have been baptized into Christ's death and resurrection may die to sin and rise to newness of life, and that through the grave and gate of death we may pass with him to our joyful resurrection" (BCP,

480). The baptismal life, with its pivotal metaphors of dying to sin and walking in newness of life, is the path to eternal life.

But the connection is more than sequential. Death may provide a decisive point of entry into eternal life as the consummation of the baptismal life, but the Scriptures suggest a great deal more continuity between our living out of newness of life here and entering into life beyond death. In a reading from the Gospel of John, Jesus promises that "anyone who hears my word and believes him who sent me has eternal life, and does not come under judgment, but has passed from death to life" (Jn 5:24). The verb tenses here are striking. Hearing Christ's word and trusting it to be the revelation of God's own will (and responding accordingly) means the present possession of eternal life, a life we begin to live now as we walk in line with Jesus' word, a life we continue to live beyond death. While this is immediately tempered in the next verse, where Jesus speaks of the future resurrection of those who are in the grave, at no point is the idea of possessing eternal life *now* retracted.

We could dismiss this as a quirk of John's theology, but other voices from Scripture paint a similar picture. The author of 1 Peter talks about a new, imperishable life quickening within us as a result of hearing and responding to God's word (see 1 Pet 1:23-25). The life of the new person is, in effect, the beginning of our experience of eternal life and the kernel of who we are and will be for eternity. It gives us roots in a life beyond death. Paul also senses this new person growing daily within him, and, with it, his connection with eternity (see 2 Cor 4:16, 18).

From this perspective, it becomes somewhat problematic to speak of life beyond death as "after-life." The term assumes that this life is the norm, the standard, in some sense more worthy to be called "life" than anything that waits for us beyond death. It also assumes discontinuity between our experience of life here and what lies on the other side of death. While death is still a crucial transition, eternal life—living beyond death—is something that begins and blossoms as we live out our baptism, not something for which we must wait until after death.

At each funeral, we are taken back to the centrality of living out the baptismal life so that we may enjoy the end and goal of that life:

> Raise us, we humbly pray, from the death of sin to the life of
> righteousness; that when we depart this life we may rest in him,
> and at the resurrection receive that blessing which your well-
> beloved Son shall then pronounce: "Come, you blessed of my Fa-
> ther, receive the kingdom prepared for you." (BCP, 505)

Dying to sin and to self and living anew for God and his righteousness is the essence of our baptismal covenant. As we give ourselves away
for the good of others like people who have an endless supply of life and
as we invest ourselves more and more in embodying God's righteousness and justice, we find ourselves ever more securely tethered to the life
beyond death.

PUTTING IT INTO PRACTICE

As you think about your relationships, your hang-ups, your professional and personal pursuits, what are the greatest challenges that you
face living from the new person? To what desires and drives that you
know are impeding your ability to love, serve and walk like Jesus are you
having the most difficulty "dying"?

Ask the Holy Spirit to help you select one of these challenges to focus
on. Ask for help to see the challenge, and the alternatives of pleasing
Christ and pleasing yourself, in the light of eternity. Pray for the assurance and strength you need to respond in a way that is in line with your
baptismal covenant (spending some time in adoration may be of great
help here). Be attentive to ways in which you feel more closely connected
with God and with eternity as you move forward in this direction.

Since the baptismal journey is a life of growing out from the old person
into the life of the new person, reflect on how your new person has grown
from your baptism to this point. Write, however briefly, a spiritual auto-
biography of significant episodes that have called the new person more

and more into being or have challenged or threatened its growth.

If you are more inclined toward the visual arts, you might create a portrait or sculpture of your new person reflective of its health and vitality at the moment. Then spend some time in silent contemplation, and listen for the Spirit's word to you concerning the next step in this journey.

43

Affirmation Worth Seeking

❧

Psychologists tell us that affirmation is vital for the development of a healthy self-image. This is particularly true in our formative years, when a lack of affirmation can contribute to the distortion of personality and the resultant deformation of life itself. The child can become a people pleaser, so desperately in need of affirmation that he would compromise his own value system rather than risk criticism. The child can become an overachiever or workaholic, throwing herself endlessly into completing projects or winning cases in the hope of experiencing that affirmation that she used to get as a child only when she "produced."

Our dependence on the affirmation of others for our own identity formation often subtly derails our ability to follow where Christ leads, for the people around us often give their affirmation for what is contrary to the call of discipleship. People receive affirmation of their worth when they get a promotion or pay raise, not when they empty themselves and take a lower station so as to better serve those in need, as did Christ (see Phil 2:5-11).

The burial rites call our attention to that word of affirmation that will have the most significant impact on our identity formation, and, indeed, our future: Jesus' word, "Well done" (see Mt 25:20-23). Our attention is drawn to those who have lived out their love for God as we ask for grace to follow their example of steadfast obedience, so that "at the day of the general resurrection we . . . may be set on his right hand, and hear that his most joyful voice: 'Come, ye blessed of my Father, inherit the kingdom prepared for you'" (BCP, 487; reciting Mt 25:34).

The prayer calls us to follow in the steps of those who have been in step with Jesus, so that we, too, may receive the grant of eternal affirmation of our investment of our short time on this earth. The good news is that we do not need to wait for the last judgment to enjoy that affirmation, which comes from God's own Spirit testifying within us to God's pleasure as we reach out in his love and reflect the mind of his Son, from those people around us who value growth in discipleship and from our own conscience as we see our lives reflecting more and more the heart of Jesus. As we place Christ's affirmation above all others, we find ourselves walking with greater integrity in regard to our faith convictions and in greater freedom from the fear of human disapproval of our faithful choices.

Scripture is, of course, full of guidance concerning what kind of life enjoys Jesus' commendation, and we have explored many different facets of this already. If we look more closely here at the context of Jesus' word of approval, "Come, you blessed of my Father," we find that, as in so much of Jesus' teaching, the approval of heaven comes on those who use their time, resources and energies to relieve the needs of their neighbor, insofar as they have the ability. Feeding the hungry, giving drink to the thirsty, clothing those who are exposed to the elements, welcoming the stranger, caring for the sick, visiting the prisoner—these are wise investments of our resources (see Mt 25:31-46). Where God gives prosperity and a person responds by building up a bigger barn or investment portfolio, the response from heaven is still "You fool!" Living as people who would pass through death into eternity poses for us the challenge of investing ourselves now so as to be "rich toward God," and not simply rich. (See Lk 12:13-21.)

Henry and Maria were really struck by that parable, which they heard read in the morning Eucharist just days after meeting with their financial adviser to tweak their portfolio. Although they knew that, in a roundabout way, their invested money was helping companies to keep running and providing jobs, they wanted to put their money to work for people more directly. They liquidated over half their portfolio. With part, they supported a missionary organization that worked to provide safe drinking water and teach more productive agricultural practices in Africa. With the rest, they bought three older homes in their small town outright and used them to provide housing for families who had lost their income after two major businesses had closed. While the families looked for and got established in other jobs, they would "pay" rent by helping to renovate the houses. In time, Henry and Maria hoped to sell the homes for a profit and use the proceeds to buy more houses to offer families between jobs or to respond to new needs that arose.

In a verse read at the opening of the burial service, a voice from heaven proclaims, "Blessed are the dead who die in the Lord; even so saith the Spirit, for they rest from their labors, for their deeds follow them" (BCP, 469; reciting Rev 14:13). What will follow us into eternity? What deeds, what commitments, what sacrifices will have value before God's throne and result in the affirmation of the company of heaven?

Human approval is short-lived indeed, but God's affirmation is constant and lasts forever. As Paul reflected on the time of this life as absence from the Lord and on death as the homecoming for which he longed, he and his coworkers lived for the approval of the Lord who would receive them into eternity: "whether we are at home or away, we make it our aim to please him" (2 Cor 5:9). Living now in the hope of the resurrection means looking to please Christ in all that we do. This is the ultimate leap of faith—spending our short span of life as an investment for eternity.

PUTTING IT INTO PRACTICE

What is your understanding of what Jesus really wants to see in your heart and to observe in your actions? As you look at how you spend your time and your resources, how much of this is directed toward endeavors that will delight the Lord compared to endeavors that you undertake for your own satisfaction or to satisfy the expectations of others?

If you are married, discuss with your spouse and family the adjustments you might consider making so as to make Christ's approval a more central and significant aim of your endeavors. Invite them also into the process of discerning and envisioning the adjustments you all might make as a family. If you are single, seek the discernment of trusted friends.

44

Freed for
Costly Discipleship

❦

Will we keep walking in the baptismal life when it becomes costly, when our renunciations of Satan, the domination systems of this world and our own gratification bring us into places of deprivation, hardship, even peril? This is where our ability to see in death "the gate of eternal life" becomes really important. It was a make-or-break issue for the apostle Paul. "If for this life only we have hoped in Christ," he would be ready to disavow his entire apostolic experience (1 Cor 15:19). "Why are we putting ourselves in danger every hour? . . . If the dead are not raised, 'let us eat and drink, for tomorrow we die'" (1 Cor 15:30, 32).

For Paul it is a matter of course that Jesus leads his followers into places of sacrifice, of conflict with the power of this age, of dying to the desires and gratification of the self. Will we follow Jesus when it becomes costly rather than tolerable or even advantageous? If our mind is set on living for this life only, we will not be faithful disciples in the difficult choices. We will not pass by the pleasures and gains we think ourselves entitled to enjoy in life's fleeting moments, nor embrace adverse conditions in order to walk consistently after Christ's example and in service to God's cause in the world.

Paul and his team expend their physical well-being in service to the gospel. As they carry their countercultural message from city to city, challenging public discourse about empire and threatening the economic practices built on the ideology of empire, they are subjected to imprisonment, beatings and mob violence (see Acts 16:20-21; 19:23-27). The startling thing is that they persist. They embrace the costs of obedience to God's call to die to themselves and bear witness to the new life in word and deed. They can accept the wear and tear on their bodies because they experience the life of the Spirit growing within—the new person taking shape inside them and growing up into the resurrection body (see 2 Cor 4:16-18). They know that the shedding of this mortal body means being invested with the fuller clothing of the immortal body (see 2 Cor 5:1-5). In this same hope, Paul can encourage us to "be steadfast, immovable, always excelling in the work of the Lord, because you know that in the Lord your labor is not in vain" (1 Cor 15:58). As we sow this life to the Spirit, it grows into an eternal harvest.

Revelation 7:9-17, the epistle lesson provided for services of burial that gave us our sharpest vision of the church triumphant on the other side of "the great ordeal," was in fact written not to console mourners, but to embolden disciples to engage the contest of this life with all its challenges to faithfulness. I would want to challenge any notion that this "great ordeal" or "great tribulation" refers to some "seven last years," a view that the Left Behind series has made popular. It is rather the whole of our earthly existence, the contest in which we are called to overcome every obstacle to our faithfulness to Christ and our obedience to the Spirit of God. For some, like our sisters and brothers in nations where the expression of Christian faith is now severely restricted and even openly persecuted, this "great tribulation" is considerably more acute. But the contest simply to remain centered on God in the face of the lures of the world, the flesh and the devil requires strenuous vigilance and exertion as well.

John provides his glorious visions of triumph beyond death to embolden his hearers to walk fully in line with God's commands and values, no matter what the cost in terms of this world's goods, comforts, even life itself. His words not only provide comfort and hope to the grieving gathered around a casket, but also instill boldness and willingness to invest ourselves fully in the baptismal life.

Thomas found this courage to witness against the injustice of racism. He was no rebel. His parents had raised him to believe that white people were naturally better than blacks (though his parents used another term). He even believed it himself until he started preparing a sermon on Galatians 3:28: "There is no longer Jew or Greek, there is no longer slave or free, there is no longer male and female; for all of you are one in Christ Jesus." For the first time, he really heard the challenge of this text and knew that he could not continue to call himself a Christ-follower while making distinctions between white and black (and always to the detriment of the latter).

Even though the wheels of desegregation were beginning to turn in his region, there was no question of where most of his old-school parishioners and neighbors would stand on the issue. But he knew he had to bear witness to the word God had spoken to him and challenge the beliefs he and so many others had accepted as God's divine order. He was taken aside after his sermon and warned not to rock the boat. When he continued to challenge segregation as an affront to the gospel, he lost his pulpit and his livelihood. But a small group from the church gathered at his house one night and said they had been having the same doubts about how they had been raised. Many of them would go on to become advocates for desegregation in the face of burning crosses on their lawn and death threats to their family and would help build bridges with their sisters and brothers in "black" churches.

From the perspective of God's desires for human community, Western society needs to be challenged yet on many other fronts. Disciples are called to rescue the name of God from being used to legitimate violence and to perpetuate domination systems. Assumptions about wealth and lifestyle need to be challenged so that all of God's children can share in his bounty. And we are still a long way from allowing Paul's vision for the unity of the people of Christ to come to life above our ethnic, nationalistic and gender-related prejudices. Jesus boldly confronted all of these obstructions to God's kingdom in the course of his witness, as those who follow his path through life, through death, to eternal life are called to do. "Grant to your servants to follow in faith where you have led the way, that we may at length fall asleep peacefully in you and wake up in your likeness" (BCP, 504).

❋ ❋

PUTTING IT INTO PRACTICE

Think of a time in which you succeeded in choosing faithfulness to God's righteous standards in the face of a threatening situation. Think also of a time when you failed. What was different? What considerations were guiding you each time? How did each "feel" in regard to the health and vitality of your inner person?

Using any resources available to you—the web, a seminary, an "international" church in your area, a missionary—learn more about the situation of Christians in a country where Christian faith and practice is restricted or prohibited. If at all possible, get to know a Christian from such a country personally (if you are near a seminary, the chances will be good that you will find one among its international student population). What are the costs of discipleship and challenges to living out the baptismal life there? What empowers a believer there to embrace those costs for the sake of the new life he or she has in Christ?

45

Dying As Those
Who Go Forth to Live

※

We began this book by looking closely at the baptismal life as a "dying life," a life of *choosing* death to our own selfish passions and self-interests, to the sick systems of our world and to the deceptions of Satan so that we might become free to walk in newness of life. We are emboldened to embrace this dying to self and to swim against the currents of our society both by the promise of the resurrection and by the assurance that the new person within us that comes alive to the Spirit of God lives forever. It is the promise of eternal life that allows us to live out the baptismal life fully, without hedging our bets. It is this promise that allows us to live fully within the economy of receiving from God and giving ourselves away to others in his love, without grasping here and there for our own wants and entitlements.

And it is a giving away, not a throwing away. When Paul chooses a life of moving from city to city, often as a refugee, often being slandered and beaten by the people who just will not give up the world's promises for the sake of God's, he does not do it because he devalues life in this body. In fact, he places the *highest* value on life in this body, treating it as the seed of his own immortality. Convinced of Jesus' resurrection, and therefore that death was not the final word in his story, Paul is empowered to live no longer for this life only, but for the resurrected life: He wants "to know Christ and the power of his resurrection and the sharing of his sufferings by becoming like him in his death, if somehow I may attain the resurrection from the dead" (Phil 3:10-11). The promise of the resurrection empowers the journey toward Christlikeness in this life—and necessitates it, if we hope to encounter death as a portal rather than a brick wall. This is the mystery that Jesus tried to communicate to his disciples: those who try to secure their own lives will lose them; those who give away their lives in acts of love, service and witness for Jesus' sake will secure them for eternity (see Mk 8:35).

If we know that we will live forever and if we know that living now in conformity with the self-giving pattern of Jesus is the way to life beyond death, what new possibilities for this life open up? You're in a relationship and, rather than deciding whether or not to keep investing in it on the basis of *your* satisfaction, you are able to seek God's leading concerning how you might best nurture and invest in the other's growth toward wholeness. You're making some serious money and, rather than channeling those funds into the acquisition of more goods for your own enjoyment or into your retirement plan, you are able to see the needs of another person, near or far away, and include that one in your care. You're hiding behind a public image of yourself that you want to project so as to be valued and, rather than keep withering behind the pretense, you allow yourself to be open and vulnerable with a brother or sister in Christ who can help you find the courage and freedom to work on who you *are* rather than *seem to be.* You think more about a rival's need for nurture than your own impulse to come out on top. You invest yourself in a colleague's development rather than focusing only on your own. You give the gift of honesty and prophetic witness to God's values, even when the person to whom you are speaking could hurt you. You lay down your pride to seek reconciliation. You lay down your ambitions to serve the people around you right now.

The Book of Common Prayer discovers the meaning of both baptism and burial in the Paschal mystery, the death and resurrection of Jesus. This mystery is that those who live forever are the ones who give themselves away to others and to God's cause in the world, who die to self by embodying the mind of Christ and following the leading of the Spirit to complete Christ's work in the world. The question we face between baptism and our own Easter is this: will we live for this mortal life, witnessing to the triumph of death over our lives, or will we live as witnesses to the triumph of Christ's resurrection, the triumph of God over death, proclaiming by our self-giving actions and courageous witness, "Where, O death, is your victory? Where, O death, is your sting?" (1 Cor 15:55).

Appendix A

The Apostles' Creed

I believe in God, the Father almighty,
creator of heaven and earth.

I believe in Jesus Christ, his only Son, our Lord.
He was conceived by the power of the Holy Spirit
and born of the Virgin Mary.
He suffered under Pontius Pilate,
was crucified, died, and was buried.
He descended to the dead.
On the third day he rose again.
He ascended into heaven,
and is seated at the right hand of the Father.
He will come again to judge the living and the dead.

I believe in the Holy Spirit,
the holy catholic Church,
the communion of saints,
the forgiveness of sins,
the resurrection of the body,
and the life everlasting.

Appendix B

The Nicene Creed

We believe in one God,
the Father, the Almighty,
maker of heaven and earth,
of all that is, seen and unseen.

We believe in one Lord, Jesus Christ,
the only Son of God,
eternally begotten of the Father,
God from God, Light from Light,
true God from true God,
begotten, not made,
of one Being with the Father.
Through him all things were made.
For us and for our salvation
he came down from heaven:
by the power of the Holy Spirit
he became incarnate from the Virgin Mary,
and was made man.
For our sake he was crucified under Pontius Pilate;
he suffered death and was buried.
On the third day he rose again
in accordance with the Scriptures;
he ascended into heaven
and is seated at the right hand of the Father.
He will come again in glory to judge the living and the dead,
and his kingdom will have no end.

We believe in the Holy Spirit, the Lord, the giver of life,
who proceeds from the Father and the Son.
With the Father and the Son he is worshiped and glorified.
He has spoken through the Prophets.
We believe in one holy catholic and apostolic Church.
We acknowledge one baptism for the forgiveness of sins.
We look for the resurrection of the dead,
and the life of the world to come. Amen. (BCP, 358-59)

Notes

Introduction

page 11 "I left the Episcopal Church": For those who may be curious, the principal reason I did, in fact, leave was that I found the United Methodist Church to offer the possibility of combining the richness of Anglican liturgy with a greater degree of liturgical creativity. This was modeled so winsomely in the chapel services at Candler School of Theology that I was won over to a new—but not too distant!—denominational affiliation during my doctoral studies at Emory University.

page 13 "Thomas Cranmer, archbishop of Canterbury": See, further, Jeffrey Lee, *Opening the Prayer Book* (Cambridge, Mass.: Cowley Publications, 1999), pp. 47-55, on the period and the development of the early editions of the Book of Common Prayer.

page 14 "A fruit of the reformation of worship": See Lee, *Opening the Prayer Book*, p. 51.

page 14 "Catholic and . . . Protestant convictions": For example, affirming that the bread and wine *are* the body and blood of Christ, while also speaking of eating the bread and wine as an act of *remembrance*. See Lee, *Opening the Prayer Book*, p. 52.

page 14 "One can still recognize": For further details on the influence of early Christian liturgies on the BCP, as well as a fuller account of the successive editions of the BCP in England and America, see Charles P. Price and Louis Weil, *Liturgy for Living* (Minneapolis: Seabury Press, 1979), pp. 65-94, 103-8, 191-96.

page 15 "available online": This website also provides access to almost every published edition of the Book of Common Prayer in the Church of England (hence, the historic prayer books from 1549 through 1662) and in the Protestant Episcopal Church (hence, the prayer books used in the American branch of the Anglican Communion from 1786 through the present), not to mention the prayer books used in Scotland, Ireland, Wales and Canada, together with selections from Anglican prayer books used throughout the world.

page 15   "a clear command of Christ": In regard to baptism, Mt 28:19-20; in regard to the Eucharist, 1 Cor 11:23-25.

page 15   "all *seven* sacraments": Baptism, Communion, reconciliation of the penitent (penance), confirmation, marriage, ordination and extreme unction, the anointing of the dying commonly called the "last rites."

page 16   "Ash Wednesday through Easter": Ash Wednesday initiates a forty-day period of self-examination, self-denial and penitence known as Lent. The forty days recall, of course, Jesus' own time of preparation and temptation in the wilderness, when he devoted himself to fasting and prayer. Lent culminates in Holy Week, the week that celebrates Jesus' entrance into Jerusalem (Palm Sunday), institution of the Lord's Supper (Maundy Thursday), death (Good Friday) and resurrection (the Easter Vigil and Easter Sunday services).

Chapter 1: Christian Life as Baptismal Life

pages 22-23   "Martin Luther wrote": Martin Luther, *The Large Catechism*, trans. Robert H. Fischer (Philadelphia: Fortress, 1959), pp. 85-86.

page 23   "The daily garment": Luther, *Large Catechism*, p. 90. This is "to receive baptism rightly," as asserted in the "Articles of Religion," the principal doctrinal statement of the Episcopal Church (BCP, 873). We "receive baptism rightly" when we strive each new day to embody its significance for our lives a little more.

page 24   "we are entering": Green, *Baptism*, p. 123, quoting a letter from a Baptist missionary who later became an Anglican nun.

Chapter 3: New Birth, New Life

page 29   "mis-shaping process": See, further, David deSilva, "1 Peter: Strategies for Counseling Individuals on the Way to a New Heritage," *Ashland Theological Journal* 32 (2000): 33-52.

page 31   "oil of Chrism": The term *Chrism* comes from the Greek word *chrisma*, "anointing," the term used by John the Elder to speak of the Holy Spirit, given to believers from above to guide them into

God's truth (see 1 Jn 2:20, 26-28).

page 31   "sealed . . . and marked": This climactic statement draws on language from Paul (2 Cor 1:20-22; 5:1-5), in which the Holy Spirit is God's "down payment" or "pledge" that he will fulfill all his promises to us in Christ. It also draws on language from John the Seer (Rev 7:3), in which the seal of God is placed on the foreheads of those who are his, who are destined to stand among the redeemed from every people, nation and language.

Chapter 4: Union with Christ

page 33   "the Christian mystery": Charles P. Price and Louis Weil, *Liturgy for Living* (Minneapolis: Seabury Press, 1979), p. 102.

page 33   "letters of Paul": Rom 6:3-11 is an especially important text in this regard.

page 34   "laying down our lives . . . as Jesus loved us": See Jn 15:12-13; 1 Jn 3:16-17. On this subject, see the further discussion in D. A. deSilva, *New Testament Themes* (St. Louis: Chalice Press, 2001), pp. 51-63.

page 35   "Death *means* death": Michael Green, *Baptism* (London: Hodder & Stoughton, 1987), p. 49.

page 35   "consecrated to a crucified Messiah": John Durel, *The Liturgy of the Church of England Asserted (1662)*, quoted in *Prayer Book Spirituality: A Devotional Companion to the* Book of Common Prayer *Compiled from Classical Anglican Sources*, ed. J. Robert Wright (New York: Church Hymnal Corporation, 1989), p. 236.

page 35   "The more completely you die": Thomas à Kempis *The Imitation of Christ* 2.12.

page 36   "in actual practice": Green, *Baptism*, p. 49.

Chapter 5: A New Exodus

page 38   "the spiritual meaning": Leonel L. Mitchell, *Praying Shapes Believing: A Theological Commentary on the* Book of Common Prayer (Harrisburg, Penn.: Morehouse Publishing, 1985), p. 89.

Chapter 6: We Renounce All That Is Not from God

page 41   "As early as the third century": These details come from the baptismal service described by Hippolytus of Rome in book eight of the *Apostolic Tradition*. See also Charles P. Price and Louis Weil, *Liturgy for Living* (Minneapolis: Seabury Press, 1979), p. 106.

page 42   "two equal and opposite errors": C. S. Lewis, *The Screwtape Letters* (San Francisco: Harper Collins, 2001), preface.

page 42   "Scripture presents Satan as": For the Scriptural background undergirding this paragraph, see Jn 12:31; 14:30; 16:11; 1 Cor 7:5; 2 Cor 2:10-11; 4:4; 11:3; 1 Thess 3:4-5; Rev 12:9; 13:4.

page 43   "You may be sure": Thomas à Kempis *The Imitation of Christ* 3.6.

page 44   "domination systems": C. Dale White, *Making a Just Peace: Human Rights and Domination Systems* (Nashville: Abingdon, 1998), is perhaps the most helpful "primer" on this subject. See also the celebrated trio of books by Walter Wink, *Naming the Powers* (Minneapolis: Augsburg Fortress, 1983); *Unmasking the Powers* (Minneapolis: Augsburg Fortress, 1986); *Engaging the Powers* (Minneapolis: Augsburg Fortress, 1992), as well as Wes Howard-Brook and Anthony Gwyther, *Unveiling Empire: Reading Revelation Then and Now* (Maryknoll, N.Y.: Orbis, 1999), a striking interpretation of Revelation as a clarion call to disciples to take up a stance of prophetic witness and distance from these domination systems.

page 45   "diseased spirituality": White, *Making a Just Peace*, p. 26.

page 45   "Rev 18:4-5": See, further, D. A. deSilva, "The Revelation of John and the Practice of Christian Counseling," *Asbury Theological Journal* 60 (2005): 67-87, esp. 74-75, 83-85.

page 46   "Those who made their living": Price and Weil, *Liturgy for Living*, p. 105.

Chapter 7: We Reach Out for All That Is from God

page 53   "If through weakness": Thomas à Kempis *The Imitation of Christ* 3.6.

Chapter 8: We Journey Together Toward Christlikeness

page 55   "As many as are persuaded" Justin Martyr *First Apology* 61, emphasis added.

page 57   "resist such intervention": Jesus himself anticipates that his followers would not always accept correction from a few fellow believers and that some might even cling to their old self in the face of the correction of the entire assembly (see Mt 18:15-17).

page 57   "who faced persecution": Heb 13:3. On the subject of reaching-ing out to persecuted Christians, see D. A. deSilva, *Perseverance in Gratitude: A Socio-rhetorical Commentary on the Epistle "to the Hebrews"* (Grand Rapids: Eerdmans, 2000), pp. 488-89, 521-23, and the literature and Internet sites therein noted.

page 58   "The voices that speak": See Eph 6:18-20; Col 3:16; 4:2-4; 1 Thess 4:18; 5:11. Notably, the reminders of our common faith and hope are meant not only to help us find strength in the face of grief (see 1 Thess 4:13-18) but also to help us not buy into the way the domination systems around us would have us think about our lives in this world (see 1 Thess 5:1-11).

Chapter 9: We Promise to Live Out Our Baptism in "Real Life"

pages 60-61 "Believing does not mean": From *The Whole Duty of Man* (1657), adapted from J. Robert Wright, ed., *Prayer Book Spirituality: A Devotional Companion to the* Book of Common Prayer *Compiled from Classical Anglican Sources* (New York: Church Hymnal Corporation, 1989), pp. 230-31.

page 61   "a body of spiritual disciplines": For a fuller introduction to these and other spiritual disciplines, see Richard J. Foster, *The Celebration of Discipline: The Path to Spiritual Growth*, rev. ed. (San Francisco: HarperSanFrancisco, 1998).

page 63   "The collects": The "collect" is a short prayer, generally offered by the minister or priest, that "gathers" and focuses the prayers of the assembled congregation. In the BCP, one can find a cycle of collects for use throughout the church year, a different prayer for every Sunday and special "feast day" (for example, Ascension Day, days for commemorating particular saints and the like), as well as other collects sprinkled in various liturgies, such as the "Collect for Purity" that begins the service of Holy Communion.

page 64   "Evangelism is one beggar": D. T. Niles, quoted in the *New York Times*, May 11, 1986.

page 65   "You have made all people": As paraphrased in D. A. deSilva, *Praying with John Wesley* (Nashville: Discipleship Resources, 2001), p. 17.

Chapter 10: A Sevenfold Prayer for the Baptismal Life

page 69   "the *Didache* and the *Epistle of Barnabas*": These are two texts from the "mainstream" of early Christianity and can be found in the (modern) collection known as "The Apostolic Fathers" or "The Post-apostolic Fathers." *Barnabas* is a lengthy interpretation of the major symbols and rites of Judaism, explaining their allegorical significance for Christians. It was so influential, it even appears in one fourth-century codex of the Septuagint (the Christian "Bible" containing a Greek translation of the Old Testament and the Greek New Testament). Both texts contain a form of ethical instruction known as the "two ways," a form also known from early Jewish literature.

page 70   "Let your love": Thomas à Kempis *The Imitation of Christ* 3.5.

page 72   "when a person": Thomas à Kempis *The Imitation of Christ* 3.5.

Chapter 11: Encountering Jesus in the Eucharist

page 77   "Shepherd of souls": *The Hymnal 1982*, no. 343, v. 1 (New York: The Church Hymnal Corporation, 1985).

page 77   "the health of soul and body": Thomas à Kempis *Imitation of Christ* 4.4.

page 77   "frequent receiving": Robert Nelson, *The Great Duty of Frequenting the Christian Sacrifice* (1706), as quoted in *Prayer Book Spirituality: A Devotional Companion to the* Book of Common Prayer *Compiled from Classical Anglican Sources*, ed. Robert Wright (New York: Church Hymnal Corporation, 1989), p. 309. John Wesley recommends the same in the "General Rules" that he developed for his Anglican renewal movement.

page 79   "epistle to the Hebrews": See especially Heb 8:1—10:18; a detailed discussion can be found in D. A. deSilva, *Perseverance in Gratitude: A Socio-rhetorical Commentary on the Epistle "to the Hebrews"* (Grand Rapids: Eerdmans, 2000), pp. 284-331.

Chapter 13: The Host Who Is the Feast

page 84   "came forth from Egypt": *Mishnah Pesachim* 10:5.

pages 84-85 "We share the table": Compare Paul's expectation that worshipers would actually share a table with the One or ones they worshiped, whether the Lord or the demons that he regarded as the gods of the nations (see I Cor 10:21).

page 85   "extending his or her arms": Anglican liturgy communicates not just by means of words, but also often by accompanying actions that make the impression more vivid.

page 85   "all thoughts of bread": William Beveridge, *The Great Necessity and Advantage of Public Prayer and Frequent Communion* (1708), as quoted in *Prayer Book Spirituality: A Devotional Companion to the* Book of Common Prayer *Compiled from Classical Anglican Sources,* ed. Robert Wright (New York: Church Hymnal Corporation, 1989), p. 312.

Chapter 14: A Family Meal

page 87   "As Christ breaks bread": *The Hymnal 1982,* no. 304, v. 2 (New York: The Church Hymnal Corporation, 1985).

page 88   "social divisions": See Gerd Theissen, *The Social Setting of Pauline Christianity* (Philadelphia: Fortress, 1982), pp. 145-74; Bruce Winter, *After Paul Left Corinth* (Grand Rapids: Eerdmans, 2001), pp. 142-58.

Chapter 15: An Appetizer

page 90   "now scattered . . . will yet be gathered": This is beautifully captured in the *Didache,* which preserves an early second-century Eucharistic prayer: "Just as this piece of bread had been scattered over the mountains and, gathered together, became one, in this way let your church be gathered from the corners of the earth into your kingdom" (*Didache* 9.4).

page 90   "to proclaim our hope": Each of the eucharistic prayers in the BCP includes a declaration of the "mystery of faith" focusing on Christ's death, resurrection and coming again in glory, most often spoken in unison by the congregation.

page 91   "In that consummation": The following images are taken from Rev 21:23-24; 22:5.

Chapter 16: Self-Examination and Confession

page 95   "People from many different cultures": See, further, D. A. deSilva, *Honor, Patronage, Kinship & Purity: Unlocking New Testament Culture*

(Downers Grove, Ill.: InterVarsity Press, 2000), chaps. 7 and 8.

page 96   "A constant part": Leonel L. Mitchell, *Praying Shapes Believing: A Theological Commentary on the* Book of Common Prayer (Harrisburg, Penn.: Morehouse Publishing, 1985), p. 133.

Chapter 17: The Confession of Sin

page 101   "Do you master": From Thomas à Kempis *Imitation of Christ* 4.6, freely adapted.

page 101   "Prayers for Daily Use": For a modern adaptation of this classic resource, see David deSilva, *Praying with John Wesley* (Nashville: Discipleship Resources, 2001).

page 102   "Israel's call to 'be holy'": See Lev 19:2. This is the opening "thesis statement" that is developed throughout Lev 19, including the command to love one's neighbor as oneself.

page 104   "Who can now walk away": Jesus similarly extends the ethical territory covered by the seventh commandment, the prohibition of adultery, to include lustful glances and thoughts (see Mt 5:27-28).

page 105   "While Jesus dines": The story is found in Lk 7:36-50.

page 105   "Godly sorrow . . . that leads to repentance": See 2 Cor 7:8-11, where Paul helpfully distinguishes between the kind of regret that leads to amendment of life and, ultimately, restoration, and the kind that drags a person down into despair.

Chapter 18: Solidarity in Sin, Solidarity in Forgiveness

page 109   "solidarity in corporate sinfulness": Leonel L. Mitchell, *Praying Shapes Believing: A Theological Commentary on the* Book of Common Prayer (Harrisburg, Penn.: Morehouse Publishing, 1985), p. 139.

page 111   "suspicion, ill-feeling" and "Sacrifice of Peace": Thomas à Kempis *Imitation of Christ* 4.9 (p. 200, modified).

Chapter 19: Prayer and Intercession

page 114   "He wants to make us more like Jesus": This is the real message of Rom 8:28-29. It is not simply that "all things work together for good" for disciples in the sense that "everything will turn out alright," but that this "good" toward which all things are working is the fulfillment of our destiny of being "conformed to the image of [God's] Son."

page 115   "to spend . . . on our own desires": See James 4:1-3.

Chapter 20: The Collects of the Day

page 118   "You have prepared": Collect for the Sixth Sunday of Easter (BCP, 225).

page 118   "run without stumbling": Collect for Proper 26 (BCP, 235). This image also appears in the Collect for Proper 21 (BCP, 234), where we are set "running to obtain [God's] promises."

page 119   "Grant us, Lord": Collect for Proper 20 (BCP, 234).

page 119   "clouds . . . hide from us": Collect for the Eighth Sunday after Epiphany (BCP, 217).

page 119   "Grant us so perfectly": Collect for the Fifth Sunday of Easter (BCP, 225) drawing on 1 Pet 2:21; see also the collects for Proper 15 (BCP, 232) and Proper 27 (BCP, 236).

page 120   "that we may be devoted . . . united": Collect for Proper 9 (BCP, 230-31).

page 120   "joined together . . . a holy temple": Collect for Proper 8 (BCP, 230), drawing on an image from 1 Pet 2:4-5.

page 120   "gathered together . . . show forth": Collect for Proper 16 (BCP, 232).

page 121   "in our weakness": Collect for the Sixth Sunday after Epiphany (BCP, 216).

page 121   "Give us grace": See the collects for First and Second Advent; Seventh Epiphany; Third Lent; Sixth Easter; Propers 1, 5, 14, 15, 19, 23 and 26.

Chapter 21: Prayers of the People

page 130   "pray even 'for our enemies'": As Jesus himself instructed his disciples to do (see Mt 5:44-45).

page 131   "greater degree of continuity": This has perhaps nowhere been more masterfully expressed than in C. S. Lewis's *The Great Divorce* (New York: Macmillan, 1963).

page 132   "cloud of witnesses": The author of Hebrews calls to mind the men and women who exemplified faithfulness to God and to seeking his promises throughout Hebrews 11 in order to assemble this company, as it were, as a crowd of spectators watching his congregation's own "race" along the course of discipleship (Heb 12:1), encouraging them by their example, but also putting on the pressure to live up to their achievement.

Chapter 22: The Lord's Prayer

page 137   "plunders . . . and calls it": This sentence borrows language from the Roman historian Tacitus (*Agricola* 30), specifically from a speech placed on the lips of a British chieftain critiquing Roman imperialism.

page 141   "adding this doxology": The doxology appears in neither of the forms of the Lord's Prayer found in the Gospels (Mt 6:9-13; Lk 11:2-4), although the scribes who copied the Gospels began adding it, conforming the text to the customs in worship, as early as the fifth century. The doxology first appears (in a slightly shorter form) in the early second-century text known as the *Didache*, the "Teaching," our earliest church manual. It bears a striking resemblance to 1 Chron 29:11, the opening of David's last song of praise, from which it may have been derived.

Chapter 23: Adoration

page 145   "Fair are the meadows": *The Hymnal 1982*, no. 383, vv. 2-3 (New York: The Church Hymnal Corporation, 1985).

pages 146-47 "I'll praise my maker": *The Hymnal 1982*, no. 429, v. 1.

page 149   "lost in wonder": This is the closing line of Charles Wesley's hymn, "Love Divine, All Loves Excelling," *The Hymnal 1982*, no. 657.

Chapter 24: Idolatry, Then and Now

page 153   "warn against . . . idols": See especially Is 2:17-21; 44:8-21; Jer 10:1-16; Ezek 6:2-14; 14:3-8; 20:6-31; 1 Cor 8:1-11; 10:14-22; and also the apocryphal texts Wis 13:1—14:21; Letter of Jeremiah.

page 154   "Jesus calls us": *The Hymnal 1982*, no. 550, v. 3 (New York: The Church Hymnal Corporation, 1985).

Chapter 25: What Gift Shall We Bring?

page 158   "expresses symbolically": Leonel L. Mitchell, *Praying Shapes Believ-*

ing: A Theological Commentary on the Book of Common Prayer (Harrisburg, Penn.: Morehouse Publishing, 1985), p. 149.

Chapter 26: Through the Open Door

page 160   "Scenes of adoration and other liturgical acts": See especially Rev 4:I—5:I4; 7:9-17; 8:3-5; II:I5-19; 15:2-4; 16:5-7; 19:I-8.

page 160   "serious persecution and testing": Tellingly, this view arose in the English-speaking West, which has not known any such serious time of testing in the whole of the modern period. That we should read Revelation as a promise that we should be spared some time of testing makes a mockery of the experience of our sisters and brothers across the globe, for many of whom the *present* moment is the "great tribulation" out of which they hope to come with their faithfulness to Jesus Christ intact, so as to stand in God's presence *on the other side* of testing (see Rev 7:I3-I7).

page 161   "the *Sursum Corda*": This opening dialogue between priest and people has been a part of the church's entry into the Lord's presence in the sacrament at least since the early decades of the third century, as attested in Hippolytus's *Apostolic Tradition.*

page 162   "Rank on rank": *The Hymnal 1982,* no. 324, v. 3 (New York: The Church Hymnal Corporation, 1985).

page 164   "A man after God's own heart": See I Sam 13:14.

page 164   "One promises that": The song is "Turn Your Eyes upon Jesus," by Helen H. Lemmel (found, for example, in *The United Methodist Hymnal* [Nashville: United Methodist Publishing House, 1989], no. 349).

Chapter 27: Shaped by the Story of God's Self-Giving

page 167   "*We* were slaves": See Deut 26:5-10, the "creed" that each Israelite would recite when bringing the offering of the first fruits of the land at the temple.

page 170   "Reading and reflecting on Scripture": Resources for further exploration of how Scripture shapes our lives as disciples include M. Robert Mulholland, *Shaped by the Word* (Nashville: Upper Room Books, 1986); Victor H. Matthews, *Old Testament Themes* (St. Louis: Chalice Press, 2000); and David A. deSilva, *New Testament Themes* (St. Louis: Chalice Press, 2001).

Chapter 28: The Nicene Creed

page 174　　"too much with us": The phrase is borrowed from William Wordsworth's poem, "The World Is Too Much with Us."

page 177　　"the soul . . . of the body": Compare Eph 4:4, which speaks of "one body and one Spirit."

Chapter 29: The Great Thanksgiving

page 180　　"Hippolytus . . . Basil": Jeffrey Lee, *Opening the Prayer Book* (Cambridge, Mass.: Cowley Publications, 1999), p. 111.

page 184　　"Faith still receives": *The Hymnal 1982*, no. 306 (New York: The Church Hymnal Corporation, 1985).

page 185　　"Now the silence": *The Hymnal 1982*, no. 333.

page 185　　"No less vigilance": Thomas à Kempis *Imitation of Christ* 4.12.

Chapter 30: Send Us Out

page 188　　"Tongues that have sung": This sentence is based on a line from the hymn "Strength for service, Lord," *The Hymnal 1982*, no. 312 (New York: The Church Hymnal Corporation, 1985).

Chapter 31: Marriage Made in Heaven

page 196　　"inherent in the process of creation": Among the readings from the Old Testament suggested for the marriage service stand both Gen 1:26-28 and Gen 2:4-9, 15-24, selections from the two creation stories that begin the Scriptures. Creation and creation stories are places to which people tend to go to discover something of God's "order" or his "purpose" for the world, and it is not surprising to find both creation stories addressing the question of his purpose for what has become perhaps *the* fundamental unit of societal order.°

page 196　　"The stories of Genesis": See especially Gen 1:28; 2:18. The opening statement of the ceremony resonates with and extends these images from Genesis: "The union of husband and wife in heart, body, and mind is intended by God for their mutual joy; for the help and comfort given one another in prosperity and adversity; and, when it is God's will, for the procreation of children and their nurture in the knowledge and love of the Lord" (BCP, 423).

Chapter 33: Made Within Community, Made for Mission

page 208   "The celebrant prays": The prayers quoted in this and the follow-
               ing paragraph come from BCP, 429.

Chapter 34: Bringing the "New Person" to the Marriage

page 213   "I Pet 3:7": Most modern translations of this verse are inade-
               quate representations of the Greek, suggesting that husbands pay
               "honor to the woman as the weaker sex" (NRSV). But that is not
               the basis that the author holds forward as the ground for respect-
               ing one's wife, and it smacks of condescension.

page 216   "the way of the cross . . . the way of life": These phrases are taken
               from the "Collect for Fridays" in the order for Morning Prayer
               (BCP, 99).

Chapter 35: Bringing God to the Marriage

page 219   "the book of Tobit": See Tob 8:5-8 (for the list of recommended
               readings for weddings, see BCP, 426).

Chapter 36: Facing Death As a People of Hope

page 227   "liturgies help us visualize": The images in this paragraph punc-
               tuate the burial service. See BCP, 465, 466, 481, 484.

page 227   "a glimpse of the church triumphant": See Rev 7:9-17, one of the
               epistle readings recommended for services of burial in the BCP.

page 228   "we liturgically enact": "Into thy hands, O merciful Savior, we
               commend thy servant N. . . . Receive *him* into the arms of thy
               mercy" (BCP, 483); "Into your hands, O Lord, we commend our
               brother (sister)," spoken five times as a response in the "Prayers
               for a Vigil" (BCP, 465-66).

page 229   "belong to God": "Whether we live, therefore, or die, we are the
               Lord's" (BCP, 469, reciting Rom 14:8).

page 229   "liturgical act of committing": This is captured vividly by the
               minister's declaration by the graveside: "In sure and certain hope
               of the resurrection to eternal life, . . . we commit *his* body to the
               ground" (BCP, 485).

page 229   "source of consolation": This ongoing connection is a stabilizing
               anchor in the midst of the disorientation of grief: "Help us, we

pray, in the midst of things we cannot understand, to believe and trust in the communion of saints" (BCP, 481).

Chapter 37: In the Shelter of the Most High

page 231   "The congregation's prayer": The minister leads the congregation in prayer that the grief-stricken will find "a sure confidence in thy fatherly care, that, casting all their grief on thee, they may know the consolation of thy love" (BCP, 481). The minister prays that God will "surround *them* with your love, that *they* may not be overwhelmed by their loss, but have confidence in your goodness, and strength to meet the days to come" (BCP, 494).

page 231   "psalms appointed for funerals": Praying the psalms is a staple of liturgical worship. The burial rites include the full printed texts of Ps 42, 46, 90, 121, 130 and 139 as especially appropriate for finding a voice in the face of death. Quotations and allusions in this paragraph come from Ps 42:3; 121:1-2; 42:1-2; 130:5; 42:5.

page 232   "Jesus . . . begins to weep": Jn 11:33-37 is an essential part of the story for us to hear in our own grief.

Chapter 38: Growing Through Grief

page 235   "example of the departed": See, for example, the following prayers: "Almighty God, . . . we give you heartfelt thanks for the good examples of all your servants, who, having finished their course in faith, now find rest and refreshment" (BCP, 503); "Give us grace . . . to follow the example of their steadfastness in thy faith, and obedience to thy holy commandments" (BCP, 487); "We pray that, encouraged by their examples, . . . we also may be partakers of the inheritance of the saints in light; through the merits of your Son Jesus Christ our Lord" (BCP, 504).

Chapter 39: Reminders of Our Mortality

page 240   "to suffer without knowing why": From Sophocles' *Oedipus* trilogy to Victor Frankl's *Man's Search for Meaning* (1959), this has been a recognized fact of human experience.

Chapter 40: Some Dead Ends

page 244   "the resurrection of the body": A tenet of the Apostles' Creed.

Chapter 41: Smashing Down the Wall

page 248   "even at the grave": BCP, 499, incorporating a funeral anthem in
use in the eastern churches since the ninth century,

Chapter 42: Living Like You'll Live Forever

page 252   "John Donne": E. M. Simpson and G. R. Potter, eds., *The Sermons of
John Donne* (Berkeley: University of California Press, 1953-1962),
3.13.514.

Chapter 43: Affirmation Worth Seeking

page 258   "absence from the Lord": See 2 Corinthians 5:6

Chapter 44: Freed for Costly Discipleship

page 261   "I would want to challenge": On this alternative reading of
Revelation and the methodological considerations on which it
is based, see D. A. deSilva, *An Introduction to the New Testament:
Contexts, Methods and Ministry Formation* (Downers Grove, Ill.: InterVarsity Press, 2004), pp. 885–932.

Chapter 45: Dying As Those Who Go Forth to Live

page 265   "to complete Christ's work": The language comes from BCP,
374.

Index of References to the *Book of Common Prayer*

Scripture Index